Lecture Notes in Computer Science 6707

Commenced Publication in 1973
Founding and Former Series Editors:
Gerhard Goos, Juris Hartmanis, and Jan van Leeuwen

T0224085

Jordi Cabot
Eelco Visser (Eds.)

Theory and Practice
of Model Transformations

4th International Conference, ICMT 2011
Zurich, Switzerland, June 27-28, 2011
Proceedings

 Springer

Volume Editors

Jordi Cabot
INRIA / École des Mines de Nantes
4, rue Alfred Kastler
44307 Nantes
France
E-mail: jordi.cabot@inria.fr

Eelco Visser
Delft University of Technology
Faculty Electrical Engineering,
Mathematics and Computer Science
Mekelweg 4
2628 CD Delft
The Netherlands
E-mail: e.visser@tudelft.nl

ISSN 0302-9743   e-ISSN 1611-3349
ISBN 978-3-642-21731-9   e-ISBN 978-3-642-21732-6
DOI 10.1007/978-3-642-21732-6
Springer Heidelberg Dordrecht London New York

Library of Congress Control Number: 2011929224

CR Subject Classification (1998): D.2, F.3, D.3, C.2, K.6, D.2.4

LNCS Sublibrary: SL 2 – Programming and Software Engineering

Typesetting: Camera-ready by author, data conversion by Scientific Publishing Services, Chennai, India

Printed on acid-free paper

Springer is part of Springer Science+Business Media (www.springer.com)

Preface

This volume contains the papers presented at the International Conference on Model Transformation (ICMT 2011) held during June 27–28, 2011 in Zürich, Switzerland.

Modeling is a key element in reducing the complexity of software systems during their development and maintenance. Model transformations are essential for elevating models from documentation elements to first-class artifacts of the development process. Model transformation includes model-to-text transformation to generate code from models, text-to-model transformations to parse textual representations to model representations, model extraction to derive higher-level models from legacy code, and model-to-model transformations to normalize, weave, optimize, and refactor models, as well as to translate between modeling languages.

Model transformation encompasses a variety of technical spaces, including modelware, grammarware, and XML-ware, a variety of transformation representations including graphs, trees, and DAGs, and a variety of transformation paradigms including rule-based graph transformation, term rewriting, and implementations in general-purpose programming languages.

The study of model transformation includes foundations, semantics, structuring mechanisms, and properties (such as modularity, composability, and parameterization) of transformations, transformation languages, techniques, and tools. An important goal of the field is the development of high-level declarative model transformation languages, providing model representations of transformations that are amenable to 'higher-order' model transformation. To achieve an impact on software engineering practice, tools and methodologies to integrate model transformation into existing development environments and processes are required.

ICMT is the premier forum for the presentation of contributions that advance the state of the art in the field of model transformation and aims to bring together researchers from all areas of model transformation.

This was the fourth edition of the conference. We received 62 abstracts, of which 51 materialized as full papers, and 14 were eventually selected — a 27% acceptance rate. Each submission was reviewed by at least three Program Committee members and on average by four Program Committee members. One of the submitted papers was also submitted to TOOLS Europe 2011 and was rejected by both conferences without reviews. Three papers were first conditionally accepted and subjected to a review of the revision taking into account reviewer comments. The program also included an invited talk and paper by Alexander Egyed, who unfolded his research agenda for smart assistance in interactive model transformation.

A conference such as ICMT is made possible by the collaboration of many people. We were supported by a great team. As Publicity Chair, Dimitris Kolovos worked the mailing lists and designed a stylish poster. Davide Di Ruscio maintained the website using the model-driven becontent Web application tool. The Steering Committee provided advice when we needed it. We thank the TOOLS teams headed by Bertrand Meyer for taking care of the organization of the conference. We used EasyChair to manage the submission process and the production of the proceedings. Finally, we like to thank the authors, Program Committee members, and external reviewers who did the real work that makes a conference.

April 2011   Jordi Cabot
                                                                                Eelco Visser

Organization

Program Committee

Paolo Atzeni	Università Roma Tre, Italy
Marco Brambilla	Politecnico di Milano, Italy
Jordi Cabot	INRIA-École des Mines de Nantes, France
Antonio Cicchetti	Mälardalen University, Sweden
Tony Clark	Middlesex University, UK
James R. Cordy	School of Computing, Queen's University, UK
Krzysztof Czarnecki	University of Waterloo, Canada
Juan De Lara	Universidad Autonoma de Madrid, Spain
Gregor Engels	University of Paderborn, Germany
Jean-Marie Favre	University of Grenoble, France
Nate Foster	Cornell University, USA
Jesus Garcia-Molina	Universidad de Murcia, Spain
Reiko Heckel	University of Leicester, UK
Zhenjiang Hu	National Institute of Informatics, Japan
Jendrik Johannes	Technische Universität Dresden, Germany
Gerti Kappel	Vienna University of Technology, Austria
Günter Kniesel	University of Bonn, Germany
Thomas Kuehne	Victoria University of Wellington, New Zealand
Ivan Kurtev	University of Twente, The Netherlands
Ralf Laemmel	Universität Koblenz-Landau, Germany
Oscar Nierstrasz	University of Bern, Switzerland
Bernhard Rumpe	RWTH Aachen University, Germany
Andy Schürr	TU Darmstadt, Germany
Perdita Stevens	University of Edinburgh, UK
Simon Thompson	University of Kent, UK
Mark Van Den Brand	Eindhoven University of Technology, The Netherlands
Pieter Van Gorp	Eindhoven University of Technology, The Netherlands
Eric Van Wyk	University of Minnesota, USA
Hans Vangheluwe	McGill University, School of Computer Science, Canada
Daniel Varro	Budapest University of Technology and Economics, Hungary
Jurgen Vinju	Centrum Wiskunde en Informatica, The Netherlands
Eelco Visser	Delft University of Technology, The Netherlands
Janis Voigtländer	University of Bonn, Germany
Dennis Wagelaar	Vrije Universiteit Brussel, Belgium

Additional Reviewers

A

Alalfi, Manar
Andova, Suzana

B

Bak, Kacper
Basten, Bas
Bencomo, Nelly
Branco, Moises
Brosch, Petra

C

Canovas, Javier Luis
Christ, Fabian
Cleophas, Loek

D

De Jonge, Maartje

E

Engelen, Luc

G

Gldali, Baris
Groenewegen, Danny

H

Hildebrandt, Roland
Horváth, Ákos

K

Khan, Tamim
Kurpick, Thomas

L

Langer, Philip
Legros, Elodie
Lungu, Mircea

M

Martel, Matthieu
Meyers, Bart
Mezei, Gergely

N

Nagy, Istvan
Navarro Perez, Antonio

P

Perin, Fabrizio
Pinkernell, Claas

Q

Qayum, Fawad

R

Rendel, Holger
Ressia, Jorge
Rossini, Alessandro
Ráth, István

S

Schwarz, Niko
Seidl, Martina
Semenyak, Maria
Serebrenik, Alexander
Soltenborn, Christian
Stephan, Matthew
Stevenson, Andrew
Syriani, Eugene
Sánchez Cuadrado, Jesús
Sánchez Ramón, Óscar

V

Van Amstel, Marcel
Van Der Storm, Tijs
Van Der Straeten, Ragnhild
Varro, Gergely
Verwaest, Toon

W

Wachsmuth, Guido
Wang, Meng
Weisemoeller, Ingo
Wernli, Erwann
Wieber, Martin
Wimmer, Manuel

Table of Contents

Fine-Tuning Model Transformation: Change Propagation in Context of Consistency, Completeness, and Human Guidance

Alexander Egyed, Andreas Demuth, Achraf Ghabi, Roberto Lopez-Herrejon, Patrick Mäder, Alexander Nöhrer, and Alexander Reder

Institute for Systems Engineering and Automation
Johannes Kepler University
Altenbergerstr. 69, 4040 Linz, Austria
`firstname.lastname@jku.at`

Abstract. An important role of model transformation is in exchanging modeling information among diverse modeling languages. However, while a model is typically constrained by other models, additional information is often necessary to transform said models entirely. This dilemma poses unique challenges for the model transformation community. To counter this problem we require a smart transformation assistant. Such an assistant should be able to combine information from diverse models, react incrementally to enable transformation as information becomes available, and accept human guidance – from direct queries to understanding the designer(s) intentions. Such an assistant should embrace variability to explicitly express and constrain uncertainties during transformation – for example, by transforming alternatives (if no unique transformation result is computable) and constraining these alternatives during subsequent modeling. We would want this smart assistant to optimize how it seeks guidance, perhaps by asking the most beneficial questions first while avoiding asking questions at inappropriate times. Finally, we would want to ensure that such an assistant produces correct transformation results despite the presence of inconsistencies. Inconsistencies are often tolerated yet we have to understand that their presence may inadvertently trigger erroneous transformations, thus requiring backtracking and/or sandboxing of transformation results. This paper explores these and other issues concerning model transformation and sketches challenges and opportunities.

Keywords: change propagation, transformation, consistency, variability, constraints, impact of a change.

1 Introduction

There are many benefits to software and systems modeling but these benefits hinge on the fact that models must be internally consistent. However, for models to be consistent, changes (additions, removals, and modifications) must be propagated correctly and completely with reasonable effort. Unfortunately, a change is rarely a localized event. On the code level, changes tend to affect seemingly unrelated parts [1], considering the

J. Cabot and E. Visser (Eds.): ICMT 2011, LNCS 6707, pp. 1–14, 2011.

wider dimension of software engineering, changes affect everything from requirements, models, code, test scenarios, documentation, and more [2, 3]. Considering the even wider dimension of systems, changes in one discipline (and its models) affect other disciplines (and their models). Unfortunately, when it comes to change, designers simply lack the engineering principles to guide them. Model transformation provides the means for propagating knowledge from one model to another. It is intuitive to think of change propagation as a series of model transformations where either the changed model is re-transformed to other models or only the change itself is transformed. Yet, transformation methods have to overcome a range of challenges to support change propagation.

In this paper, we discuss the challenge of change propagation in software and systems models from the perspective of transformation. It should be noted that we do not believe that change propagation is fully automatable since creativity is a major part of this process – and being creative is what humans do best. But a human should enter a modeling fact once only. If knowledge is replicated across multiple models then this knowledge should be propagated automatically. If this knowledge is changed then it should be updated. Unfortunately, the diversity and inter-disciplinary nature of models rarely sees model elements to be replicated directly. Moreover, models typically do not (just) replicate knowledge from other models but also add their own, unique information. This implies that model transformation is rarely fully automatable. A simple analogy is the blueprint for a house. While the side view of a house cannot be derived from the front view (no automatic transformation), it is obvious that the height of the house must be the same in both views - a restriction that two modeling views impose on each other. This is intuitive because if models were derivable through other models then one modeling language could replace another (or one discipline with its models could replace another discipline with their models) – which is not desirable. The sole purpose of diverse modeling languages (with separate structure, behavior, scenarios, and more) is to depict modeling information from different points of views that may overlap in the knowledge they include but are meant to have unique parts also.

It is the objective of this paper to highlight challenges on how to automatically propagate changes across diverse, inter-disciplinary design models – an unsolved problem of vital interest to software and systems engineering disciplines. If during change propagation, the information needed is already present in the model (perhaps in a semantically different, distributed form) then a goal of change propagation is to transform that information (if possible) or to restrict possible changes in other models. If some information needed is not present in the model then the goal of change propagation is to elicit this missing information from the human designer in ways that do not obstruct/interrupt their work. The role of the designer is thus to instigate change propagation and guide it. The role of automation should be to reason about the logical implications of changes in context of diverse models.

2   Illustration and Problem

Figure 1 introduces a small example to illustrate change propagation in context of three UML diagrams. The class diagram (left) represents the structure of a movie player: a *Display* used for visualizing movies and receiving user input and a *Streamer* for decoding movies. The sequence diagram (right) describes the process of selecting a movie and playing it. A sequence diagram contains interactions among instances of classes (vertical life lines), here a user invoking *select* (a message) on the display lifeline of type *Display* which then invokes *connect* on the *streamer* lifeline of type *Streamer*. The movie starts playing once the *playOrStop* message occurs which is followed by *stream*. The state machine (middle) describes the allowed behavior of the *Streamer* class. It is depicted that after *connect*, the *Streamer* should toggle between the *stopped* and *playing* states. Change propagation can only be automated to the degree that failure to propagate changes is observable. Indeed, we believe that model constraints are the perfect foundation to understand failure to propagate [4] and change propagation should leverage from knowledge about constraints [5]. For example, imagine that the designer changes the model, say, by splitting the single *playOrStop* operation in the class diagram into two separate operations called *play* and *stop* (see top left of Figure 1). This change in the class diagram causes inconsistencies with the state machine and sequence diagram due to their continuing use of the old names. Such inconsistencies are the result of violations of constraints which govern the correctness within and among such diagrams (note that we use the terms *model* and *diagram* interchangeably). Table 1 depicts three such constraints, the first of which is described in more detail using the OCL constraint language [6]. It defines that the name of a message must match at least one operation in the class diagram – not just any operation but the one on the receiving end of the message (arrow head).

Table 1. Constraints are useful for Change Propagation

Constraint 1	**Name of message must match an operation in receiver's class** context Message inv: self.receiveEvent.covered->forAll(Lifeline lll.represents.type.ownedOperation->exists(Operation olo.name=self.name))
Constraint 2	**Name of statemachine action must match an operation in owner's class**
Constraint 3	**Sequence of messages must match allowed sequence of actions in state machine**

This paper suggests that knowledge about changes, combined with knowledge about possible transformations and constraints that govern the correctness of the models, results in a better understanding of change propagation. The example also makes it obvious that transformation must be possible partially or in form of alternatives if no unique answer is computable. Take for example the implication of the designer change onto the state machine. The two transitions *playOrStop* have to be changed – at least in name – however, it is not possible to automatically transform this change in the state machine because the designer has not provided enough information to infer this.

Which *playOrStop* transition should be named *play*, which one *stop?* All we know is that with the *playOrStop* method gone, the same named transitions in the state machine are affected. It is our opinion that it is not useful to propagate "likely" changes and we advocate strongly against any approach that is not generic. As such,

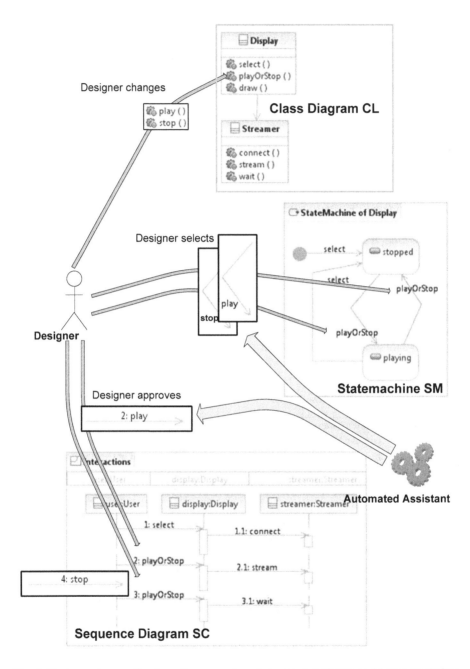

Fig. 1. Engineer changes the class diagram and an Automated Assistant could suggest choices for how to change the state machine (partial automation). After the engineer selects one of these choices, the Assistant could change the sequence diagram by itself (complete automation).

approaches that were to propagate changes based on a heuristic, such as minimizing the number of inconsistencies caused by change propagation, would be incorrect quite often. A trivial proof is the simple undo. The undo is likely the most effective way of eliminating an inconsistency (all we need to do is to undo the last change which apparently caused the inconsistency). While the undo would immediately "solve" the inconsistency, the undo would conflict with the designer's intention most times. Of course, in case of the undo, this conflict between change propagation on one hand and quick inconsistency resolution is obvious. This issue, however, becomes trickier in context of changes that carry across multiple models. What we need is thus a generic mechanism to propagate precise and complete changes or, if not possible, to propagate precise and complete restrictions (=other kinds of constraints). That is, we may not know exactly how to change the state machine; however, we can reason precisely in what ways not to change the state machine. We could even compute a list of alternative, reasonable changes: for example, automated change propagation may suggest renaming the transitions in the state machine to either *play* or *stop* which the designer must then do manually by choosing between them. The designer then complements the inferable changes from the class diagram with missing information.

The same is true for the two messages in the sequence diagram in the right. Given the changes in the class diagram, we also cannot decide exactly how to rename the messages (if renaming is the designer's way of resolving this inconsistency which is but one option). It is thus vital to combine knowledge from transformation (including alternatives and restrictions) across multiple models and knowledge of all inputs provided by the designer to understand his/her intentions. With every change made by the designer and with every intervention, the designer's intention becomes increasingly better known. For example, if the designer selects one of the choices on how to rename the transitions in the state machine then, combined with the knowledge how the designer changed the class diagram, we can automatically infer what changes must happen to the sequence diagram. Concretely, if the designer selects the name *play* for the left *playOrStop* transition and *stop* for the right one then, based on the given constraints and the restrictions of both designer changes, we can automatically decide that the top *playOrStop* message in the sequence diagram must be renamed to *play* and the bottom one to *stop*. This conclusion would be the only one that would satisfy all constraints imposed in Table 1 because the state machine defines that the *play* transition must happen after either the *connect* or *stop* transition and the sequence diagram list the *connect* message before the *playOrStop* message.

Our goal should thus be an automated assistant with a well-defined methodology for reasoning about changes, their interpretations, and their combined propagation. The benefit of such an assistant was to request human intervention only when necessary to complement the already given information and not to require the same knowledge to be re-entered repeatedly. This benefits the automatic maintenance of correctness across the many modeling languages used (provided the dependencies among these models could be formalized in form of constraints which is already common practice in many domains). Such an assistant would facilitate change and counter the single biggest reason for software engineering failure: the inability to propagate changes correctly and completely.

3 Fine-Tuning Transformations

In this section, we sketch in more detail the challenges that an automated assistant for change propagation should address – a challenge in which transformation plays a key role.

The classical textbook definition of a model transformation is to convert a source model into a target model where both source and target models have well-defined syntax and semantics. In the engineering of software systems, it is quite common to attribute different models (or modeling languages) to different engineers (or engineering disciplines) and their needs. Figure 2 depicts a simple pipeline where an engineer may create a model in a language most suitable for his/her work and then transform it to another model in a language most suitable for the work of another engineer who is meant to add to the knowledge provided by the first engineer. Engineering may be seen as a set of sequential or parallel transformation steps where the engineers manipulate models and transformations propagate knowledge embedded in these models for the benefit of others.

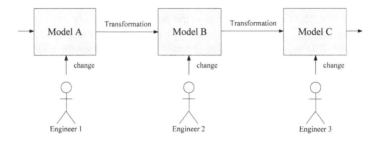

Fig. 2. Transformation to Avoid Re-Entering Knowledge

In this context, transformation can have a range of different roles, such as:

1) *Transformation as translation:* translate a model from one language to another, usually with the intent of preserving the semantics of the model such that the engineer may benefit from reasoning or automations available in context of the target model (e.g., analysis or synthesis methods).
2) *Transformation as a simplification/abstraction*: simplify a source model by depicting only parts that are relevant to a concern, engineer, or discipline. The target model can be a true subset of the source model or some transformation thereof.
3) *Transformation as a merger:* combine various source models to provide a more comprehensive, integrated target model where different, separately modeled concerns are depicted together.

There are other roles of transformation of course [7], but in context of design modeling and propagating information among models and engineers, these are the most common in our experience. There is also no clear separation of the roles. Instead, transformation typically follows multiple such roles (e.g., merging and filtering go hand-in-hand). However, in all cases, *transformation propagates knowledge – knowledge that originally must have come from human engineers.* While transformation can have many roles, the main purpose of transformation is to avoid having engineers re-enter knowledge if that knowledge is already available in another model. The intent is not only to save effort but also to ensure that knowledge is propagated correctly and completely from those that create it to those that require it. Making sure that transformations are correctly chained or composed is a topic that deserves further attention [8, 9].

3.1 Transformation and Redundancies

Transformations would not be possible if models would not overlap. However, if we could compute one model entirely from another (or set of other models) then the model would not contribute new knowledge. The less knowledge a model adds, the less likely this model is going to be used during engineering as there is no value added (except for cases where model transformations are necessary to integrate tools or technologies but in the bigger context of change propagation these kinds of transformations are implementation details). Models are thus typically partially overlapping only – intentionally diverse to ensure that each model contributes new knowledge. This implies that transformation is not able to (nor meant to) compute a target model in its entirety but only fragments thereof – the parts that can be inferred from other (source) models while the remaining, new knowledge must come from the engineers or other models. The degree of overlap can vary: from no overlap (disjoint models) where no transformation is possible to partial overlaps, subsets, and complete overlaps. The "overlapping" area is either outright replication of modeling elements (physical overlap) or a re-interpretation thereof (semantic overlap). The more obscure the re-interpretation, the more complex the transformation.

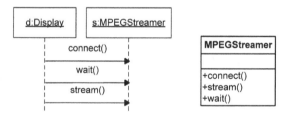

Fig. 3. Semantic Overlap: A Method with the Name of the Message must be defined in the Message Receiver's Class. The method and the message are distinct model elements but they share knowledge, such as their names.

An example of a relatively simple re-interpretation of modeling elements is given in Figure 3 (based on the example introduced in the illustration in Figure 1). The message in the sequence diagram (left) is a different kind of model element than the method in the class diagram (right). Semantically, the method defines functionality whereas the message represents a specific invocation of that functionality. While these two model elements are quite distinct elements in terms of their syntax, they share knowledge: (1) the message defines the location of the method through the message receiver (e.g., message *stream()* identifies object *s* of type *Streamer*) and (2) the message defines the name of the method through the message's name. However, the message does not define the parameters of said method nor, in case of inheritance, whether the method should be in the location referenced or one of its parents. There may be heuristics for choosing among these uncertainties but again we like to point out that heuristics can be wrong and advocate against using them.

3.2 Transformation Conflict

Transformation propagates knowledge and, once propagated, this knowledge exists redundantly (in the source model and the target model). We know that redundant knowledge must be kept consistent over time. We define the source model to be consistent with the target model if all knowledge transformable from the source model to a target model is equal to the knowledge in the target model (and vice versa). If the transformation is correct then the source and target models must be consistent initially. However, what if the model changes?

If a model changes then we first need to remember all past transformations that included the changed model because the (target) models derived from these models may need to change also. This requires *traceability*, the knowledge where knowledge came from and where it was being used. See "Past Transformation" trace in Figure 4 (left).

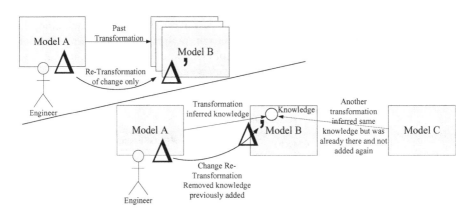

Fig. 4. Changing a model requires updating all models to which knowledge was transformed. Transformation interactions occur when later transformations are affected by the results of earlier transformations.

To support change propagation, a transformation needs to be precise in that, ideally, only the change is re-transformed and not the entire model. This is particularly important if the transformation requires manual intervention:

- during transformation by the engineer providing additional knowledge not inferable from the source model.
- after transformation in form of changes to the target model.

Here we encounter different forms of change propagation problems. Consider that one transformation method inferred some knowledge in context of a model (e.g., knowledge inferred in model B based on transformation from model A in Figure 4 right). If the same knowledge would also be derivable through another transformation (e.g., from model C) then obviously this knowledge is not created twice in the target model (model B) but rather the first transformation creates it and the second one simply terminates without creating anything. What if the source model of the first transformation changes such that it no longer infers that knowledge? If change propagation would just undo the creation of the knowledge in model B then the result would be incorrect. The knowledge should remain because there is another model that still supports it.

Such transformation interactions not only happen between automated transformations. The engineer is also a (manual) transformation engine and Figure 5 illustrates a simple dilemma that involves undesirable interactions between an engineer and a transformation. For the above illustration, we know that a method should be added to a class or its parents if a message is created. Obviously, the method should only be added if such a method does not exist but if the class also has parents then additional guidance by the engineer is necessary to specify where to add the method – to the class or to one of its parents (manual guidance). However, imagine that the message was transformed at a time where the parent did not exist. Obviously, the transformation placed the method at the only class available *at that time* – which was a correct decision that did not require human intervention. A change to, say, the message name, should then update the corresponding method (propagation). Yet, if a parent class was introduced since then, the re-transformation should not just transform the change, the name, but it should also understand that the premise of the initial transformation is no longer valid. Indeed, one might argue that this premise should already be questioned at the time the parent class is introduced.

For change propagation, the sequence of changes cannot be taken strictly. If the source and target models are manipulated by different engineers then it is largely irrelevant who made what change first. In other words, the initial transformation of the *stream()* method was correct only until the introduction of the parent class in the target model. This problem is analogous to race conditions.

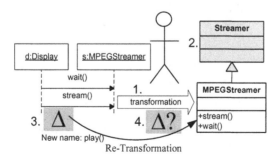

Fig. 5. For Change Propagation, Transformations have an "Expiration Time Stamp". Here, the initial transformation of the *stream()* message to the *stream()* method was correct because there was no parent. The later introduction of the parent class potentially invalidates the initial transformation.

For change propagation, we obviously require fine-grained traceability to remember where to transform to. However, we also need mechanisms for triggering re-transformation to avoid race conditions in when/how transformations happened and when/how models where changed (by transformations or engineers).

3.3 One-Directional Transformation but Bi-directional Change Propagation

A change is neutral in terms of the transformation direction; however, often transformation is one-directional only. If an engineer likes to change some model elements and these elements were (in part) computed through transformation from other model elements then this change may cause inconsistencies. Again, we need to remember past transformation results – but this time from the perspective of the target model. Still, this problem is different from the above. If the model element we like to change was computed through a one-directional transformation method then how are we to propagate this change? We would either have to manually update both the target model(s) and the source model(s) with the same knowledge (this is not desirable) or we would need to change the source model such that the re-transformed source model causes the desired model change in the target model - a nearly impossible task in context of complex transformations (Figure 6).

The basic implication is that we need bi-directional transformation [10]. However, bi-directional transformations often do not occur in practice. Even in context of the trivial transformation from messages to methods above, it is hard to imagine how to reverse transform a method to a message. It is clear that a method should be invoked in form of messages but how many such invocations should exist or where/when they should exist is not inferable. The answer here is in partial transformation. In this simple example, many modeling tools may suggest the name of a method once a message is created. This conception of model completion is an area ripe for research on transformation [11].

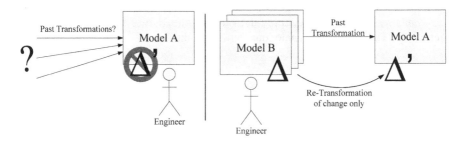

Fig. 6. Change Propagation cannot be solved with One-Directional Transformation. Here: if transformation can propagate the change from model B to model A only then the engineer must either update a model A change in model B manually or attempt to change model B such that it causes the desired change in model A through transformation.

3.4 Multiple Transformation Steps and Change Propagation

Change propagation must follow redundant knowledge. If a model changes then the knowledge that was inferred from it must be re-transformed a s must be the knowledge that was inferred [12, 13]. However, a change must be re-transformed only for as long as the knowledge produced during the re-transformation is different from before (Figure 7). We thus require knowledge of data differences before and after transformation [14]. Re-transformation terminates if the target model does not change.

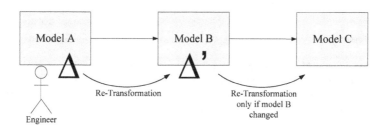

Fig 7. Re-transformation of a sequence of model transformations ends once the re-transformation does not change the targer model (here, if the re-transformation of model A to model B does not change model B then no further transformation is necessary)

Re-transforming sequentially is particularly then problematic if seen together with the problem of transformation interactions discussed above: where some but not all re-transformations unfold in the same manner

- Problem 1: what if the initial transformation required human intervention? Should re-transformation replay the human intervention? What if the source model changed in a manner were the original human intervention was no longer valid?
- Problem 2: what if the changes would trigger a different kind of transformation? Imagine that distinct transformations exist and which transformation to use depends on the contents of the source model. A change to the source model may then also change what transformation to use. It follows that re-transformation cannot blindly repeat past transformations.

3.5 Merging Transformation Results

The motivating example in Figure 1 showed that the combined changes in the class and the statechart diagrams make it possible to automatically change the sequence diagram. This is the result of combining the impact of changes from two models where each model individually would not have contained enough information for transformation to propagate the change further but together they have all information needed (not unlike parallel transformation [15] and merging [16]). Figure 8 illustrates this problem. On the surface, this problem may seem solvable by allowing multiple source models for a given transformation; thus in effect combining transformations to more complex transformations. However, in context of change propagation there may be too many transformation interactions to consider. We thus requires a different handling – one where transformations are standalone but with knowledge on how to merge results (Figure 8).

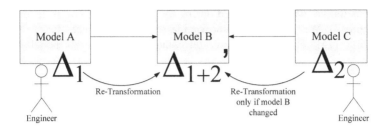

Fig. 8. A Model (or its Model Elements) may sometimes be computable through the merging of multiple source models only. The dilemma: should distinct transformations be merged to single, more comprehensive transformation involving multiple sources or should transformations remain small, diverse but require explicit mechanisms for merging their results whenever necessary?

3.6 Trusting Transformation

Finally, in addition to all of the above, we have to understand that modeling implies the presence of errors (inconsistencies [17]). Indeed, a change is only necessary if the current model is no longer consistent with the engineers intention. After all, the very essence of modeling implies accepting and living with inconsistencies. Given that engineers may tolerate any number of inconsistencies, the final question is about trustworthiness of transformation (results) if we know that neither source models nor target models are complete or correct. In part, we addressed this problem in section 3.2 above when we spoke of transformations having an "expiration date." However, should we treat transformation results differently if we know that they are based on model elements known to be contributing to inconsistencies? Works like [18, 19] are able to compute whether model elements contribute to inconsistencies. Any (subset of) transformation results that are directly or indirectly based on such "contributing" model elements have to be flagged such that the engineers are spared follow-on errors elsewhere. That is, model elements contributing to inconsistencies must identified and flagged such that engineers are aware of them in the model(s) they contributed to and in all their transformed forms.

4 Conclusions

The role of a smart assistant during change propagation is to guide the human engineer in a manner that is correct and complete. Change propagation can only be automated to the degree that 1) failure to propagate changes is observable and 2) suitable transformation methods exist to propagate knowledge. A smart assistant for change propagation thus requires the integration of consistency checking technologies and transformation technologies. Transformations are needed to move knowledge between models and consistency checking is needed for understanding when and how to transform that knowledge. The focus of this paper was specifically on the role of transformation. We discussed major transformation capabilities needed to support change propagation ranging from support for bi-directional transformation to understanding the validity of transformation results and correspondingly the need for re-transformation. We believe that transformation for change propagation is only partially automatable; hence the need for incremental transformation and the transformation of partial results (e.g., variability in form of choices and alternatives). This paper explored these and other issues, and sketched challenges and opportunities.

Acknowledgments

We would like to gratefully acknowledge the Austrian Science Fund (FWF) through grants P21321-N15 and M1268-N23, and the EU Marie Curie Actions – Intra European Fellowship (IEF) through project number 254965.

References

[1] Gall, H., Lanza, M.: Software evolution: analysis and visualization. In: Proceedings of the International Conference on Software Engineering, pp. 1055–1056 (2006)

[2] Tarr, P., Osher, H., Harrison, W., Sutton Jr., S.M.: N Degrees of Separation: Multi-Dimensional Separation of Concerns. In: Proceedings of the 21st International Conference on Software Engineering (ICSE 21), pp. 107–119 (1999)

[3] Bohner, S.A., Arnold, R.S.: Software Change Impact Analysis. IEEE Computer Society Press, Los Alamitos (1991)

[4] Cabot, J., Clarisó, R., Guerra, E., de Lara, J.: Analysing Graph Transformation Rules through OCL. In: 1st International Conference on Theory and Practice of Model Transformations (ICMT), Zürich, Switzerland, pp. 229–244 (June 2008)

[5] Egyed, A.: Automatically Detecting and Tracking Inconsistencies in Software Design Models. IEEE Transactions on Software Engineering (TSE) 37, 188–204 (2011)

[6] Warmer, J.K.A.: The Object Constraint Language. Addison Wesley, Reading (1999)

[7] Mens, T., Czarnecki, K., Gorp, P.V.: 04101 Discussion - A Taxonomy of Model Transformations. In: Language Engineering for Model-Driven Software Development, Dagstuhl Seminar Proceedings. Schloss Dagstuhl, Germany (2005)

[8] Heidenreich, F., Kopcsek, J., Aßmann, U.: Safe Composition of Transformations. In: 3rd International Conference on Theory and Practice of Model Transformations (ICMT), Malaga, Spain, pp. 108–122 (June 2010)

[9] Hettel, T., Lawley, M., Raymond, K.: Model Synchronisation: Definitions for Round-Trip Engineering. In: 1st International Conference on Theory and Practice of Model Transformations (ICMT), Zürich, Switzerland, pp. 31–45 (June 2008)

[10] Czarnecki, K., et al.: Bidirectional Transformations: A Cross-Discipline Perspective. In: 2nd International Conference on Theory and Practice of Model Transformations (ICMT), Zurich, Switzerland, pp. 260–283 (June 2009)

[11] Sen, S., Baudry, B., Vangheluwe, H.: Towards Domain-specific Model Editors with Automatic Model Completion. Journal of Simulation 86, 109–126 (2010)

[12] Jouault, F., Tisi, M.: Towards Incremental Execution of ATL Transformations. In: 3rd International Conference on Theory and Practice of Model Transformations (ICMT), Malaga, Spain, pp. 123–137 (June 2010)

[13] Shen, W., Wang, K., Egyed, A.: An Efficient and Scalable Approach to Correct Class Model Refinement. IEEE Transactions on Software Engineering (TSE) 35, 515–533 (2009)

[14] Hemel, Z., Groenewegen, D.M., Kats, L.C.L., Visser, E.: Static consistency checking of web applications with WebDSL. Journal of Symbolic Computation 46, 150–182 (2011)

[15] Cicchetti, A., Ruscio, D.D., Pierantonio, A.: Managing Dependent Changes in Coupled Evolution. In: 2nd International Conference on Theory and Practice of Model Transformations (ICMT), Zürich, Switzerland, pp. 35–51 (June 2009)

[16] Xiong, Y., Song, H., Hu, Z., Takeichi, M.: Supporting Parallel Updates with Bidirectional Model Transformations. In: 3rd International Conference on Theory and Practice of Model Transformations (ICMT), Malaga, Spain, pp. 213–228 (June 2010)

[17] Balzer, R.: Tolerating Inconsistency. In: Proceedings of 13th International Conference on Software Engineering (ICSE), pp. 158–165 (1991)

[18] Egyed, A.: Fixing Inconsistencies in UML Design Models. In: Proceedings of the 29th International Conference on Software Engineering, Minneapolis, MN, pp. 292–301 (2007)

[19] Nentwich, C., Emmerich, W., Finkelstein, A.: Consistency Management with Repair Actions. In: Proceedings of the 25th International Conference on Software Engineering (ICSE), Portland, Oregon, USA, pp. 455–464 (2003)

Optimization of Visitor Performance by Reflection-Based Analysis

Markus Lepper[1] and Baltasar Trancón y Widemann[2]

[1] <semantics/> GmbH, Berlin
post@markuslepper.eu
[2] Universität Bayreuth
Baltasar.Trancon@uni-bayreuth.de

Abstract. Visitors are a well-known and powerful design pattern for processing regular data structures and for combining declarative and imperative coding styles. The authors' umod model generator creates Java data models from a concise and algebraic notation. It is primarily used to model intermediate representations of computer languages. The user defines visitor code by extending skeleton classes, which are generated according to traversal annotations in the model. Since the generated code on its own executes the pure traversal and no semantic side-effects, traversals are redundant unless some user-overridden method is eventually invoked. We present a reflection-based control flow analysis to detect this situation and prune the traversal transparently. With a well-stratified model, this may lead to substantial increase in performance.

Keywords: Visitor Pattern, Generative Programming, Control Flow Analysis, Reflection.

1 Introduction

1.1 Visitors

Visitors are a well-known and powerful design pattern for processing regular data structures and for combining declarative and imperative coding styles [3]. The principle is as follows: For evaluating or transforming a certain *instance* of a *data model definition* (existing in a certain *hosting* computer language, normally an object-oriented one), there is some *visitor class* definition (in a strict sense "external" to the model itself) which executes a *traversal* of the model instance. This means that one or more methods (defined in this visitor class) with reserved names are called recursively with all or some of the objects that make up the *elements* of the model instance. The selection and sequential order of these method incarnations follows the graph of the model instance, as defined and realized by the references among the model elements.

There are many different variants of this principle, see Sect. 5. In particular, different phases or transformation steps of the visiting process can be identified by distinct method names. Commonly, the *base visitor code* performs only the

J. Cabot and E. Visser (Eds.): ICMT 2011, LNCS 6707, pp. 15–30, 2011.

traversal, nothing more. Intended *semantics* (i.e. evaluation or transformation of the model) are realized by deriving user-defined, specialized visitors from these base classes, overriding the appropriate method definitions.

1.2   Optimization and Generative Programming

The base class(es) for the visitors are general-purpose traversal code, and do not "know" which subgraphs of a given model instance really need to be visited for a certain user-defined visitor. The optimization algorithm presented here prunes all paths which *surely do not reach any user-defined code*, and consequently do not contribute to the custom semantics of the visitor.

This principle can of course also be applied manually, and indeed often is, e.g. by defining different base visitors for different traversal situations, or by explicitly overriding descending code with a "no-operation". But as the example in Sect. 4.1 will show, the effects of these manipulations can possibly turn out to be very surprising. Hence evolution, incremental definition and refactoring of models may become impossible in a safe and efficient way.

In general, maintenance and evolution of models and the related visitor classes can be made especially safe and efficient if the code for both is *generated* automatically from some concise model definition. The authors' umod is a tool for this kind of generative programming. It generates multiple base visitor classes, each combining a certain *kind of processing* with a user-definable *traversal directive*. In this context, the optimization is based on traversal directive information extracted in the model *compilation* phase, combined with the collection of method signatures specific to the user-defined, derived visitor classes, extracted at *class-initialization* time via *reflection*.

2   The Algorithm in General

2.1   Prerequisites for the Algorithm

Our algorithm is suitable for all modeling frameworks where (1) the class collection for a certain model is finite and structured by references and inheritance, (2) visitors with a certain semantics are defined by deriving from basic visitors which realize mere traversal, and (3) the visiting sequence of the latter is defined by a sequence of field selections per class. This applies to our own umod implementation, as described in the Sect. 3.2, to many other modeling frameworks, and to XML document type definition languages, see Sect. 4.3.

The following subsections describe these prerequisites and the algorithm in a semi-formal way. A survey of the employed notation is found appendix A.

2.2   Models

Let $\mathcal{C}_0$ be a finite set of predefined, external classes. Any certain model M defines a finite set of classes C_M, the *model element classes*, i.e. the classes of the objects which make up the model instances. C_M is disjoint from $\mathcal{C}_0$. There is a total superclass function $\texttt{extends} : C_M \rightarrow (C_M \cup \mathcal{C}_0)$, which must be free of cycles, as usual.

Let ident be the (infinite) set of valid identifiers. Each class definition from C_M is assigned a finite set of *field definitions* by $fieldDefs : C_M \rightarrow (\mathsf{ident} \nrightarrow \mathcal{T})$. Assume there is no shadowing of field names. Then the inheritance closure of this map, denoted by $fieldTypes$, is defined recursively as

$$fieldTypes(c) = \begin{cases} \{\} & \text{if } c \in \mathcal{C}_0 \\ fieldDefs(c) \cup fieldTypes(\texttt{extends}(c)) & \text{otherwise} \end{cases}$$

The set of types $\mathcal{T}$ contains primitive predefined types and reference types to external classes from $\mathcal{C}_0$, which are not relevant to our topic. But $\mathcal{T}$ of course also includes simple references to one single instance of a certain model class from C_M, and also to aggregate types referring to more than one instance of more than one model class, like "$\texttt{MAP } T_1 \texttt{ TO } (T_2 \texttt{*} T_3)$". The cycle from class definitions via field types back to classes is closed by a relation $containedClasses : \mathcal{T} \leftrightarrow C_M$ which relates each type to all model classes appearing in its definition.

The *set of all field definitions* of a certain model M can be represented by set of pairs $F_M : C_M \leftrightarrow \mathsf{ident}$ which is defined by simply forgetting the types of the defined fields:

$$F_M = fieldDefs \,\mathring{\,}\, \mathsf{dom}$$

Let Q_M be a certain *model instance* of the model M. In practice, this is realized by a finite collection of objects of the underlying programming language which complies to the structural declarations in M. By the actual values of all those fields which point to instances of element classes, this collection describes an *arbitrarily shaped, labeled directed graph*.

2.3   Visitors

A *visitor* is an imperative program construct which reads and modifies some Q_M, enhanced by some *arbitrary state space* S. Transformations of S may include local visitor fields updates, local side-effects, or even global side-effects like I/O.[1] For our optimization it is required that visitors with semantic actions are derived by method overriding from *basic visitors*. Each of these does not perform any transformation of the state space, but realize only one certain traversal of the model instance, i.e. the successive visiting of the model objects. Its behavior is thus equivalent to a *traversal selection*, which is simply the selection of those fields, the visitor will follow[2], given as a subrelation $R_n \subseteq F_M$. Let V_n^G be the basic visitor corresponding to R_n.

---

[1] In the following formulae, the modification of Q_M is restricted not to modify the traversed fields, because this would make the mathematical modeling unnecessarily complicated. But in theory, there is no real difference for the optimization algorithm.

[2] Indeed, in most frameworks the user defines a *sequential order* of traversal, but we can abstract from this for the purpose of this paper.

From V_n^{G}, the user defines the semantic transformations by deriving one or more *user-defined visitors* $V_n^{\mathrm{U0}}, V_n^{\mathrm{U1}}, \ldots$ by subclassing, i.e. method overriding. Let the collection of all possible visitors of the model M be V_M, and V_n all those based on R_n.

$$
\begin{aligned}
transformationType &= V_M \times Q_M \to (\mathcal{S} \nrightarrow \mathcal{S}) \\
\mathtt{match}, \mathtt{descend} &: \; transformationType \\
getAction &\quad : V_M \to (C_M \to transformationType) \\
\mathtt{getClass} &\quad : Q_M \to C_M \\
\mathtt{match}\,(v, q) &\; = \big(getAction(v)(\mathtt{getClass}(q))\big)(v, q)
\end{aligned}
$$

The purpose of simple visitors is to evaluate a state transformation $(s \mapsto s') \in \mathtt{match}(v, q)$. The transformation operation $\mathtt{match}(v, q)$ depends on the lookup function $getAction(v)$. This function delivers the transformation for a certain visitor and a certain model element class.

In case of the basic visitors, this "transformation" is nothing more than a complicated construction of the "identity"; for all $c \in C_M$, we have

$$
getAction(V_n^{\mathrm{G}})(c) = \mathtt{descend}_{c,n}
$$

The operation $\mathtt{descend}_{c,n}$ of *transformationType* realizes the traversal of the model, following all fields selected by R_n in class definitions c.

Let $f_1, f_2, \ldots, f_k$ be the sequence of field identifiers from the traversal selection R_n, restricted to *fieldDefs*(c), i.e., to all fields appearing in a certain class definition. Let $\mathtt{get}(q, f)$ be the semantic operation to look up the current value of a certain field named f in a model element instance q. This value is of type *fieldTypes*$(\mathtt{getClass}(q))f$, and can be a direct reference to a model element, or of some aggregate type like $\mathtt{SET}$ or $\mathtt{REL}$, referring to model elements indirectly. Let $q_{f,1}, q_{f,2}, \ldots, q_{f,m}$ be all the model element instances which are referred to in this value. Then the code for traversing the model is specified by

$$
\begin{aligned}
\mathtt{descend}_{c,n}(v_n, q) = \; &\mathtt{descend}_{\mathtt{extends}(c),n}(v_n, q) \\
&\mathbin{\raisebox{0.2ex}{$\substack{\circ\\\circ}$}} \mathtt{match}\big(v_n, \mathtt{get}(q, f_1)\big) \mathbin{\raisebox{0.2ex}{$\substack{\circ\\\circ}$}} \ldots \mathbin{\raisebox{0.2ex}{$\substack{\circ\\\circ}$}} \mathtt{match}\big(v_n, \mathtt{get}(q, f_k)\big)
\end{aligned}
$$

where $\mathtt{match}\big(v_n, \mathtt{get}(q, f)\big)$ is just an abbreviation for the aggregated operation $\mathtt{match}(v_n, q_{f,1}) \mathbin{\raisebox{0.2ex}{$\substack{\circ\\\circ}$}} \mathtt{match}(v_n, q_{f,2}) \mathbin{\raisebox{0.2ex}{$\substack{\circ\\\circ}$}} \ldots \mathbin{\raisebox{0.2ex}{$\substack{\circ\\\circ}$}} \mathtt{match}(v_n, q_{f,k})$. This code constitutes *a first axis of inheritance*, namely on the model's element classes which serve as *arguments* of the visitor methods.

Some important properties of the **basic visitors' code** can directly be concluded:

(1) If the selected traversal sequence applied to a certain model instance Q_M leads to any *cycles* in the traversal path, then the top-level $\mathtt{match}$ will not terminate.
(2) But if there are no cycles, it *will* terminate, because $\mathtt{get}()$ and $getAction()$ are *total* functions.

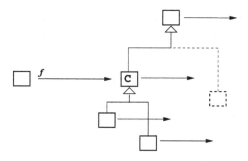

Fig. 1. Inheritance of Associations and Paths

(3) The state variable $s : S$ is not changed at all, but simply passed through. So each generated visitor V_n^G does not perform any useful work on its own. See the next section for the far-reaching optimization potential that arises from this deceivingly simple property.

A **user-defined visitor** is specified as

$$V_n^{\mathrm{U}m} : V_n \times (C_M \nrightarrow transformation\,Type)$$

The projection functions $\mathtt{baseVisitor} : V_n^{\mathrm{U}m} \to V_n$ and $actionDefs : V_n^{\mathrm{U}m} \to (C_M \nrightarrow transformation\,Type)$ return its first or second component, resp. Its purpose is to re-define the transformations only on the model element classes to be analyzed or modified. This is accomplished by completing the equation system above by

$$getAction(V_n^{\mathrm{U}m}) = getAction\big(\mathtt{baseVisitor}(V_n^{\mathrm{U}m})\big) \oplus actionDefs(V_n^{\mathrm{U}m})$$

This constitutes *a second axis of inheritance*, namely w.r.t. the hierarchy of user-defined visitors, rooted at the basic visitors. Again, the inheritance relation must be free of cycles, as usual.

Of course, in all implementations following this scheme, the code delivered by *actionDefs* can make use of ("call") the `match` code of the super-class visitor, including the `descend` of the basic visitor.

2.4   Optimization

Due to observation (3) from the list above basic visitors never change the state, only user-defined code does. Therefore **it is sound to prune all paths on which no user-defined code will ever be executed for any model instance.** So the optimization aims at eliminating the redundant calls to `descend()` that will never reach any user-defined code, for a given Visitor $V_n^{\mathrm{U}m}$. It is necessary to follow a certain field f, iff at least one class appears in the domain of $getAction(V_n^{\mathrm{U}m})$, an instance of which is reachable through f, either directly or indirectly.

To decide this question, we have to consider *inheritance*, as depicted in Fig. 1: The field f as declared pointing to an instance q_c of some model element class c (any "association" in UML nomenclature) may point, in a certain model instance, to an instance of any subclass of c. So, in a first step, all subclasses and all superclasses must be tested whether they appear in the domain of *actionDefs* of any V_n^{Um}, which means that the corresponding action method is overridden by the user. Furthermore, all relevant fields of all subclasses of c, and of all superclasses of c must be included for extending the possible paths which start at f and which have to be checked recursively for user code. Associations starting from "siblings" and "nephews" of the declared target of f need not be considered, see the dotted lines in Fig. 1, since the declaration of the field as of type c does not allow instances of those classes in any valid model instance.

In other words: As soon as the $c \in C_M$ are no longer seen as one level of declaration, but interpreted as an *extensional collection*, i.e., as representatives for all possible run-time objects q for which "q instanceof c" holds, then the fields of all super- and subclasses must be included when constructing their connectivity graph. This graph is the first basis for the further search for classes subject to user code. It is calculated as

$$includeFieldsOf : C_M \leftrightarrow C_M$$
$$includeFieldsOf = \texttt{extends}^* \cup (\texttt{extends}^*)^\sim$$

Please note that the transitive and symmetric closure must be applied in exactly this nesting order, for including all ancestors and descendants while excluding siblings and nephews. We consider this the central "trick" of our algorithm.

Independent from this relation is the question which class *declarations* are related by association through fields. This is the second basis for the search paths. It depends on the selected traversal R_n and is calculated by

$$decClassToDecClass_n : C_M \leftrightarrow C_M$$
$$relevantFields_n = F_M \cap R_n$$
$$relevantTypes_n = \left\{ \left(c, fieldTypes(c)(i)\right) \mid (c,i) \in relevantFields_n \right\}$$
$$decClassToDecClass_n = relevantTypes_n \,\text{\r{,}}\, containedClasses$$

where *containedClasses*(t) is simply the set of all model classes which appear in a certain field type t, as defined in Sect. 2.2.

Composing these two axes, we obtain a finite adjacency relation which is subject to standard SCC analysis.[3] Each of the recognized *strongly connected components* is represented simply by some natural number:

---

[3] A strongly connected component (SCC) is a maximal nonempty subgraph in which there is a path between each pair of members. In this context, the SCC analysis serves as "data compression" to minimize the information which has to be carried over from compile-time to run-time. It is orthogonal to the semantics of the optimization because no two classes in one and the same SCC can behave differently w.r.t. the algorithm. SCC analysis can be performed by standard algorithms like TARJAN's or GABOW's, in linear time w.r.t. the number of edges.

$$
\begin{aligned}
connected_n &\quad:\ C_M \leftrightarrow C_M \\
connected_n &\ =\ includeFieldsOf \ \mathring{,}\ decClassToDecClass_n \ \mathring{,}\ includeFieldsOf \\
\texttt{class2scc}_n &\quad:\ C_M \rightarrow \mathbb{N} \quad // \ partition \\
sccToScc_n &\quad:\ \mathbb{N} \leftrightarrow \mathbb{N} \quad // \ quotient \ of \ the \ SCC \ analysis \ of \ connected_n \\
\texttt{field2sccs}_n &\quad:\ F_M \leftrightarrow \mathbb{N} \\
\texttt{field2sccs}_n &\ =\ fieldTypes \ \mathring{,}\ containedClasses \ \mathring{,}\ \texttt{class2scc}_n
\end{aligned}
$$

Up to this point, the analysis uses only information from model class definitions and the traversal selections for the basic visitors (R_n). Its results are identical for all semantic visitors based on the same R_n.

The next step of analysis requires the knowledge of the semantic visitors:

$$
\begin{aligned}
defedClasses &\quad:\ V_M \leftrightarrow C_M \\
defedClasses &\ =\ (actionDefs \ \mathring{,}\ \mathrm{dom}) \cup (\texttt{baseVisitor} \ \mathring{,}\ defedClasses) \\
\texttt{fieldFlags} &\quad:\ V_M \leftrightarrow F_M \\
\texttt{fieldFlags} &\ =\ defedClasses \ \mathring{,}\ \texttt{class2scc} \ \mathring{,}\ \texttt{field2sccs}_n^{\sim}
\end{aligned}
$$

So $defedClasses(v)$ is the set of all model element classes which appear as an argument to some `action()` method overwritten by the user, i.e. the set of those an action method has been "defined for". From this set, the set of all overwritten SCCs is inferred, and from this the set of fields that need to be followed. The traversal code contained in V_n^{G} is instrumented with corresponding conditionals, so that it only calls "$\texttt{match}\bigl(V_n^{\mathrm{U}m}, \texttt{get}(\dots, f)\bigr)$" if $(V_n^{\mathrm{U}m}, f) \in \texttt{fieldFlags}$.

3 Implementation

3.1 The ^meta-tools Context

^meta-tools [15] is a collection of Java and XML-based tools for generative programming, compiler generation, text processing etc. The basic philosophy of all components is to relieve the programmer from tedious and error-prone routine by generating code from semantic models, but at the same time preserving the freedom of arbitrary usage of the underlying programming language as far as possible, for smooth integration with a wide range of tools and software development processes. Hand-written code and generated code are not woven together, but cooperate using the conventional language features for modularization, in particular inheritance.

Typical components of ^meta-tools are `format` (a framework for human-readable text and code layout, enhancing HUGHES's pretty-printing combinators [5] substantially), `metajava` (seamlessly integrated counterpart of Java reflection for *generating* source code), `tdom` (a *strictly typed* XML document object model [16]), or `option` (compiler for command-line style and GUI style parametrization of applications). These tools have been successfully employed in a variety of mid-scale projects.

3.2   The umod Tool

Among these tools the umod compiler is a central means for generating Java code for general-purpose data models. This includes the classes for the model's elements, safe constructors and setter methods (primarily w.r.t. the illegal value null), various methods for visualization and (de-)serialization and different kinds of visitors. Fig. 2 shows a simple model definition source file[4], presenting the most important features of the compiler:

- The syntax of the model definition is designed for compactness.
- Source code of model element classes is generated for

      abstract class A extends java.lang.Object
      class B1 extends A
      class B2 extends A
      class D extends java.lang.Object

- Class B1 has algebraic semantics: the equals() predicate and the corresponding hashCode() are defined structurally by field-wise recursion, and all instances are *immutable*—no set() methods will be generated, but instead with() methods that create a modified copy.
- These classes have fields which point to different types of containers (maps, relations, sequences), for which empty instances are created automatically, and which have setter functions checking for illegal null values.
- The directive "C 0/0" following a field declaration generates constructor code which initializes this field. Constructor code is *inherited*, and 0-ary constructors are provided whenever appropriate.

3.3   umod Visitors

The basic visitors V_n^G from Sect. 2.3 are also generated by the tool.

Visitor strategies are defined in the same source document with the model, to ensure the consistency of necessary changes as required by certain software development processes. e.g. rapid prototyping. and by later maintenance. In the generated code however, model classes do not depend on visitor classes.

Visitor code generation is controlled by the "VISITOR ..." statements, as in Fig. 2. This syntax combines a *traversal directive* and a *visitor kind*.

The traversal directive n is constructed by annotating a field definition with "V n/...". It specifies the field references a visitor shall follow when traversing the model, i.e. it defines the traversal selection R_n which is employed in definition of the basic visitor's behavior in Sec. 2.3.

Fig. 3 shows a simplified realization of the visitor class Simple, as defined in the model. (The actual code generated by umod looks slightly different.) The visitor *kind* distinguishes between simple visitors, multi-phase visitors, rewriters, co-rewriters (which can deal with cycles), printers, Swing tree builders for visualization, XML encoders, etc. Only basic visitors are generated by the tool.

---

[4] Please ignore the graying-out of two text lines until reading Sect. 4.1.

```
MODEL M =
   VISITOR  0 Simple ;
   VISITOR  1 Rewrite IS REWRITER ;
   VISITOR  2 Visitor2 ;

TOPLEVEL CLASS
  A ABSTRACT
       a1   int <-> B1     !        V 0/0 1/0 2/0 ;
       a2   A              ! C 0/0 V          2/1 ;
   | B1 ALGEBRAIC
       b1   OPT A          !        V     1/0     ;
       b1b SEQ B1          !        V 0/0         ;
   | B2
       b2   int -> D       !        V 0/0 1/0 2/0 ;
       b2b OPT B2          !        V 0/1 1/1     ;
  D
       d    int  = "17"
END MODEL
```

Fig. 2. A simple example model definition

```
public class Simple {                    protected void action(A x) {
  public void match(Object x) {            for (B1 sub : x.a1.range())
    if (x instanceof A)                      match(sub);
      match((A)x);                         match(x.a2);
    else if (x instanceof D)             }
      match((D)x);                       protected void action(B1 x) {
    else                                   action((A)x);
      action_foreignObject(x);             for (B1 sub : x.b1b)
  }                                          match(sub);
  public void match(A x) {              }
    if (x instanceof B1)                 protected void action(B2 x) {
      match((B1)x);                        action((A)x);
    match((B2)x);  // closed world         for (D sub : x.b2.values())
  }                                          match(sub);
  public void match(B1 x) {               if (x.b2b != null)
    action(x);                             match(x.b2b);
  }                                      }
  public void match(B2 x) {              protected void action(D x) {}
    action(x);                           //no call of match() for "int"
  }                                      protected void
  public void match(D x) {                action_foreignObject(Object x)
    action(x);                            {}
  }                                    }//class Simple
```

Fig. 3. Generated code for a simple visitor according to traversal directive "V 0/.."

The subsequent definition of the semantic visitors $(V_n^{\mathrm{U}m})$ is done on source-text level, using the normal Java inheritance techniques, and tools and processes of the user's choice.

3.4   Implementation of the Visitor Optimization Algorithm

All analysis up to the calculation of $\mathtt{class2scc}_n$ and $scc\,ToScc_n$ is done at **model code-generation time**. Every model class is part of an SCC, and every field is linked to the SCC that constitutes the root of the subgraph of classes which can be potentially reached by following the actual value of this field. Using the "ops" libraries of ^{meta}-tools for high-level algebraic programming, the specifications from Sect. 2.4 are implemented almost literally. The results are encoded into appropriate `static final` data structures, and passed over to the Java compiler, and thus to **execution time**.

At class loading the analysis is completed, since the calculation of *defedClasses* and `fieldFlags` requires the knowledge of the user-defined semantic visitor code. In our framework, this code can come from any source, could even be generated on the fly, therefore the byte code must be analyzed. Since the interaction between generated and user-defined code is restricted to method overriding, *reflection* is sufficient. When the first instance of the visitor class $V_n^{\mathrm{U}m}$ is constructed, its Java class object is queried via reflection for all methods with a matching signature. Whenever such a method is recognized as defined at an inheritance level lower than that of the *generated* basic visitor, then it is classified as user-defined and recorded in *defedClasses*. From this set, the set of all overwritten SCCs is inferred, and from this the set of fields that need to be followed.

The results are stored in a central cache, and retrieved on each subsequent constructor call. The values of these sets vary with every user defined visitor class. Since these are written independently from the tool, this little overhead of copying constant bitset values from a dynamic storage is required.

4   Examples

4.1   Simple Example, Continued

Returning to the toy model definition presented in Fig. 2, assume there is a user-defined visitor $V_n^{\mathrm{U}1}$ which only overrides the method for `action(D)`, and it has to be decided whether a call to `match(A.get_a1())` is necessary. Note that this call could be rather expensive, since `a1` can contain references to an unknown number of `B1` objects. The relevant associations are depicted in Fig. 4.

If $n = 0$, meaning that the visitor is derived from V_0^{G}, the base visitor generated from traversal code 0, then this match *does not* need to be called: The only way to reach an object of class `D` is via `B2.b2`, but all associations starting from any `B1`, namely `B1.b1b` and `A.a1`, stay in the collection of `B1` objects. This is different when deriving from V_1^{G} and V_2^{G}, for different reasons: $V_1^{\mathrm{U}m}$ follows additionally field `B1.b1` of type `A`. The actual value of this field *could* be of type `B2`, thus `action(D)` can be reached.

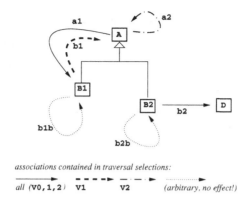

associations contained in traversal selections:

all (V0,1,2)   V1   V2   (arbitrary, no effect!)

Fig. 4. The associations in the example model

The consequence of adding A.a2 with traversal code 2 may seem somehow surprising at a first glance: While the "loops" at the "leaf classes" B1.b1b and B2.b2b are totally irrelevant for the analysis (indicated by the graying-out of the source text lines and the dotted arrows in the graphic!), a loop at a non-leaf class is *not*: of course, the current visited object is already an instance of A (remember, we are discussing whether match(A.get_a1()) needs to be executed). But this new association A.a1 does not only add some redundant self-reference, but also a way to reach a B2 from any instance of B1, which changes the graph of possible paths dramatically. This illustrates that applying this kind of optimization *manually* would be rather error-prone, esp. when later maintenance requires adaption of the model's structure.

4.2   A Real-World Application

We have applied the optimization to a real-world programming language compiler created with extensive use of the ^meta^-tools: The Tofu language is a pure functional language with a powerful type system based on the *calculus of constructions*. It features polymorphism, type-level functions and dependent types, but is still *total*: All well-typed functions terminate for all inputs. Tofu is intended as executable semantics, and hence prototype implementation and test oracle, for mathematically rigorous software documentation (cf. [17]). The Tofu compiler uses a generated parser and a umod-generated semantical model of the language. All compiler passes are implemented as visitor-style transformations on the model (mostly of the rewriter kind). The compiler translates Tofu to a low-level, untyped applicative intermediate representation (functional "assembly language") and eventually to Java using the facilities of metajava.

The structure of the internal umod-model of Tofu makes it a natural test case for visitor optimization: The model is, in its current version, strictly 2-stratified, with references from a *namespace* level (modules, declarations, definitions) to an *expression* level (terms, function abstractions, types), but not vice versa. In total there are 33 classes with 44 declared fields (not counting inheritance) in the model.

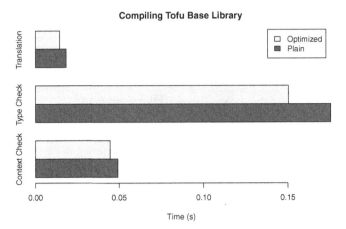

Fig. 5. Run times for major phases of the Tofu compiler, compiling the Tofu base library. Shown figures are means of real durations (`System.nanoTime`) of 100 runs after a warm-up phase of 10 runs. Relative improvement is approx. 9% (Context Check), 14% (Type Check) and 21% (Translation), resp. (14% cumulatively). A total of 5639 subtrees are pruned per run.

Fig. 5 shows some benchmark results. They were obtained on an Athlon 64 X2 5000 dual-core machine and the Sun JDK 1.6.0_13 client VM with 200MiB of heap space. The execution times of the following phases have been measured: *Context Check* – removes syntactic sugar, resolves references, establishes scoping of variables. *Type Check* – verifies type consistency (including termination) of all function definitions, infers implicit type parameters. *Translation* – performs type erasure, constant folding, inlining and lambda lifting; generates low-level (LISP-like) functional code.

All of these rely heavily on the visitor pattern, invoking 21 user-defined visitor classes. Invoked on the Tofu base library (757 lines of code), a total of 3625 visitors are instantiated. The measurements show consistent improvement of the optimized version of the generated visitor code over the plain version of approximately 14%. The overhead of a dynamic check of `fieldFlags` for each field value is included in the calculation. The check allows to prune the traversal of a subtree of unknown size in 5693 cases. The additional overhead of the execution-time phase of our algorithm is difficult to measure exactly because of its interference with class loading, but can be estimated as at most 4 ms, i.e. 5% of execution time.

The measurements have been obtained as the real execution times (as reported by successive calls to `System.nanoTime()`) of the respective compiler phase. To reduce the impact of system load and random effects, the compilation has been repeated $K + N$ times, interspersed with calls to `System.gc()`. The first $K = 10$ runs served as a warm-up phase for the class loader and JIT compiler. The following $N = 100$ runs were averaged.

We conclude that the achieved gain in efficiency is satisfactory. Most of the pruned subtrees are subgraphs that represent Tofu expressions, traversed by visitors that only provide custom actions for the namespace level of Tofu. While the same efficiency (and even more, considering the overhead of dynamic pruning checks) can be achieved by user-controlled explicit pruning, the automatic optimization is superior from the software-engineering perspective, because the stratification properties of the Tofu model could be altered, or ruined entirely, even by small changes (cf. "A.a2" in Fig. 4). For a model of realistic size, the transparency provided by automatic visitor optimization is a valuable feature.

4.3 Possible Applications on Other Stratified Data

The amount of stratification and unidirectional references in a model is an indicator for the expected gain from applying our algorithm. Our analysis of two wide-spread XML models has shown significant potential. We have recorded the number of SCCs and the maximal path length in the SCC graph (generation count), which serve as measures of stratification in relation to the number of elements.

Document Type	Path Length	SCCs	Elements
XHMTL 1.0	6	22	77
DocBook 5.0	18	77	362

5 Related Work

The related work we have found is either rather narrow or rather broad, depending on the criterion: There is only one work dealing with automated pruning ([8]) and few dealing with pruning by programming. On the other hand there are many approaches to automated visitor code generation, very different and hardly comparable. We decided to give here the broader view, because all these papers contribute valuable aspects.

The "visitor pattern" itself appears to have risen out of folklore, with [3] being the first publication to use this term explicitly. In [1] there is a more recent and more exact description.

In [10] "Walkabout" is presented, a versatile extension of the visitor pattern, avoiding the need of the "closed-world assumption". It uses Java reflection for run-time inquiry and even for *method invocation*, being substantially less efficient than generated code. We did not find practical applications. A combinator library for visitors is presented in [14]. It allows, among other useful things, explicit and hand-coded pruning of subtrees. It contains combinators like "Choice(v1,v2) — Try v1. If it fails, try v2". This catalog could be a valuable suggestion for further evolution of the umod output. A more recent paper on "strategic programming" is [6], which discusses the need of a language-independent traversal control very thoroughly. Automated pruning is not discussed, but could be integrated into this context in a rather natural way.

The only paper we found which addresses (among more general questions of traversal control) a very similar topic, namely automated pruning of visiting sequences directed by constraints, is [8]. Its context is the Demeter system [7], which translates graph models into Java code and other programming languages. It resembles our umod approach w.r.t. compactness and algebraic flavor. Belonging to aspect-oriented programming, this approach is independent from a particular language as back-end and includes proprietary language constructs for visiting strategies and algorithms. Our approach leaves this intentionally to Java constructs, while supporting also non-syntactic data types like sets and maps, with their Java-specific semantics.

Based again on a standard programming language is the approach in [4]: an architecture based on C++ template instantiations and the "standard template library" (STL) for re-using visitor code for translating domain specific models into different back-ends. This meets our approach w.r.t. re-using traversal code and separating phases and tasks. The issue of automated pruning is not addressed there.

The approaches in [9] and in [13] are even more similar to ours, since Java code is generated. The main difference is that umod visitors are generated as part of generated Java source, but in [9] the visitors are generated to operate with independently created Java classes. Consequently, the visitor description language is much more complicated and deals with details (e.g. calculation results and method signatures) which our tool leaves to the subsequent "manual" refinement process, using plain Java language means.

Another ambitious visitor code generation system is presented in [13], together with formal semantics and corresponding proofs. Again, we do less (w.r.t. verification and provable correctness), but allow more (namely arbitrary transformations in the course of $S \nrightarrow S$, e.g. I/O). In [11], all possible execution sequences of a certain visitor are translated into a context-free grammar. In a second step, this approach would also allow automated pruning, but this is not addressed in the paper. The approach in [2] resembles our umod code generation, but is again more versatile on the back-end (not focused on a single programming language) and less versatile on the front-end (models must be "trees"). Whether the visitors perform any optimization is not clear from the documentation.

As a **conclusion**, our approach seems to take a middle road between the others: One one hand, it has exact algebraic specification of the data model, and computability of certain model properties needed for the optimization. On the other hand, it is not a self-contained language for the complete definition of models and their transformations, but a pragmatic solution for generating "smart boilerplate" model code in Java, leaving open all the possibilities of the language the programmer is accustomed to use freely.

Acknowledgments

Many thanks to the anonymous reviewers for valuable hints. These have helped to improve the text substantially.

References

1. Buchlovsky, P., Thielecke, H.: A Type-theoretic Reconstruction of the Visitor Pattern. In: Mathematical Foundations of Programming Semantics (MFPS 2005). ENTCS, vol. 155. Elsevier, Amsterdam (2006)
2. Demakov, A.: TreeDL (2007), http://treedl.org/
3. Gamma, E., et al.: Design Patterns: Elements of Reusable Object-Oriented Software. Addison Wesley, Reading (1995)
4. Hill, J.H., Gokhale, A.: Using Generative Programming to Enhance Reuse in Visitor Pattern-based DSML Model Interpreters. Tech. rep. IEEE Trans. SP (2007)
5. Hughes, J.: The Design of a Pretty-printing Library. In: Advanced Functional Programming, pp. 53–96. Springer, Heidelberg (1995)
6. Lämmel, R., Visser, E., Visser, J.: The Essence of Strategic Programming (2002)
7. Lieberherr, K.: Demeter: Aspect-Oriented Software Development, http://www.ccs.neu.edu/research/demeter/
8. Lieberherr, K., Patt-Shamir, B., Orleans, D.: Traversals of object structures: Specification and Efficient Implementation. ACM Trans. Program. Lang. Syst. 26(2), 370–412 (2004)
9. Ovlinger, J., Wand, M.: A language for specifying recursive traversals of object structures". In: ACM SIGPLAN Notices, vol. 34 (October 1999)
10. Palsberg, J., Jay, C.B.: The Essence of the Visitor Pattern (1997)
11. Schordan, M.: The Language of the Visitor Design Pattern. Journal of Universal Computer Science 12(7), 849–867 (2006)
12. Spivey, J.: The Z Notation: A Reference Manual. Prentice Hall, Englewood Cliffs (1988), http://spivey.oriel.ox.ac.uk/~mike/zrm/
13. van Drunen, T., Palsberg, J.: Visitor-oriented programming. In: Proc. FOOL-11 (2004)
14. Visser, J.: Visitor Combination and Traversal Control. In: Proc. OOPSLA 2001, pp. 270–282. ACM Press, New York (2001)
15. Trancón y Widemann, B., Lepper, M.: The BandM Meta-Tools User Documentation. (2010), http://bandm.eu/metatools/docs/usage/
16. Trancón y Widemann, B., Lepper, M., Wieland, J.: Automatic Construction of XML-based Tools seen as Meta-programming. Automated Software Engineering 10(1), 23–38 (2003)
17. Trancón y Widemann, B., Parnas, D.L.: Tabular Expressions and Total Functional Programming. In: IFL 2007 Revised Selected Papers, pp. 219–236. Springer, Heidelberg (2008)

A   Mathematical Notation

The employed mathematical notation is fairly standard, inspired by the Z notation [12]. The following table lists some details:

$A \to B$	The type of the *total* functions from A to B.
$A \nrightarrow B$	The type of the *partial* functions from A to B.
$A \nrightarrow\!\!\!\!\rightarrow B$	The type of the *partial and finite* functions from A to B.
$A \leftrightarrow B$	The type of the relations from A to B.
ran a, dom a	Range and domain of a function or relation.
$r^{\sim}$	The inverse of a relation
r^*	The reflexive-transitive closure of a relation
$r \, \mathbin{\raise.1ex\hbox{$\circ$}\kern-.35em\lower.6ex\hbox{$,$}} \, s$	The composition of two relations: the smallest relation s.t. $a\,r\,b \wedge b\,s\,c \Rightarrow a\,(r \, \mathbin{\raise.1ex\hbox{$\circ$}\kern-.35em\lower.6ex\hbox{$,$}} \, s)\,c$
$r \oplus s$	Overriding of function or relation r by s. Pairs from r are shadowed by pairs from s: $r \oplus s = \left(r \setminus (\text{dom } s \times \text{ran } r)\right) \cup s$

Functions are considered as special relations, i.e. sets of pairs, like in "$f \cup g$".

A Comparison of Rule Inheritance in Model-to-Model Transformation Languages*

Manuel Wimmer[1], Gerti Kappel[1], Angelika Kusel[2],
Werner Retschitzegger[2], Johannes Schönböck,[1], Wieland Schwinger[2],
Dimitris Kolovos[3], Richard Paige[3], Marius Lauder[4], Andy Schürr[4], and Dennis
Wagelaar[5],**

[1] Vienna University of Technology, Austria
[2] Johannes Kepler University Linz, Austria
[3] University of York, United Kingdom
[4] Darmstadt University of Technology, Germany
[5] AtlanMod (INRIA & École des Mines de Nantes), France

Abstract. Although model transformations presumably play a major role in Model-Driven Engineering, reuse mechanisms such as inheritance have received little attention so far. In this paper, we propose a comparison framework for rule inheritance in declarative model-to-model transformation languages, and provide an in-depth evaluation of three prominent representatives thereof, namely ATL, ETL (declarative subsets thereof), and TGGs. The framework provides criteria for comparison along orthogonal dimensions, covering *static aspects*, which indicate whether a set of inheriting transformation rules is well-formed at compile-time, and *dynamic aspects*, which describe how inheriting rules behave at run-time. The application of this framework to dedicated transformation languages shows that, while providing similar syntactical inheritance concepts, they exhibit different dynamic inheritance semantics and offer basic support for checking static inheritance semantics, only.

Keywords: Rule Inheritance, Model Transformations, Comparison.

1 Introduction

Model-Driven Engineering (MDE) defines models as first-class artifacts throughout the software lifecycle, which leads to a shift from the "everything is an object" paradigm to the "everything is a model" paradigm [5]. In this context, model transformations are crucial for the success of MDE, being comparable in role and importance to compilers for high-level programming languages. Support for large transformation scenarios is still in its infancy, since reuse mechanisms such as inheritance have received little attention so far [10], although the concept of inheritance plays a major role in metamodels, as revealed, e.g., by the evolution of the UML standard [13]. As inheritance is employed in metamodels to reuse feature definitions from previously defined classes, inheritance between

---

* This work has been funded by the FWF under grant P21374-N13.
** The author's work is funded by a postdoctoral research grant provided by the Institute for the Promotion of Innovation by Science and Technology in Flanders.

J. Cabot and E. Visser (Eds.): ICMT 2011, LNCS 6707, pp. 31–46, 2011.

transformation rules is indispensable in order to avoid code duplication and consequently maintenance problems. Although this need has been recognized by developers of transformation languages, the design rationales underlying individual transformation languages are not comparable at first sight. This makes it difficult to understand how these constructs are to be used.

Therefore, we propose a comparison framework for rule inheritance in declarative model-to-model transformation languages that makes explicit the hidden design rationales. The proposed framework categorizes the comparison criteria along three orthogonal dimensions analogous to the three primary building blocks of programming languages [2]. The first two dimensions comprise *static criteria*: (i) the *syntax* a transformation language defines with respect to inheritance and (ii) *static semantics*, which indicates whether a set of inheriting transformation rules is well-formed at compile-time. The third dimension of the comparison framework describes how inheriting rules interact at run-time, i.e, *dynamic semantics*. On the basis of this framework, inheritance mechanisms in dedicated transformation languages (ATL [9], ETL [11], TGGs (MOFLON) [10]) are compared. The results show that the inheritance semantics of these languages differ, which has profound consequences for the design of transformation rules.

Outline. Section 2 provides the rationale of this work, and Section 3 presents the comparison framework with its three dimensions. In Section 4, we compare the inheritance mechanisms of ATL, ETL and TGGs and present lessons learned. Finally, Section 5 gives an overview on related work, and Section 6 concludes.

2   Motivation

When developing a framework for comparing rule inheritance in transformation languages, one starting point is to look at the well-known model transformation pattern (cf. Fig. 1) and to examine where the introduction of inheritance would play a role. Obviously, a transformation language must define syntactic concepts (cf. question 1 in Fig. 1), which leads to the first dimension of our comparison framework, namely *syntax*. In this respect, the following questions are of interest:

- *Which types of inheritance are supported?* Does the transformation language support only single or multiple inheritance?
- *Are abstract rules supported?* Is it possible to specify transformation behavior that is purely inherited?

In addition to syntax, further well-formedness constraints on the transformation rules must hold (cf. question 2 in Fig. 1), which represents the second dimension, namely *static semantics*. Thereby, the following questions may arise:

- *In which way may a subrule modify a superrule?* For instance, how may the types of input and output elements be changed in subrules such that they may be interpreted in a meaningful way?
- *When is a set of inheriting rules defined unambiguously?* Are there sets of rule definitions that do not allow selecting a single rule?

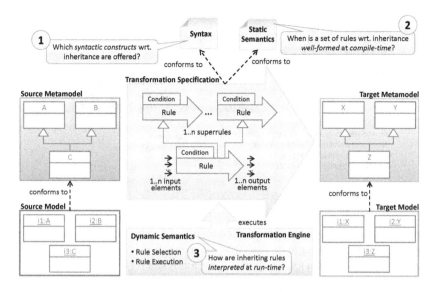

Fig. 1. Model-to-Model Transformation Pattern

A transformation specification is usually compiled into executable code, which is interpreted by a transformation engine that takes a source model and tries to select and execute rules in order to generate a target model. Again several questions concerning the interpretation of inheritance at run-time arise (cf. question 3 in Fig. 1), which leads to the third dimension, namely *dynamic semantics*:

- *Which instances are matched by which rule?* If a rule is defined for a supertype, are the instances of the subtype also affected by this rule?
- *How are inheriting rules executed?* Either top down or bottom up in the rule inheritance hierarchy?

3   Comparison Framework

This section presents our framework for comparing inheritance support in declarative transformation languages which are used to describe transformations between object-oriented metamodels, conforming to, e.g., Ecore or MOF2. Although metamodeling languages such as MOF2 support refinements between associations, e.g., subsets or redefines, these are out of scope of this paper. As shown in Fig. 2, the comparison criteria can be divided into the three dimensions of (i) *syntax*, (ii) *static semantics*, and (iii) *dynamic semantics*. These dimensions and the corresponding sub-criteria are described in the following.

3.1   Syntax

This subsection provides criteria for comparing transformation languages in terms of syntactic concepts that they support. We consider both general criteria

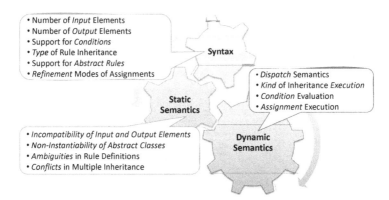

- Number of *Input* Elements
- Number of *Output* Elements
- Support for *Conditions*
- *Type* of Rule Inheritance
- Support for *Abstract Rules*
- *Refinement* Modes of Assignments

Syntax

- *Dispatch* Semantics
- *Kind* of Inheritance *Execution*
- *Condition* Evaluation
- *Assignment* Execution

Static Semantics

- *Incompatibility of Input and Output Elements*
- *Non-Instantiability of Abstract Classes*
- *Ambiguities* in Rule Definitions
- *Conflicts* in Multiple Inheritance

Dynamic Semantics

Fig. 2. Overview on the Comparison Framework

(e.g., the numbers of input and output elements of a rule) and inheritance-related criteria (e.g., whether single or multiple inheritance is supported).

To identify the criteria for comparison, we analyzed (i) the features of transformation languages and (ii) the classification of model transformation approaches presented in [7]. The identified features are expressed in a metamodel (MM), shown in Fig. 3 illustrating the core concepts of transformation languages. A `Transformation` typically consists of several `TransformationRules`, including an `InPattern`, referring to `InputElements` of the source MM, and an `OutPattern`, referring to `OutputElements` of the target MM. Please note that programmed graph transformations and TGGs distinguish between (i) rule parameters and (ii) input/output elements, whereby we consider only the latter. A general distinguishing criterion is the *allowed number of input and output elements*. Furthermore, transformation languages typically support the definition of a `Condition`, which may be interpreted in different ways (cf. Section 3.3). Finally, they provide the possibility of setting the values for target features by means of `Assignments`.

In the context of inheritance-related aspects, three criteria are relevant. First, a `TransformationRule` may inherit from either one or multiple other transformation rules, depending on whether *single or multiple inheritance* is supported. Second, the concept of `abstract` *rules* may be supported in order to specify that a certain rule is not executable per se but provides core behavior that can be reused in subrules. Finally, one can distinguish between different *refinement modes* by which inherited parts are incorporated into inheriting rules (cf. enumeration `RefinementMode` in Fig. 3). First, *override* implies that when a subrule refines an assignment of a superrule, the assignment of the subrule is executed together with those assignments in the superrule which are not overridden. In the refinement mode *inherit* first the overridden assignments are executed, and then the overriding assignment may alter the resulting intermediate result (such as by initializing some state by a supercall and then altering this intermediate result). Third, *merge* means that again both assignments are executed, but first the assignments of the subrule and then the overridden assignments of the superrule are executed. Finally, the refinement mode *extend* induces that inherited

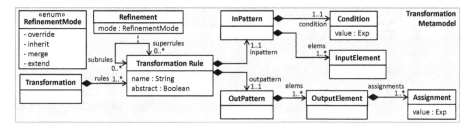

Fig. 3. Inheritance-Related Concepts of Transformation Languages

assignments may not be changed at all. For consistency reasons, all assignments in a single rule should follow the same refinement mode (cf. class `Refinement`).

3.2 Static Semantics

In the previous subsection, we identified criteria targeting the comparison of syntactic concepts. Here we elaborate on criteria relevant for checking the static semantics of inheritance. These criteria reflect the following semantic constraints: (i) incompatibility of input and output elements of subrules and superrules in terms of type and number, (ii) non-instantiability of abstract classes, (iii) ambiguities in rule definitions, and (iv) conflicts in multiple inheritance.

Incompatibility of Input and Output Elements. In the context of transformation rules, both feature assignments and conditions should be inheritable to subrules. Thus, it has to be ensured that the *types* of the input and output elements of subrules have at least the features of the types of the elements of the superrule. Thus, types of the input and output elements of a subrule might become more specific than those of the overridden rule. The inheritance hierarchy of the transformation rules must therefore have the same structure as the inheritance hierarchy of the MMs. This means that co-variance for input and output elements is demanded, conforming to the principle of *specialization inheritance* in object-oriented programming. This is in contrast to popular design rules for object-oriented programming languages, where a contra-variant refinement of input parameters and a co-variant refinement of output parameters of methods is required to yield type substitutability, also known as *specification inheritance* [12]. Additionally, the *number* of input and output elements should be extensible. Therefore, four cases of potential variations of input elements in type and number can be distinguished:

- **Same number, different types (a).** As an example, Fig. 4(a) shows two rules A2X and B2Y that are bound to the source base classes A and B and to the target base classes X and Y, where both rules simply copy the contained features. Since source class C inherits from both classes A and B and the target class Z from the classes X and Y, the rule C2Z may inherit from the rules A2X and B2Y. Thus, the feature assignments of the superrules are reused (cf. grey assignments in Fig. 4(a)).
- **Same number, equal (source or target) types (b).** This case (cf. Fig. 4(b)) may be counterintuitive, since inheritance is usually used to

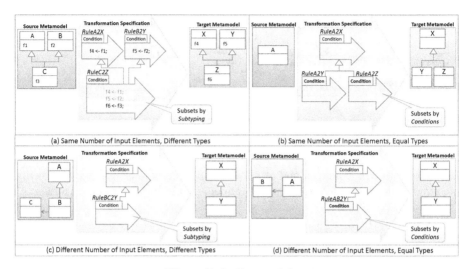

Fig. 4. Rule Compatibility

specialize some core behavior for subsets of instances, and subtypes are typically used to construct these subsets. In this case – at first sight – no subsets (according to *specialization inheritance*) are built, and it is unclear which rule should be executed for a combination of instances. Therefore, the subsets needed must be built by applying corresponding disjoint conditions to the subrules in case of equal source types. In case the target type remains equal, feature assignments refer to target elements of the superrule. These scenarios occur if either the source or the target metamodel makes use of inheritance.

- **Different number, different types (c).** Here, the subsets needed are built through the specialization of at least one input element (cf. Fig. 4(c)).
- **Different number, equal types (d).** In this case, only the number of input or output elements is extended, but the types of elements bound in subrules remain the same. Thereby, the same problem as in case (b) arises, where the subsets must be realized by means of conditions which may require certain relationships between the matched input elements (cf. Fig. 4(d)).

One interesting question in the context of cases (b) and (d) is whether the instances that do not fulfill any of the conditions of the subrules are matched by the superrule (provided that the superrule is concrete). Since this question is closely related to dynamic semantics, we further discuss it in Section 3.3.

Non-Instantiability of Abstract Classes. Since abstract classes cannot be instantiated, it must be ensured statically that no concrete rule tries to create instances of an abstract target class as output. Only abstract rules are allowed in this case, since they are not themselves executed but must be refined by a subrule. The situation is different for abstract source classes: although an abstract source class cannot have any direct instances, indirect instances may be affected by the transformation rule.

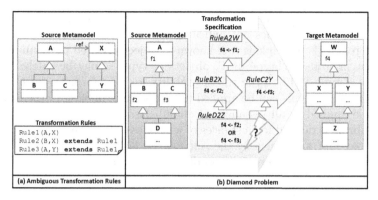

Fig. 5. Examples of Static Constraints: (a) Rule Ambiguity and (b) Diamond Problem

Ambiguities in Rule Definitions. An ambiguity between inheriting transformation rules may arise if a rule requires multiple input elements, and if there is no single rule for which the match in run-time types is closer than all the other rules. This is analogous to the problem that arises in multiple dispatching as needed for multi-methods (cf. [1,6]), since choosing a method requires the run-time type not of a *single* input element, but of a *set* of input elements. Thus, the method whose run-time types most closely match the statically specified types should be dispatched at run-time. A simple example of such a problem is depicted in Fig. 5(a). Three transformation rules are specified taking two input elements of different MM types, respectively. Now, suppose that a pair of instances (b,y) of type B and Y is transformed, and let us assume that the rules might also match indirect instances. The transformation engine should now look for a rule whose arguments *most closely match* the pair (b,y). In this case, no single rule can be determined, since **Rule2** and **Rule3** are equally good matches. Thus, the set of defined transformation rules is ambiguous.

Conflicts in Multiple Inheritance. The *diamond problem* [16], also referred to as *fork-join* inheritance [15], arises, when contradicting assignments are inherited via different inheritance paths. Consider, for instance, the common superrule A2W in Fig. 5(b), which contains an assignment for copying a feature value. This assignment is overridden within the transformation rules B2X and C2Y. Thus, it cannot be decided in the rule D2Z which assignment should be applied, unless assistance is given by the transformation designer.

3.3 Dynamic Semantics

Now we shift our focus from static to dynamic semantics, i.e., how transformation specifications may be interpreted at run-time. In this context, two main aspects are investigated: (i) which rules apply to which instances, i.e., *dispatch semantics* and (ii) how a set of inheriting rules gets executed, i.e., *execution semantics*.

Dispatch Semantics. In order to execute transformation specifications, it must be determined which rules apply to which instances, i.e., transformation rules must be dispatched for source model instances. In [7], potential strategies and scheduling variations of rules were discussed, but without any focus on inheritance. Thus, literature does not indicate, whether *type substitutability* should be considered. This principle is well-known in object-oriented programming and states that, if S is a subtype of T, objects of type T may be safely replaced by objects of type S [12]. Type substitutability for transformation rules would, thus, mean that if a rule can be applied to all instances of class T, then this rule can also be applied to all instances of all subclasses of T. Consequently, if no specific subrule is defined for instances of a subclass, then these instances of the subclass may be transformed by the rule defined for the superclass.

Concerning the evaluation of the condition two main strategies can be followed during dispatching. First, the condition is part of the matching process, i.e., if the condition fails, the rule is not applicable, but a superrule might be applied (*rule applicability* semantics). Second, the condition is not part of the matching process, i.e., the matching takes only place on the specified types of the input elements and thus, those elements, which do not fulfill the condition, are filtered, but never matched by a superrule anymore (*filter* semantics).

Execution Semantics. After having determined which rules are applicable to which source model instances, the question arises how a set of inheriting rules is executed. A first distinguishing criterion is, whether the concept of inheritance is directly supported by the execution engine or whether it is first flattened to ordinary transformation code in a pre-processing step. Independent of whether the inheritance hierarchy is flattened or not, various strategies may be applied to evaluate conditions and to execute assignments. This raises questions such as "Are conditions of a superrule also evaluated?" and "Are the assignments of a superrule executed before the assignments of a subrule?". Hence, we investigated the main characteristics of executing methods in an inheritance hierarchy in object-oriented programming [16]: (i) the *completion of the message lookup*, i.e., whether only the first matching method is executed (*asymmetric*) or all matching methods along the inheritance hierarchy are executed (*composing*), and (ii) the *direction of the message lookup*, i.e., whether a method lookup starts in the subclass (*descendant-driven*) or in the superclass (*parent-driven*).

4   Comparison of Transformation Languages

In this section we use the criteria introduced in the previous sections to compare inheritance support in model-to-model transformation languages. The results are based on a carefully developed test set, which includes at least one test case for each criterion. These documented test cases, including the example code, the MMs, and source models, can be downloaded from our project homepage[1].

Comparison Setup. For the comparison we considered common model-to-model transformation languages which offer dedicated inheritance support and allow relationships between source and target models to be specified in a declarative way. We examined the declarative subsets of the hybrid transformation

---

[1] http://www.modeltransformation.net

languages ATL (version 3.1.0) and ETL (version 0.9.0). There are different implementations of TGGs, whereby our comparison bases on the one of MOFLON. Although MOFLON's current implementation of the execution engine of TGGs (MOFLON 1.5.1) does not yet support inheritance, TGGs were included, since specific literature concerning inheritance support exists [10]. In order to compare the bidirectional TGG-based model transformation approach with the unidirectional languages ATL and ETL, we considered only the unidirectional forward translation. Although the QVT standard specifies the declarative transformation language QVT Relations, it is not included in this survey, since QVT Relations support only redefinition of whole rules, i.e., they do not allow the reuse of original rule definitions, and no inheritance between rules is offered, as is the focus of our framework. Actual mapping refinement is only mentioned in the QVT Core part, which leaves the transfer to QVT Relations open. Fig. 6 shows an example of the differences between the languages when transforming UML Statemachines into Petri Nets. The rule `State2Place` transforms `State` instances that are not of the kind `initial` into corresponding `Place` instances, while inheriting from the rule `ModelElem2Element`, which specifies the `name` assignment.

Table 1. Comparison of Syntax

Rule Part	Values	ATL	ETL	TGGs
Input Elements	1 | 1...n	1..n	1	1..n
Output Elements	1 | 1...n	1..n	1..n	1..n
Condition	Yes | No	Yes	Yes	Yes
Type of Rule Inheritance	Single | Multiple	Single	Multiple	Multiple
Abstract Rules	Yes | No	Yes	Yes	Yes
Refinement Modes of Assignments	Override | Inherit | Merge | Extend	Override (implicit)	Override (implicit)	Extend

4.1   Comparison of Syntax

When comparing the supported language features (cf. Table 1), differences in the *number of allowed input elements* can be detected. Whereas ATL (multiple elements in `from` pattern) and TGGs (source object graph) allow several input elements to be bound to a rule, this is not possible in ETL (cf. single variable after `transform` keyword in Fig. 6). However, all of the languages evaluated support multiple *output elements* (multiple elements in `to` pattern in ATL and ETL, target object graph in TGGs). Finally, all transformation languages allow for the specification of *conditions* (OCL expressions in ATL and TGGs, and a `guard` in ETL). ETL and TGGs support multiple inheritance, whereas ATL is restricted to single inheritance (keyword `extends` in ATL and ETL, inheritance arrow on type level of TGGs). All languages provide means to define abstract rules (keyword `abstract` in ATL, annotation `@abstract` in ETL, property `abstract` in TGGs). Finally, concerning potential *refinement modes of assignments*, none

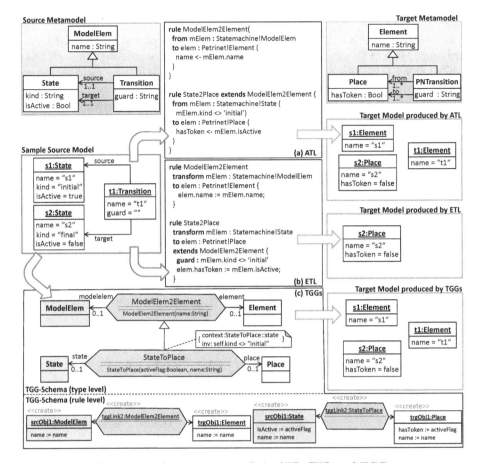

Fig. 6. Transformation example in ATL, ETL and TGGs

of the approaches evaluated provide specific keywords for explicitly choosing the semantics to be applied. Instead, ATL and ETL implicitly assume *override* semantics, and TGGs support the refinement mode *extend* since only new assignments may be added, but existing ones must not be modified.

In summary, all of the approaches evaluated support similar syntactic concepts in terms of inheritance. The main differences lie in the type of inheritance supported and the implicitly assumed refinement modes of assignments.

4.2   Comparison of Static Semantics

This part of the comparison evaluates to which extent the static semantics of inheritance is checked in each transformation language (cf. Table 2). Concerning *input and output elements*, in ATL a violation of co-variance is detected at run-time, since missing features result in a "feature not found" exception. In ETL no error is reported, and a target model with invalid features is created. In TGGs

Table 2. Comparison of Static Semantics with respect to Inheritance

Verification Target	Fault	Values	ATL	ETL	TGGs
Input Elements	Non-co-variant Type Change	[Compile-Time|Run-Time|No] Error	Run-Time Error	No Error (invalid target model)	Compile-Time Error
	Restriction in Number	[Compile-Time|Run-Time|No] Error	Run-Time Error (also with extension)	n.a. (cf. syntax)	Compile-Time Error
Output Elements	Non-co-variant Type Change	[Compile-Time|Run-Time|No] Error	Run-Time Error	No Error (invalid target model)	Compile-Time Error
	Restriction in Number	[Compile-Time|Run-Time|No] Error	n.a. (output elements are still produced even if not specified again)	Run-Time Error	Compile-Time Error (except of output to input modification)
Abstract Target Classes	Concrete Rules for Abstract Target Classes	[Compile-Time|Run-Time|No] Error	Run-Time Error	Run-Time Error	Run-Time Error (application fails)
Rule Ambiguity		[Compile-Time|Run-Time|No] Error	No Error (first matching rule in file wins)	n.a. (cf. syntax)	Run-Time Error
Diamond Problem		[Compile-Time|Run-Time|No] Error	n.a. (cf. syntax)	Compile-Time Error	Compile-Time Error

this results in a compile-time error in the upcoming implementation, since the main principle is that applying the subrule should guarantee the existence of the subgraph created by the superrule. Concerning the number of input elements, in ATL a run-time error also occurs, if the number is changed in any way, i.e., ATL prohibits to extend number of input elements. ATL does not raise any exception if the number of output elements is restricted, since they are produced even if they are not respecified. In ETL, the restriction of the number of input elements is not applicable, since ETL restricts the number of input elements to exactly one anyway. In ETL a run-time error ("index out of bound" exception) is raised if the number of output elements is restricted. In TGGs, to conform to the main principle that applying the subrule should guarantee the existence of the subgraph created by the superrule, only an extension of the number of input and output elements is allowed, which is again ensured statically.

None of the languages evaluated detect *concrete rules referencing abstract classes* at compile-time, but run-time errors are thrown. ATL does not throw exceptions for *ambiguous rule definitions* – neither at compile-time nor at run-time. Instead, the first matching rule defined in the file is executed. In ETL, the problem of ambiguous rule definitions cannot arise, since multiple input elements are not supported. In TGGs, a run-time error is thrown. It must be noted that in the area of multi-methods, there are approaches for explicit disambiguation (e.g., [3] proposes a minimal set of method redefinitions necessary for disambiguation), which could be reused in transformation languages. The *diamond problem in multiple inheritance* does not apply to ATL, since multiple inheritance is not supported. Although the diamond problem is detected in ETL at compile-time, it is checked on a coarse-grained level, i.e., diamonds that do not include ambiguous assignments also cause errors. In TGGs, this problem is checked statically. Analogously to the explicit disambiguation of rule definitions, the transformation designer could be supported by proposals which assignments must be overridden in order to achieve unambiguous assignment definitions.

In summary, ATL and ETL provide limited support for static inheritance checks. Only the diamond problem gets statically checked by ETL. In contrast, the TGG-related publication lists a number of static checks that will be considered in the upcoming implementation of rule inheritance.

4.3   Comparison of Dynamic Semantics

In order to compare the dynamic semantics, the *dispatch semantics* and the *execution semantics* are investigated (cf. Table 3). Considering the *dispatch semantics*, one can see that the output models produced by ATL and TGGs (Fig. 6(a) and (c)) include only one `Place` instance, since only the `State` s2 fulfills the specified condition in the subrule. As ATL and TGGs support *type substitutability* and *rule applicability* semantics for conditions, instance s1 is matched by the more general superrule `ModelElem2Element`, and therefore creates the target `Element` s1. Also the indirect instance t1 is matched by the superrule, and therefore the target `Element` t1 is created. In contrast, ETL does not support *type substitutability* by default. Thus, although the specifications in ETL and ATL are syntactically similar, the produced target models are quite different. ETL's target model contains only a `Place` s2 produced by the rule `State2Place`. The dispatch semantics may be modified by annotating rules with `@greedy` in ETL. Such rules also match indirect instances, but the interpretation is different to ATL and TGGs, since the superrule still regards all instances irrespective of whether the instances have already been matched by subrules or not. Adding the `@greedy` annotation to the rule `ModelElem2Element` in our example would therefore create four instances in total: three `Elements` s1, s2, and t1 produced by the superrule `ModelElem2Element`, and one `Place` s2 produced by the subrule `State2Place`. Even if type substitutability is enabled in ETL, the result of the condition evaluation does not influence the dispatch semantics because the superrule always matches all direct and indirect instances, disregarding subrules.

Regarding the inheritance support in the engine, in ATL inherited rules are flattened during compilation and can thus use optimization strategies, i.e., the

Table 3. Comparison of Dynamic Semantics of Inheritance

	Criterion	Subcriterion	Values	ATL	ETL	TGGs
	Dispatch semantics	Type Substitutability	Yes | No	Yes	User-Definable	Yes
		Condition Semantics	Filter | Rule Applicability	Rule Applicability	n.a.	Rule Applicability
Execution Semantics	Inheritance Support	-	Flattened | Direct engine support	Flattened	Direct engine support	n.a. (since flattened in patterns already)
	Condition	Completion of lookup	Asymmetric | Composing	Composing	Composing	Composing (by copy)
		Direction of lookup	Parent-driven | Descendent-driven	Parent-driven	Descendent-driven	n.a.
	Assignments	Completion of lookup	Asymmetric | Composing	Optimized Composing	Composing	Composing (by copy)
		Direction of lookup	Parent-driven | Descendent-driven	Descendent-driven	Parent-driven	n.a.

ATL compiler inlines the assignments of a superrule. In contrast, ETL supports inheritance in the execution engine, which reduces the amount of code generated. In TGGs, this criterion is not applicable, since an inheriting TGG rule contains a copy of the superrules, which causes code duplication. Concerning the evaluation of the *conditions*, all transformation languages we compared exhibit a *composing* completion of the lookup, i.e., an instance processed by a subrule must fulfill all the specified conditions up the inheritance hierarchy. The actual evaluation is parent-driven in ATL and descendent-driven in ETL. In TGGs, this criterion is not applicable, since a subrule lists all its inherited conditions. Concerning *assignments* the same strategy as for conditions is applied. Thus, in ATL (i) the assignments of the superrule, which are not overridden, (ii) the overridden assignments, and (iii) new assignments specified in the subrule are executed realizing the optimization strategy. In contrast, in ETL, (i) the assignments of the superrule, and (ii) the assignments of the subrule are executed. In TGGs this is again not applicable. More specifically, TGGs enforce composition already in the syntax, which causes code duplication.

In summary, the main difference in terms of dynamic semantics lies in the application of type substitutability, which is user-definable in ETL, but interpreted in a different way than in ATL and TGGs. ETL has the disadvantage that several target instances for a single source instance are created when a superrule is annotated with @greedy. Moreover, all of the transformation languages implement a *composing* behavior for conditions and assignments. Thus, the lookup direction does not influence the result of the transformation.

4.4   Lessons Learned

This subsection presents lessons learned from our comparison.

Similar Syntax, Different Semantics. As the example in Fig. 6 reveals, similar syntax (cf. ATL and ETL) does not necessarily lead to the same results, which implies different dynamic semantics. This is undesirable, since the dynamic semantics is not made explicit by any syntactical elements to the transformation designer. Thus, the transformation designer must know the design decisions taken in each transformation language in order to obtain the desired result. Therefore, the current situation concerning rule inheritance is comparable to the situation in the early stages of object-oriented programming, where no common agreements on the dynamic semantics of inheritance had been reached.

Limited Support for Static Semantics. Currently, support for checking the static semantics is limited. This gives rise to run-time errors or – even worse – to erroneous target instances with no error message. Thus, the tedious task of checking the static semantics is left entirely to the transformation designer.

Fixed Dynamic Semantics. As introduced above, different kinds of refinement modes may be desirable. The evaluation of the languages has shown, that each of them assumes a certain refinement mode, but none of them allows the transformation designer to choose between different options. Thus, the languages support only fixed dynamic semantics for rule inheritance. Since different dynamic semantics are suitable for different transformation scenarios, the transformation designer should be enabled to alter the dynamic semantics. The introduction of a **super** reference as in object-oriented programming languages would enable the transformation designer to express different refinement modes.

Consequences for Transformation Interoperability. The discovered differences in the interpretation of inheritance lead to profound consequences for transformation development, and thus, for transformation interoperability. Concerning ATL, the main restriction is the support for single inheritance only. Although multiple inheritance can be achieved by simulation, this leads to code duplication reducing the advantages of the concept of inheritance significantly. In contrast, although TGGs and ETL allow for multiple inheritance, they exhibit other intricacies. In case of TGGs, assignments are duplicated in any case. ETL provides a different interpretation of type substitutability, leading to redundant instances. Thus, transformation interoperability demands for a detailed knowledge to achieve exactly the same outcome of a transformation expressed in different transformation languages.

5   Related Work

This section considers two threads of related work. First, we focus on inheritance support in transformation languages, and second, since inheritance is mainly a reuse mechanism, we broaden the scope to other reuse facilities.

Inheritance Support in Transformation Languages. Although inheritance plays a vital role in object-oriented modeling, and thus also in model transformations, no dedicated survey exists to the best of our knowledge. Only a small number of publications mention inheritance explicitly. Inheritance support in ATL is briefly described in [9], and that in ETL in [11], but rather on a syntactical level, while the actual execution semantics are left open. A detailed discussion of static semantics that must be considered in TGG rule inheritance may be found in [10]. For graph transformations in general, Bardohl et. al [4] introduced type substitutability when executing graph transformation rules, i.e., (abstract) supertypes may be used in patterns which are then applicable to subtypes at run-time. Finally, in the QVT standard [14] detailed semantics with respect to inheritance is defined only for QVT Operational.

Reuse Facilities in Model Transformations. General work has been done in composing transformations. Wagelaar et. al. [18] proposed a superimposition mechanism of transformations to build the union of all transformation rules. Thereby rules can be added and redefined (i.e., replacing a rule by a new one), whereby it is impossible to refer to the original rule. This is similar to the mechanism in QVT Relations, in which a transformation can extend another transformation and redefine existing rules [14]. Another reuse mechanism is to provide predefined transformations that can be adapted to specific MMs. Varró et al. [17] introduced generic transformations in VIATRA2 which in fact resembles the concept of templates in programming languages. Another approach to generic transformations was proposed in [8], where transformations are designed between generic "concepts models". These transformations can be bound to concrete MMs, but only if they have the same structure. Finally, Wimmer et. al. [19] presented mapping operators which allow to specify model transformations by means of reusable components, similar to mappings known in data engineering.

In summary, only basic approaches for reuse are available, which confront the transformation designer with code duplication and maintenance problems.

6 Conclusion and Future Work

In this paper, we have presented a systematic comparison of inheritance support in the transformation languages ATL, ETL, and TGGs. We (i) identified syntactic concepts required for inheritance, (ii) elaborated on static semantics that should be checked between inheriting rules, and (iii) investigated potential dynamic semantics of rule inheritance. Thus, the design rationales behind the realizations have been made explicit. Since we have considered declarative model-to-model transformations only, future work will comprise an investigation of inheritance support in imperative transformation languages, including also the imperative parts of hybrid transformation languages.

References

1. Agrawal, R., Demichiel, L.G., Lindsay, B.G.: Static Type Checking of Multi-Methods. In: Proc. of OOPSLA 1991, pp. 113–128 (1991)
2. Aho, A., Sethi, R., Ullman, J.: Compilers: Principles, Techniques,and Tools. Addison-Wesley, Reading (1986)
3. Amiel, E., Dujardin, E.: Supporting explicit disambiguation of multi-methods. In: Cointe, P. (ed.) ECOOP 1996. LNCS, vol. 1098, pp. 167–188. Springer, Heidelberg (1996)
4. Bardohl, R., Ehrig, H., de Lara, J., Taentzer, G.: Integrating Meta-modelling Aspects with Graph Transformation for Efficient Visual Language Definition and Model Manipulation. In: Wermelinger, M., Margaria-Steffen, T. (eds.) FASE 2004. LNCS, vol. 2984, pp. 214–228. Springer, Heidelberg (2004)
5. Bézivin, J.: On the Unification Power of Models. SoSyM Journal 4(2) (2005)
6. Chambers, C.: Object-Oriented Multi-Methods in Cecil. In: ECOOP 1992. LNCS, vol. 615, pp. 33–56. Springer, Heidelberg (1992)
7. Czarnecki, K., Helsen, S.: Feature-based Survey of Model Transformation Approaches. IBM Systems Journal 45(3), 621–645 (2006)
8. de Lara, J., Guerra, E.: Generic meta-modelling with concepts, templates and mixin layers. In: Petriu, D.C., Rouquette, N., Haugen, Ø. (eds.) MODELS 2010. LNCS, vol. 6394, pp. 16–30. Springer, Heidelberg (2010)
9. Jouault, F., Kurtev, I.: Transforming Models with ATL. In: Proc. of the Model Transformations in Practice Workshop (2005)
10. Klar, F., Königs, A., Schürr, A.: Model transformation in the large. In: Proc. of ESEC-FSE 2007, pp. 285–294 (2007)
11. Kolovos, D., Paige, R., Polack, F.: The epsilon transformation language. In: Proc. of ICMT 2008, pp. 46–60 (2008)

12. Liskov, B., Wing, J.M.: A new definition of the subtype relation. In: Cardelli, L. (ed.) ECOOP 2003. LNCS, vol. 2743, pp. 118–141. Springer, Heidelberg (2003)
13. Ma, H., Shao, W., Zhang, L., Ma, Z., Jiang, Y.: Applying OO metrics to assess UML meta-models. In: Baar, T., Strohmeier, A., Moreira, A., Mellor, S.J. (eds.) UML 2004. LNCS, vol. 3273, pp. 12–26. Springer, Heidelberg (2004)
14. OMG. Meta Object Facility (MOF) 2.0 Query/View/Transformation Specification (2009), http://www.omg.org/spec/QVT/1.1/Beta2/PDF/
15. Sakkinen, M.: Disciplined Inheritance. In: Proc. of ECOOP 1989, pp. 39–56 (1989)
16. Taivalsaari, A.: On the notion of inheritance. ACM Comput. Surv. 28(3), 438–479 (1996)
17. Varró, D., Pataricza, A.: Generic and meta-transformations for model transformation engineering. In: Baar, T., Strohmeier, A., Moreira, A., Mellor, S.J. (eds.) UML 2004. LNCS, vol. 3273, pp. 290–304. Springer, Heidelberg (2004)
18. Wagelaar, D., Van Der Straeten, R., Deridder, D.: Module superimposition: a composition technique for rule-based model transformation languages. SoSyM Journal 9, 285–309 (2010)
19. Wimmer, M., Kappel, G., Kusel, A., Retschitzegger, W., Schoenboeck, J., Schwinger, W.: Surviving the heterogeneity jungle with composite mapping operators. In: Tratt, L., Gogolla, M. (eds.) ICMT 2010. LNCS, vol. 6142, pp. 260–275. Springer, Heidelberg (2010)

Model-Driven Development of Model Transformations

Kevin Lano and Shekoufeh Kolahdouz-Rahimi

Dept. of Informatics, King's College London, Strand, London, UK
kevin.lano@kcl.ac.uk

Abstract. In this paper we define a systematic model-driven development process for model transformations based on a precise semantics. We illustrate this process by applying it to the development and verification of the UML to relational database transformation.

1 Introduction

Model transformations are a key element of model-driven development (MDD), yet paradoxically, MDD has not itself been generally applied to systematically specify, design and evolve model transformations. At present, construction of model transformations is focussed upon the implementation of a transformation in a particular model transformation language [4], the transformation is typically described only at a relatively low level of abstraction, without a separate specification. Although languages such as QVT-R [11] and ATL [5] are declarative in style, they define transformations in terms of collections of individual transformation rules, and it may be very difficult to deduce the global effect of the transformation from these rules, which may be applied in many different alternative orders, or even concurrently.

The large number of different transformation languages also creates problems of migration and reuse of transformations from one language to another.

The solution which we propose to these problems is to adopt a general model-driven software development approach, based on UML and MOF, for model transformation development. UML provides the necessary specification notations for model transformation definition, at different levels of abstraction, and there exists established formal semantics for parts of the language [8] to support verification and the synthesis of executable code. Rule-based implementations can be used for convenience, but are additionally supported by global specifications, to provide a basis for analysis and verification of the transformation prior to implementation.

Section 2 describes the QVT-R version of the UML class diagram to relational database transformation, and the semantic problems with this transformation. Section 3 defines a general semantics for model transformations and defines concepts of correctness for model transformations. Section 4 describes the steps of our model transformation development process using UML. Section 5 describes the application of the process to the specification and design of the UML to

J. Cabot and E. Visser (Eds.): ICMT 2011, LNCS 6707, pp. 47–61, 2011.

relational database case study. Finally in Section 6 we compare our development method with other proposals for model transformation development.

2   The UML to Relational Database Model Transformation

This transformation is a well-known PIM to PSM mapping, used to map class diagram data models into data models for storage of data in a relational database. Figure 1 shows the two metamodels.

Specifications of the transformation have been defined in a number of different model transformation languages. Here we will consider the QVT-R specification of this transformation [11]. This version has a number of problems, which also occur in other specifications of the transformation:

- No logical constraints of the source or target languages are expressed, for example that cycles of inheritance cannot occur in the source language, and that the columns of a table must have distinct names, for the target language.
- There is no global specification of the transformation itself, it is defined only by individual rules.
- Without source and target language constraints, and without a global specification, it is difficult to formulate any correctness property for the transformation. The property "any model of the source language can be transformed to a model of the target language by application of the rules" fails because of non-termination issues: circularity in inheritance, or in the embedding of one class as the type of an attribute of another can lead to unbounded recursion in the rules as presented.
- It is not clear that the rules are confluent. Some rules are not complete because they do not set the *kind* attribute of created elements of the target model.
- If the source language is strengthened with constraints to exclude circularity in inheritance or embedding, and the target language is strengthened by the unique column names constraint, then the target constraint is not ensured by the rules: individual classes may have same-named attributes, or duplicate-named columns may be introduced by the rules.
- The transformation does not introduce foreign keys to represent implicit sub-associations of an association: if association r is directed from class C to class E, then there are also implicit associations to E induced by r on each subclass D of C, but these are not represented.
- A more subtle difficulty is that the transformation irrevocably loses information from the source model, even though it is intended as a refinement (towards implementation of a data model in a specific platform). In particular, the inheritance relation of the source model cannot be recovered from the transformed model, the mapping is non-injective in this respect.

The problems present in this one example are typical of current model transformation definitions: inadequate precision in defining source and target languages, particularly language constraints; the absence of a global specification of the transformation effect; the lack of proof of termination or confluence; no proof of basic syntactic or semantic correctness.

Similar problems are present in other specifications of the transformation, for example in the Viatra specification [13], the transformation may also introduce columns with duplicate names and does not deal with inheritance.

In the following sections, we describe how these issues can be addressed and solved, by using model-driven development for model transformations, based upon a formal semantics for UML and model transformations.

3   Semantic Framework for Model Transformations

3.1   Metamodelling Framework

We will consider transformations between languages specified using the Meta-Object Framework (MOF). This has four levels, with level M0 being the domain of run-time instances, M1 being the domain of user models such as specific class diagrams, M2 is the level of language definitions such as the class diagram language, and M3 is the domain of metamodelling notations, such as EMOF (Essential MOF) [12]. At each level, a model or structure can be considered to be an instance of a structure at the next higher level.

In discussing model transformation correctness, we will refer to the M2 level as the *language level* (the models define the languages which the transformation relates) and to the M1 level as the *model level* (the models which the transformation operates upon).

For each model M at levels M2 and M3, we can define (i) a logical language $\mathcal{L}_M$ that corresponds to M, and (ii) a logical theory Γ_M in $\mathcal{L}_M$, which defines the semantic meaning of M, including any internal constraints of M. If an M1 model is also a UML model, it can also be assigned such a language and theory. These are defined using the axiomatic semantics for UML given in Chapter 6 of [8], based upon structured theories and theory morphisms in a real-time temporal logic.

$\mathcal{L}_M$ consists of type symbols for each type defined in M, including primitive types such as integers, reals, booleans and strings which are normally included in models, and each classifier defined in M. There are attribute symbols $att(c : C) : T$ for each property att of type T in the feature set of C. There are attributes $\overline{C}$ to denote the instances of each classifier C (corresponding to $C.allInstances()$ in the UML object constraint language (OCL)), and action symbols $op(c : C, p : P)$ for each operation $op(p : P)$ in the features of C [7]. Collection types and operations on these and the primitive types are also included. The OCL logical operators *and*, *implies*, *forAll*, *exists* are interpreted as $\wedge$, $\Rightarrow$, $\forall$, $\exists$.

A structure interpreting $\mathcal{L}_M$ can therefore be considered as a tuple $(T_i, \overline{E_j}, f_k)$ of type interpretations, entity interpretations and feature interpretations.

Γ_M includes axioms expressing the multiplicities of association ends, the mutual inverse property of opposite association ends, deletion propagation through composite aggregations, the existence of generalisation relations, and the logical semantics of any explicit constraints in M. Structures for $\mathcal{L}_M$ which satisfy Γ_M are termed *models* of M.

For a sentence φ in $\mathcal{L}_M$, there is the usual notion of logical consequence:

$$\Gamma_M \vdash \varphi$$

means the sentence is provable from the theory of M, and so holds in M. $\vdash_L$ is used to emphasise that the deduction takes place within language L.

If M is at the M1 level and is an instance of a language L at the M2 level, then it satisfies all the properties of Γ_L, although these cannot be expressed within $\mathcal{L}_M$ itself. We use the notation $M \models \varphi$ to express satisfaction of an $\mathcal{L}_L$ sentence φ in M.

3.2 Model Transformation Semantics

Model transformations can be regarded as relations between models, in the same or in different modelling languages. Let $\mathcal{L}_1$ and $\mathcal{L}_2$ be the source and target languages. We assume these are defined as metamodels using MOF. A transformation τ then describes which models M_1 of $\mathcal{L}_1$ correspond to (transform to) which models M_2 of $\mathcal{L}_2$.

$Models_{\mathcal{L}}$ denotes the set of structures for $\mathcal{L}$ which interpret the language (metamodel) $\mathcal{L}$ and satisfy ($\models$) any logical properties defined for $\mathcal{L}$.

A model transformation τ from language $\mathcal{L}_1$ to language $\mathcal{L}_2$ can therefore be expressed as an element in the space $Models_{\mathcal{L}_1} \leftrightarrow Models_{\mathcal{L}_2}$ of relations between $Models_{\mathcal{L}_1}$ and $Models_{\mathcal{L}_2}$:

$$Rel_\tau : Models_{\mathcal{L}_1} \leftrightarrow Models_{\mathcal{L}_2}$$

3.3 Model Transformation Correctness

We can precisely define different criteria for correctness as follows for a model transformation τ from $\mathcal{L}_1$ to $\mathcal{L}_2$:

Representation. For each model which conforms to (is a model in the language) $\mathcal{L}_1$, and to which the transformation can be applied, the transformed model is a structure for $\mathcal{L}_2$, but may not satisfy its constraints:

$$\forall M_1 : Models_{\mathcal{L}_1};\ M_2 \cdot Rel_\tau(M_1, M_2)\ \Rightarrow\ M_2 \text{ is a structure for } \mathcal{L}_2$$

Syntactic correctness. For each model of $\mathcal{L}_1$, and to which the transformation can be applied, the transformed model is a model of $\mathcal{L}_2$:

$$\forall M_1 : Models_{\mathcal{L}_1};\ M_2 \cdot Rel_\tau(M_1, M_2)\ \Rightarrow\ M_2 : Models_{\mathcal{L}_2}$$

Semantic correctness

1. (Language-level correctness): each language-level property $\varphi : \mathcal{L}_{\mathcal{L}_1}$ satisfied by source model M_1 is also satisfied, under an interpretation χ on language-level expressions, in M_2:

$$\forall M_1 : Models_{\mathcal{L}_1};\ M_2 : Models_{\mathcal{L}_2} \cdot$$
$$Rel_\tau(M_1, M_2)\ \wedge\ M_1 \models \varphi\ \Rightarrow\ M_2 \models \chi(\varphi)$$

This shows that $\mathcal{L}_2$ is at least as expressive as $\mathcal{L}_1$, and that users of M_2 can continue to view it as a model of $\mathcal{L}_1$, because the data of M_1 can be expressed in terms of that of M_2. In particular, no information about M_1 is lost by τ.

2. (Model-level correctness): each model-level property $\varphi : \mathcal{L}_{M_1}$ of a source model M_1 is also true, under an interpretation ζ on model-level expressions, in M_2:

$$\forall\, M_1 : Models_{\mathcal{L}_1};\ M_2 : Models_{\mathcal{L}_2}.$$
$$Rel_\tau(M_1, M_2)\ \wedge\ \Gamma_{M_1} \vdash \varphi\ \Rightarrow\ \Gamma_{M_2} \vdash \zeta(\varphi)$$

for $\varphi \in \Gamma_{M_1}$.

This means that internal constraints of M_1 remain valid in interpreted form in M_2, for example, that subclassing in a UML model is mapped to subsetting of sets of table primary key values, in the transformation from UML to relational databases.

Representation is the most basic notion of correctness, but more advanced degrees of correctness are essential for business-critical transformations.

An important design property of a transformation is *confluence*: if different orders of application of transformation rules to a model are possible, the resulting models should be the same regardless of the order of applications.

4   Model-Driven Development Process for Model Transformations

A general model-driven development process for model transformations is as follows:

Requirements. The requirements of the transformation are defined in terms of the source and target metamodels, including which constraints need to be established (*Ens*) or preserved (*Pres*) by the transformation, and what assumptions (*Asm*) can be made about the input models. A use case diagram can be used to describe the top-level capabilities of the system, and non-functional requirements can be identified.

Abstract Specification. This formalises the requirements as constraints (in a language such as OCL). Constraints can be used to define the overall relation Rel_τ between source and target models for each use case (transformation). The precondition of a transformation (considered as a single operation) is defined as a predicate *Asm*, and the postcondition as a predicate *Cons*, both *Asm* and *Cons* may be expressed in the union of the languages of the source and target models. *Asm* defines the domain of Rel_τ, and *Cons* defines which pairs of models are in Rel_τ. Diagrams in the concrete syntax of the source and target languages can be used to explain the key aspects of this relation, as in the CGT model transformation approach [3].

It should be possible to show at this stage that *Cons* establishes the required properties *Ens* of the result models (ie., syntactic correctness):

$$Cons, \Gamma_{L1} \vdash_{\mathcal{L}_{L1 \cup L2}} Ens$$

where $L1$ is the source language, $L2$ the target language.

Likewise, *Cons* should prove that *Pres* are preserved, via a suitable interpretation χ from the source language to the target language (language-level semantic correctness):

$$Cons, Pres, \Gamma_{L1} \vdash_{\mathcal{L}_{L1 \cup L2}} \chi(Pres)$$

It should be checked that *Cons* is implementable. If *Cons* has the form of a conjunction of implications

$$s : S_i \text{ and } SCond_{i,j} \text{ implies } \exists t : T_{i,j} \cdot TCond_{i,j} \text{ and } Post_{i,j}$$

involving source language entities S_i and target language entities $T_{i,j}$, and is consistent, then there is a phased implementation of *Cons* if all the conditions are implementable, and the T_i can be ordered so that entities are defined only in terms of entities lower in the order than themselves, in the succedents of the implications.

Explicit Specification and Design. The transformation can be broken down into phases, each with its own source and target language and specification. Phases should be independent of each other, except that the assumptions of a non-initial phase should be ensured by the preceeding phase(s).

For each phase, define transformation rules (as operations specified by pre/postconditions), and an activity to specify the order of execution of the rules. For each phase, verification that the activity combination of the rules satisfies the overall specification of the phase can be carried out. It can also be checked that the rule operations are deterministic and well-defined, and that the activities are confluent and terminating under the precondition of the phase. Finally, it should be checked that the composition of the phases achieves the specified relation *Cons* and required property preservation/establishment conditions of the overall transformation:

$$\Gamma_{L1} \vdash_{\mathcal{L}_{L1 \cup L2}} Asm \Rightarrow [activity] Cons$$

where *activity* is the design decomposition of the transformation into phases. $[stat]P$ is the weakest precondition of predicate P with respect to statement/activity *stat* (Chapter 6 of [8]).

The relative independence of particular rules and phases will enhance the possibilities for reuse of these in other transformations.

Implementation. Code can be produced in a particular transformation implementation language, such as Java, ATL or Kermeta. Different phases can be implemented in different languages.

The emphasis in this development approach is on simplicity and verifiability. Even if fully formal verification is not attempted, the decomposition of a transformation into phases and activities supports the systematic composition of local pre/post specifications of individual rules to establish the specifications of phases and then of the complete transformation. The specification of the transformation can be used (independently of the details of phases) to prove the required preservation and establishment properties of the use case corresponding to the transformation.

5   Case Study: UML to Relational Database Refinement

Figure 1 shows the metamodels of the source language $L1$ and target language $L2$ of this transformation. We will carry out all reasoning in this example directly upon OCL constraints, rather than upon the formal semantics of these constraints. Such reasoning can be recast in a fully formal version.

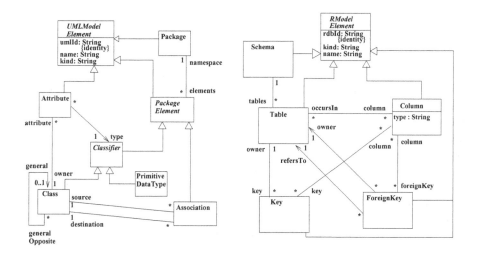

Fig. 1. UML to relational database transformation metamodels

5.1   Requirements

The requirements of the case study consist of the metamodels, and two use cases, one to check the validity of the source model and the other to carry out the mapping upon a valid model.

The assumptions $Asm1$ to $Asm10$ of the source language $L1$ are the following:

1. All associations have distinct names within their package. Associations are elements of the package of their source class.
2. All classifiers have distinct names within a package, distinct from any association name in the package.

3. The owned attributes of a class are uniquely named within their owner class and the classes it inherits.
4. There are no cycles of inheritance: $\forall c : Class \cdot c \notin c.general^+$, and the ancestors of a class are in the same package as it.
5. There is no multiple inheritance: $\forall c : Class \cdot c.general \rightarrow size() \leq 1$
6. All attributes are of a primitive data type:

$$\forall a : Attribute \cdot a.type : PrimitiveDataType$$

7. If a class is persistent so are all of its superclasses:

$$\forall c : Class \cdot c.kind = \text{`Persistent'} \; implies$$
$$\forall d : c.general \cdot d.kind = \text{`Persistent'}$$

8. If an association is persistent so are its end classes:

$$\forall a : Association \cdot a.kind = \text{`Persistent'} \; implies$$
$$a.source.kind = \text{`Persistent'} \; and \; a.destination.kind$$
$$= \text{`Persistent'}$$

9. The character "_" does not occur in any names of the source model.
10. Packages have unique names.

Assumptions 1, 2, 3, 4, 10 are usual constraints of UML class diagrams. Assumption 5 is implicitly made in the code of [11], we will consider below if it can be omitted. Assumption 6 is made because we consider that attributes of a class type should be represented as associations. Assumptions 7 and 8 are natural assumptions to make about the parts of a class diagram which are to be persistently stored.

The identity attribute *umlId* can be derived from the names of elements: for a package it is simply the name, for a package element it is *namespace.name* :: *name*, and for an attribute it is *owner.namespace.name* :: *owner.name* :: *name*.

The checking transformation has no assumptions, and should return *true* if the source model is valid (ie., it is a valid structure for $L1$, all metafeatures are defined and it satisfies the above assumptions), and *false* otherwise.

The mapping transformation has assumption *Asm* these validity conditions together with the emptiness of the target model: $RModelElement = \{\}$.

The following *Pres* property of the class diagram metamodel is to be preserved: that there are no cycles in the *general* relationship (*Asm4*).

There are three properties of the relational metamodel which should be ensured: *Ens1* is the constraint that the names of columns must be unique within each table, *Ens2* states that tables have unique names within a schema, and *Ens3* states that schemas have unique names within a model.

5.2   Abstract Specification

We will consider the mapping use case. The transformation relates attributes in the source model to columns in the target model with the same name, and likewise maps persistent classes to tables with keys, packages to schemas and persistent associations to foreign keys.

The formal specification *Cons* of the transformation as a single global relation between the source and target languages can be split into six core constraints:

C1. "For each persistent attribute in the source model there is a unique column in the target model, of corresponding type":

$$\forall\, a : Attribute \;\cdot\; a.owner.kind = \text{'}Persistent\text{'}\ implies$$
$$\exists_1\, cl : Column \cdot cl.rdbId = a.umlId\ and$$
$$cl.name = a.name\ and\ cl.kind = a.kind\ and$$
$$(a.type.name = \text{'}INTEGER\text{'}\ implies\ cl.type = \text{'}NUMBER\text{'})\ and$$
$$(a.type.name = \text{'}BOOLEAN\text{'}\ implies\ cl.type = \text{'}BOOLEAN\text{'})\ and$$
$$(a.type.name \neq \text{'}INTEGER\text{'}\ and\ a.type.name \neq \text{'}BOOLEAN\text{'}\ implies$$
$$cl.type = \text{'}VARCHAR\text{'})$$

C2. "For each persistent class in the source model, there is a unique table representing the class in the target model, with columns for each owned attribute":

$$\forall\, c : Class \;\cdot\; c.kind = \text{'}Persistent\text{'}\ implies$$
$$\exists_1\, t : Table \cdot t.rdbId = c.umlId\ and\ t.name = c.name\ and$$
$$t.kind = \text{'}Persistent\text{'}\ and$$
$$Column[c.attribute.umlId] \subseteq t.column$$

For a set x, the notation $Entity[x]$ refers to the set of *Entity* objects with primary key (in this case *rdbId*) value in x, it can be implemented in Java by maintaining a map from the key values to nodes. In OCL it would be expressed as

$$Entity.allInstances() \rightarrow select(x \rightarrow includes(id))$$

For a single value y, $Entity[y]$ denotes

$$Entity.allInstances() \rightarrow select(id\ =\ y) \rightarrow any()$$

C3. "For each root class in the source model there is a unique primary key in the target model":

$$\forall\, c : Class \;\cdot\; c.kind = \text{'}Persistent\text{'}\ and\ c.general = \{\}\ implies$$
$$\exists_1\, k : Key \cdot k.rdbId = c.umlId + \text{"}\_Pk\text{"}\ and\ k.name = c.name + \text{"}\_Pk\text{"}\ and$$
$$k.owner = Table[c.umlId]\ and\ k.kind = \text{'}PrimaryKey\text{'}\ and$$
$$\exists_1\, cl : Column \cdot cl.rdbId = c.umlId + \text{"}\_Id\text{"}\ and$$
$$cl.name = c.name + \text{"}\_Id\text{"}\ and\ cl.type = \text{'}NUMBER\text{'}\ and$$
$$cl : k.column\ and\ cl.kind = \text{'}PrimaryKey\text{'}\ and$$
$$cl : k.owner.column$$

C4. "For each association in the source model, there is a unique foreign key representing it in the target model":

$$\forall\, a : Association \text{ and } a.kind = `Persistent' \text{ implies}$$
$$\exists_1 fk : ForeignKey \cdot fk.rdbId = a.umlId + \text{"\_Fk" and}$$
$$fk.name = a.name + \text{"\_Fk" and}$$
$$fk.owner = Table[a.source.umlId] \text{ and}$$
$$fk.kind = `association' \text{ and}$$
$$fk.refersTo = Table[a.destination.umlId] \text{ and}$$
$$\exists\, cl : Column \cdot cl.rdbId = a.umlId + \text{"\_Ref" and}$$
$$cl.name = a.name + \text{"\_Ref" and}$$
$$cl : fk.column \text{ and } cl.kind = `ForeignKey' \text{ and}$$
$$cl.type = `NUMBER' \text{ and}$$
$$cl : fk.owner.column$$

C5. "If c is a subclass of d, all columns of d's table are included in c's table":

$$\forall\, c, d : Class \cdot c.kind = `Persistent' \text{ and } d : c.general \quad \text{implies}$$
$$Table[d.umlId].column \subseteq Table[c.umlId].column$$

C6. "For each package in the source model, there is a unique schema representing it in the target model":

$$\forall\, p : Package \cdot$$
$$\exists_1 s : Schema \cdot s.rdbId = p.umlId \text{ and}$$
$$s.name = p.name \text{ and } s.kind = p.kind \text{ and}$$
$$s.tables = Table[p.elements.umlId]$$

There are also dual constraints, expressing that the only elements of the target model are those derived from the source model by constraints $C1$ to $C6$. Dual constraint $C7$ expresses that the only columns of a table are those defined by $C2$, $C3$, $C4$ and $C5$.

Constraint $C8$ is the dual of $C2$, there are also dual constraints $C9$ of $C4$ and $C10$ of $C6$.

This specification is superficially similar to the rule-based description of the transformation given in [11], however the key difference is that our specification is at a higher level of abstraction, defining the intended state of the target model at completion of the transformation (independently of how the transformation is implemented). This state is defined globally, for all elements of each entity type in the model. The QVT description defines operational rules that may be applied during the transformation, locally to particular elements. There is no definition of the overall effect of the transformation.

The implementability of *Cons* can now be considered: *Table* depends on *Column*, whilst *Key*, *ForeignKey* and *Schema* depend on *Table*. However, *Table* depends upon itself (in $C5$), so the condition of strict hierarchy between $L2$ entities fails. Nevertheless, because *Table* is itself hierarchically organised, on the basis of inheritance between the source classes, *Cons* is implementable in phases (Section 5.3).

A partial logical interpretation χ from class diagram models to relational database models can be defined as follows.

$$\overline{UMLModelElement} \longmapsto \overline{RModelElement}$$
$$umlId \longmapsto rdbId$$
$$name \longmapsto name$$
$$\overline{Attribute} \longmapsto \overline{Column}$$
$$\overline{Class} \longmapsto \overline{Table}$$
$$\overline{Association} \longmapsto \{fk : \overline{ForeignKey} \mid fk.kind = \text{`}association\text{'}\}$$
$$source \longmapsto owner$$
$$destination \longmapsto refersTo$$
$$\overline{Package} \longmapsto \overline{Schema}$$
$$elements \longmapsto tables \cup \{fk : \overline{ForeignKey} \mid fk.owner \in tables\}$$

The mappings only apply to persistent classes and relationships in the source model, so only these elements of the source model are recoverable from the target model. In order for inheritance to have an interpretation in the target model, we would need to record inheritance relationships, eg., by means of foreign keys of kind 'inheritance' mapping from the subclass to the superclass. There is no inverse transformation even for source models consisting entirely of persistent elements, however, because some type information for attributes is discarded by the transformation.

The *Pres* property is true in interpreted form, if an interpretation of inheritance is provided, since the new model has an identical inheritance structure to the source model.

*Ens*1 holds because by C7 the columns of each table either correspond to attributes (inherited or owned) of the original class, and so must have distinct names (by *Asm*3), or they are the primary key of the root superclass (table) of the class, or they are foreign keys corresponding to an association whose source class is the class of the table, or an ancestor of the class (and so also in the same package as the class of the table). The primary and foreign key columns have names containing "_" and so are distinct from any of the attribute columns (by *Asm*9). They also have distinct names, since associations of the source model in the same package had distinct names (*Asm*1, *Asm*2).

*Ens*2 holds because by C8 the tables of the new model correspond to persistent classes of the source model, which have distinct names within a package by *Asm*2. Likewise, *Ens*3 holds by C10 and *Asm*10.

5.3 Explicit Specification and Design

The following phases can be defined:

1. *phase*1: map all attributes of persistent classes to corresponding columns;
2. *phase*2: for each persistent class create a corresponding table with columns for the owned attributes of the class;
3. *phase*3: for root classes create primary keys;

4. *phase*4: for associations create foreign keys;
5. *phase*5: copy all columns of tables of superclasses down to the tables of each of their subclasses, starting from root classes;
6. *phase*6: map packages to schemas.

These are composed in this order to achieve the overall mapping. The phases are all simple iterations except for the recursively defined phase 5.

Each phase can be treated as a new transformation with its own specification and design. Phase 1 establishes the constraint $C1$, phase 2 establishes $C2$, and likewise for the other phases.

In turn, a set of specific rules can be defined to carry out each phase, together with an activity which defines the order of application of the rules within the phase.

For *phase*1 the mapping of an individual attribute can be expressed by the operation (using the UML-RSDS toolset for UML [9]):

$mapAttributeToColumn()$
post:
$owner.kind\ =\ 'Persistent'\ implies$
  $\exists_1\ cl\ :\ Column\ \cdot\ cl.rdbId\ =\ umlId\ and$
  $cl.name\ =\ name\ and\ cl.kind\ =\ kind\ and$
  $(type.name\ =\ 'INTEGER'\ implies\ cl.type\ =\ 'NUMBER')\ and$
  $(type.name\ =\ 'BOOLEAN'\ implies\ cl.type\ =\ 'BOOLEAN')\ and$
  $(type.name\ \neq\ 'INTEGER'\ and\ type.name\ \neq\ 'BOOLEAN'\ implies$
    $cl.type\ =\ 'VARCHAR')$

of *Attribute*. For constraints in conjunctive-implicative form ($C1$, $C2$, $C3$, $C4$ and $C6$ in this example), such rules can be directly derived from the constraints.

The activity for this phase is a bounded iteration over all attributes:

  $for\ a : Attribute\ do\ a.mapAttributeToColumn()$

For phase 5 we have the operation

$copyColumns()$
  if $general\ =\ \{\}$
  then
    $generalOpposite.copyAllColumns(Table[umlId])$

in *Class*, where:

$copyAllColumns(t\ :\ Table)$
  $Table[umlId].addAllColumn(t.column);$
  $generalOpposite.copyAllColumns(Table[umlId])$

Reasoning in the axiomatic semantics (Chapter 6 of [8]) of UML, can be used to show that the phases do establish the constraints. This reasoning can be automated by formalising the rules in the B specification language, using the axiomatic semantics as the basis of the formalisation [9].

By composing the phases in sequence, we can establish the overall correctness of the transformation:

$$Asm \Rightarrow [phase1; \ phase2; \ phase3; \ phase4; \ phase5; \ phase6] \, Cons$$

This is the case because each phase establishes one of the core constraints $C1$ to $C6$, and no phase invalidates any of these constraints once they are established.

The dual constraints are true by construction of the phases, for example, columns for attributes are only created by phase 1.

Confluence of the phases follows by application of the syntactic rules of [9], and termination of each phase is clear, since these are based upon bounded loops, except in the case of phase 5. The recursion in this case terminates because there are no cycles in the inheritance relationship in the source model.

5.4 Limitations

The specification we have given does not cover association classes, many-many associations, multiple inheritance or qualified associations, and so these need to be removed from the class diagram before applying the transformation.

Model-level correctness of the transformation depends on the data-storage technique used in the relational database. There are two alternatives:

- If instances of a class C are stored as rows of its corresponding table, CT, but are not duplicated in superclass tables. In this case the interpretation of $\overline{C}$ is the union of the set of primary key values in CT and of each subclass table ST, because objects of these subclasses are also implicitly objects of C.
- If instances of C are stored as rows of CT and of all superclass tables, then $\overline{C}$ is interpreted as the set of primary keys of CT.

In either case, if C is a subclass of D, the axiom $\overline{C} \subseteq \overline{D}$ is true in interpreted form in the target model, by construction of the interpretation $\zeta(\overline{C})$. Attributes are interpreted as corresponding columns, and associations are interpreted using their corresponding foreign keys.

Other published specifications of the UML to relational database transformation have been defined in the Viatra [13], ATL [5] and Kermeta [6] specification languages. We can compare these by applying metrics of size and complexity to the specifications.

Table 1 compares the complexities of the different specifications, based on the total number of calls and depth of calls. Depth1 is the maximum depth of call chains not involving recursive loops, and Depth2 the maximum length of a recursive loop. The approaches are ranked by the total of recursive calls and then by Depth2, our approach (implemented in UML-RSDS) has reduced complexity compared with the QVT version by this measure. Our approach has also reduced the maximum depth of non-recursive call chains.

Table 1. Complexity of UML to relational database transformations

Approach	Total number of calls	Total recursive calls	Depth2	Total non-recursive calls	Depth1
Kermeta	22	9	2	13	4
QVT	10	4	2	6	4
UML-RSDS	14	1	1	13	3
VIATRA	16	0	0	16	3
ATL	6	0	0	6	2

The specification constraints such as $C1$ and $C2$ which are in conjunctive-implicative form correspond closely to triple-graph grammar [16] rules, which define how an incremental change (such as the creation of a new *Attribute*) in the source model should be propagated to the target model, and vice-versa.

6 Comparison with Other Approaches

The idea of applying model-driven development to model transformations has been considered by [1,2], these approaches also proposed the use of UML to specify transformations. More recently, [4] introduced a special-purpose language, transML, to support the development of model transformations. Our work provides a detailed process for model transformation specification, the separation of assumptions (*Asm*), and properties to be ensured (*Ens*) and preserved (*Pres*) by the transformation, from the global specification (*Cons*) of the transformation itself. We provide rules for the correctness of the global specification with respect to *Asm*, *Ens*, *Pres*, which can be checked at the PIM stage, prior to refinement. We also provide rules for checking the implementability of the specification at this stage. Alternative semantics for UML and OCL, such as that of [14], could be used to support formal reasoning about specifications and designs. In principle, metamodels for specifications and designs could be defined, based on characteristic structures of specifications such as the conjunctive-implicative form, to support higher-level model transformations [10].

7 Conclusions

We have defined a model-driven development process and specification technique for model transformations, using UML notations. We have used this process to rationalise and improve the definition of a well-known refinement transformation, solving the problems which we identified with its lack of precision and incompleteness.

The MDD process described here has also been applied to several large case studies, including the mapping of activities from UML 1.4 to UML 2.2, in the 2010 transformation tool competition [15], and state machine slicing [9]. Further work includes the use of proof tools, such as B, to support the automated verification of model transformation correctness.

Acknowledgement

The work presented here was carried out in the EPSRC HoRTMoDA project at King's College London.

References

1. Bezivin, J., Buttner, F., Gogolla, M., Jouault, F., Kurtev, I., Lindow, A.: Model Transformations? Transformation Models. Model-driven Engineering Languages and Systems (2006)
2. van Gorp, P.: Model-driven development of model transformations. In: Ehrig, H., Heckel, R., Rozenberg, G., Taentzer, G. (eds.) ICGT 2008. LNCS, vol. 5214, Springer, Heidelberg (2008)
3. Grønmo, R., Møller-Pedersen, B., Olsen, G.K.: Comparison of three model transformation languages. In: Paige, R.F., Hartman, A., Rensink, A. (eds.) ECMDA-FA 2009. LNCS, vol. 5562, pp. 2–17. Springer, Heidelberg (2009)
4. Guerra, E., de Lara, J., Kolovos, D.S., Paige, R.F., dos Santos, O.M.: *trans*ML: A family of languages to model model transformations. In: Petriu, D.C., Rouquette, N., Haugen, Ø. (eds.) MODELS 2010. LNCS, vol. 6394, pp. 106–120. Springer, Heidelberg (2010)
5. Jouault, F., Allilaire, F., Bezivin, J., Kurtev, I.: ATL: A model transformation tool. Science of Computer Programming 72, 31–39 (2008)
6. Kermeta (2010), http://www.kermeta.org
7. Lano, K.: A Compositional Semantics of UML-RSDS. SoSyM 8(1), 85–116 (2009)
8. Lano, K. (ed.): UML 2 Semantics and Applications. Wiley, Chichester (2009)
9. Lano, K., Kolahdouz-Rahimi, S.: Specification and verification of model transformations using UML-RSDS. In: Méry, D., Merz, S. (eds.) IFM 2010. LNCS, vol. 6396, pp. 199–214. Springer, Heidelberg (2010)
10. Lano, K., Kolahdouz-Rahimi, S., Poernomo, I., Terrell, J.: Patterns for Model Transformation Specification and Implementation. Dept. of Informatics, King's College London (2010)
11. OMG, Query/View/Transformation Specification, annex A (2010)
12. OMG, Meta Object Facility (MOF) Core Specification, OMG document formal/06-01-01 (2006)
13. OptXware, The Viatra-I Model Transformation Framework Users Guide (2010)
14. Richters, M.: A Precise Approach to Validating UML Models and OCL Constraints, PhD thesis, Universitaet Bremen (2001)
15. Rose, L., Kolovos, D., Paige, R., Polack, F.: Model Migration Case for TTC 2010. Dept. of Computer Science, University of York (2010)
16. Schurr, A.: Specification of graph translators with triple graph grammars. In: Mayr, E.W., Schmidt, G., Tinhofer, G. (eds.) WG 1994. LNCS, vol. 903, pp. 151–163. Springer, Heidelberg (1995)

Generic Model Transformations:
Write Once, Reuse Everywhere

Jesús Sánchez Cuadrado[1], Esther Guerra[2], and Juan de Lara[2]

[1] Universidad de Murcia (Spain)
jesusc@um.es
[2] Universidad Autónoma de Madrid (Spain)
{Esther.Guerra,Juan.deLara}@uam.es

Abstract. Model transformation is one of the core techniques in Model Driven Engineering. Many transformation languages exist nowadays, but few offer mechanisms directed to the reuse of whole transformations or transformation fragments in different contexts.

Taking inspiration from generic programming, in this paper we define model transformation *templates*. These templates are defined over *meta-model concepts* which later can be bound to specific meta-models. The binding mechanism is flexible as it permits mapping concepts and meta-models with certain kinds of structural heterogeneities. The approach is general and can be applied to any model transformation language. In this paper we report on its application to ATL.

1   Introduction

Model Driven Engineering (MDE) proposes the use of models as the key assets in the development, and hence all sorts of model modifications are needed. In this way, model transformations become one of the basic building blocks of MDE.

Even though MDE is being successfully applied in many scenarios, it still needs appropriate mechanisms to handle the development of complex, large-scale systems. One such mechanism is a facility to make transformations reusable, so that we can apply them to different contexts (i.e. with different meta-models). This would enable the creation of transformation patterns and idioms [3], as well as libraries of transformations addressing recurrent transformation problems. Some examples of manipulations commonly needed in different contexts are calculating the transitive closure of a relation, moving and merging nodes through a relation (like pulling up a method or an attribute), and cycle detection. Unfortunately, the definition of model transformations is normally a type-centric activity, in the sense that transformations are defined using types of specific meta-models, thus making their reuse for other meta-models difficult.

In this work, we bring into model transformation elements from generic programming in order to make model transformations reusable. In particular, we propose defining model transformation templates over concepts [6,10,17]. In generic programming, a concept expresses the requirements for a type parameter of a template. In our case, a concept is a meta-model that defines the set

J. Cabot and E. Visser (Eds.): ICMT 2011, LNCS 6707, pp. 62–77, 2011.

of requirements that a specific meta-model must fulfill to be used in a transformation. Thus, when then concept is bound to a specific meta-model satisfying the concept requirements, the transformation becomes applicable to this meta-model.

In [6] we proposed concepts as a mechanism to add genericity to models, meta-models and in-place transformations. However, we only allowed a restricted kind of binding between the concepts and the meta-models consisting in an exact embedding of the former in the latter (i.e. no structural heterogeneity was allowed). In this paper we apply concepts to model-to-model transformations, and propose a more powerful notion of binding that permits replication of elements in the concept, as well as adaptations from the structure in the concept to the structure of the meta-model. Both types of variability induce modifications in the transformation template when instantiation takes place.

As a proof of concept, we report on an implementation on top of ATL [11] where the adaptation of the transformation templates is realized by a higher-order transformation (HOT). Nonetheless, our approach is general and therefore applicable to other transformation languages.

Paper Organization. Section 2 reviews the main elements of generic programming, and outlines our approach. Section 3 introduces transformation templates, concepts and bindings. Next, Section 4 adds flexibility to our approach by providing multiple cardinality for our concepts and adapters for the bindings. Section 5 outlines our exemplary implementation on top of ATL and Section 6 presents a case study. Section 7 compares with related work and Section 8 concludes.

2   Genericity in Model Transformation

Genericity is a programming paradigm found in many languages like C++, Haskell, Eiffel or Java [8]. Its goal is to express algorithms and data structures in a broadly adaptable, interoperable form that allows their direct reuse in software construction. It involves expressing algorithms with minimal assumptions about data abstractions, as well as generalizing concrete algorithms without losing efficiency. It promotes a paradigm shift from types to algorithms' requirements, so that even unrelated types may fulfil those requirements, hence making algorithms more general and reusable [10,17].

Genericity is realized through function or class templates in many programming languages, like C++ or Java. Templates declare a number of type parameters for a given code fragment, which later can be instantiated with concrete types. Templates can also define requirements on the type parameters, so that only those concrete types fulfilling the requirements are considered valid. A unit expressing a set of requirements is called a *concept* [10], and usually declares the signature of the operations a given type needs to support in order to be acceptable in a template. Hence, templates rely on concepts to declare the requirements of their type parameters.

Based on these ideas, we have defined the approach for generic model transformations that is outlined in Fig. 1. Similar to programming templates, we build generic model transformation templates. These are transformations in which the source or the target domain (or both) is not tied to a specific meta-model, but contains *variable* types. The requirements for the variables types (needed properties, associations, etc.) are specified through a concept. A concept has the form of a meta-model as well, but its enclosing elements are interpreted as variables that need to be bound to elements of some concrete meta-model.

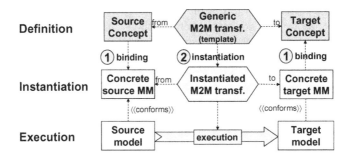

Fig. 1. Working scheme of our approach. In this case both the source and target domains are concept meta-models.

Once bindings between concepts and concrete meta-models are established (step 1 in Fig. 1), our approach automatically instantiates a concrete transformation from the template (step 2), which can be executed on regular instance models of the bound meta-models. This approach yields reusable transformations because we can bind a concept to several meta-models, so that the generic transformation is applicable to all of them. Finally, although the figure assumes a generic transformation with both domains being concepts, either the source domain or the target domain could be a concrete meta-model.

A crucial issue to increase the reuse opportunities of a transformation template is to have a flexible binding mechanism allowing concepts to be mapped to a large number of meta-models. We propose two such mechanisms: multiple cardinality (or variability of concept elements) and adaptation. As we will see, the more sophisticated the binding is, the more complex the instantiation of the transformation becomes. In this paper, the instantiation mechanism for template transformations is implemented by a HOT over ATL transformations.

3   Concepts, Bindings and Templates

A *meta-model concept* is a specification of the minimal requirements that a meta-model should fulfil to qualify for the source or target domain of a generic model-to-model transformation (or in general, of a generic model management operation [6]). From a practical point of view, a concept is just a meta-model and can be used as the source or target domain of a generic transformation template.

As an example, the upper part of Fig. 2 shows the definition of a generic transformation that populates a Java model from any object-oriented (OO) system. In this case, the domain *from* is specified by a concept, whereas the domain *to* is a concrete meta-model (a simplification of the Java meta-model). The transformation template, shown to the right with ATL syntax, generates a Java class from each OO class, and a Java field from each attribute.

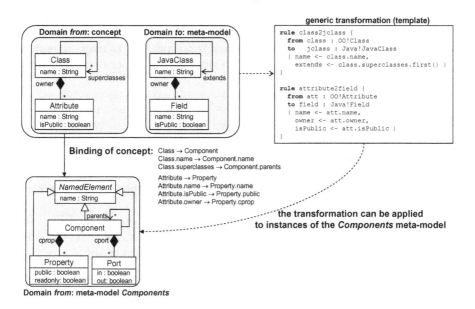

Fig. 2. Transformation template from a concept for OO systems into a fixed Java meta-model, and binding of the concept to a particular meta-model for components

In order to execute a generic transformation we have to map or bind the concepts involved in the template to specific meta-models. If one represents algebraically concepts and meta-models as attributed type graphs with inheritance [5], then, in the simplest scenario, the binding is a morphism (a function) that takes into consideration the semantics of inheritance (so-called clan-morphisms in [5]). In the following we just provide an intuition of this binding function and purposely refrain from a formalization.

In the simplest case, the binding establishes a 1-to-1 correspondence from each class in the concept to a class in the bound meta-model, from each attribute in the concept to an attribute in the meta-model, and from each association in the concept to an association in the meta-model. The binding also imposes some additional conditions to ensure the compatibility of the mapped associations and attributes, so that the operations performed in the concept can be performed in the bound meta-model types. In particular:

– the source and target classes of an association must be mapped to the source and target classes of the bound association (or to some of their subclasses).

– Attributes must be mapped to other attributes of the same type, or of a subtype. Moreover, the container classes of two mapped attributes must also be bound. There is an exception though: it is allowed to map an attribute to an inherited attribute (i.e. an attribute defined in a superclass). For instance, in Fig. 2, attribute name of Class is bound to attribute name of NamedElement, although Class is not mapped to NamedElement. Nonetheless this is allowed because Class is bound to Component, of which NamedElement is a superclass.
– if a concept represents the target of a transformation, meaning that its instances (or more precisely the instances of the bound meta-models) are being populated by the transformation, then it is not possible to map an association in the concept with an association with a lower upper bound or higher lower bound.

The binding should be a function from the set of classes, associations and attributes. Hence, we cannot map one element in the concept to two elements in the meta-model. Nonetheless, it is possible to map several elements in the concept to the same element in the meta-model (i.e. having non-injective bindings) whenever this do not lead to conflicting rules. In addition, not all elements in the meta-model need to receive a binding from the concept (i.e. non-surjective binding).

As an example, Fig. 2 shows a valid binding from a concept modelling the requirements of the source domain of a transformation (an OO system), to a particular meta-model for defining components. The binding maps classes Class and Attribute in the concept to classes Component and Property in the meta-model, associations superclasses and owner to parents and cprop, attribute name of Class to the inherited attribute name in the component, and attributes name and isPublic in class Attribute to attributes name and public in class Property. Once the binding is established, the transformation can be applied to instances of the bound meta-model, creating a Java class for each component in the meta-model instance.

From the point of view of the model transformation engine builder, there are two ways to apply a transformation template to the bound meta-model(s). The first possibility is to encode a HOT that takes as input the template, the bound meta-model(s) and the binding(s), and produces a transformation that is directly applicable to the bound meta-model(s). The HOT replaces in the template each class, association and attribute declared in the concept by elements in the concrete meta-model, as specified by the binding. For instance, the transformation generated from our example would use components and properties, but no OO classes anymore. In this way, the resulting transformation can be executed by a regular transformation engine. This is the approach we have taken in this paper. The second possibility is leaving the transformation unmodified, and including a level of indirection managed by the transformation engine. In this case, when a generic transformation is executed for a given binding and the engine finds an element defined by a concept, then it has to go through the binding to obtain the bound type. This approach is followed by tools such as [6].

4 Adding Flexibility to Concepts and Bindings

The presented binding mechanism enables a certain degree of reuse, but it lacks flexibility as the meta-model must embed the concept, that is, the concept and the bound part of the meta-model must be structurally equal.

For example, in Fig. 2 we may also want to treat Ports as Attributes to generate Java fields for them. However, we defined the binding as a function and, therefore, an element in the concept cannot be bound to several meta-model elements. In Section 4.1 we will show how to extend a concept with an interval for the cardinality of its elements so that they can be replicated and subsequently bound to more than one element in the meta-models.

Once we can bind Attribute to Port (in addition to Property), we should map attribute isPublic to some attribute in Port. However, Port does not define any meaningful attribute modelling visibility. In Section 4.2 we will show how to use binding adapters to overcome this problem. An adapter is an expression evaluated in the context of the bound meta-model, which returns a suitable element as the target of a binding. In this way, an adapter could provide a binding of isPublic to the value *true*. In general, adapters resolve structural heterogeneities between concepts and meta-models, in the style of [19].

4.1 Cardinality of Concept Elements

Our previous binding definition requires each element in the concept to be mapped to exactly one element in the bound meta-model (1-to-1 binding). However, in practice, we sometimes find that a class in a concept is modelled by several classes in the meta-model. If all these classes have a common parent, then the binding can be performed as usual by mapping the parent. The problem arises when the classes in the meta-model do not share a common parent, or when there is a common parent but it has more children than those we would like to bind, so that mapping the parent is not a suitable solution.

In order to solve this problem, we assign a cardinality to classes and associations in concepts. In this way, those elements in the concept that are allowed to be bound to one or more elements in the meta-model must define a cardinality interval "1..*" (1-to-n binding). It is also possible to specify a cardinality interval "0..1" or "0..*" if the concept element can remain unbound (i.e. it can be mapped to no meta-model element). In general, the cardinality of an element is transformation-specific, that is, the generic transformation developer must annotate a concept explicitly to enable its usage. In ATL-like languages and in our current implementation, the cardinality is restricted to be exactly 1 for classes of target concepts and for associations of source concepts.

Intuitively, a concept containing elements with cardinality annotations is equivalent to a (possibly infinite) set of "flat" concepts where the cardinality of all elements is 1. Similar to [4], the set of flat concepts is calculated by performing all possible expansions in the cardinality interval of every element in the concept. If the cardinality interval includes 0, then one of the possible expansions implies deleting such element. Fig. 3 illustrates this technique. To the left, class Attribute in the concept has been annotated with its cardinality, whereas elements without annotations have a cardinality 1. Thus, we can replicate class Attribute, together with the associations in which it participates an unbounded number of times. To the right, the figure shows the unfolded concepts without cardinality intervals in case we replicate Attribute once or twice. The concrete number of replicas must be indicated when binding a particular meta-model to the concept. For instance, in order to map Attribute to both Property and Port in the components meta-model shown in Fig. 2, we must select two replicas. Then, one can perform a 1-to-1 binding from the corresponding expanded concept to the meta-model.

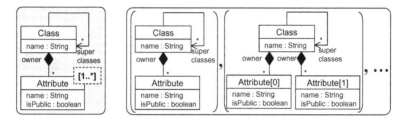

Fig. 3. Annotating a concept with cardinality (left). Set of its expansions (right).

Choosing a cardinality different from 1 for a concept element induces an adaptation of the associated transformation template. If a class in the concept is mapped to more than one element, then the rules defined for this class should be replicated for each mapping. In our example, rule *attribute2field* would be replicated twice: one with class Port in the from domain, and another one with class Property. If the cardinality is defined for an association, then the instructions assigning a value to the association should be replicated for each specified binding. For instance, if the target domain in Fig. 2 were a concept and we map relation owner to two associations, then the second line in the body of rule *attribute2field* would be duplicated.

4.2 Binding Adapters

A concept expresses requirements for a transformation. However, it also reflects a design decision which could be realized differently. For instance, the inheritance relation superclasses in the concept of Fig. 2 could be implemented with an intermediate class, as in the case of the UML meta-model [14], whereas the isPublic attribute could also be an enumerate, or a boolean with the opposite meaning (e.g. isPrivate). Since we do not want to define different concepts and templates for each design possibility, and in order to provide more reuse opportunities for a given template, a mechanism to overcome such heterogeneities is desirable.

A first solution is resorting to subtyping relations between concepts [16]. In this case, the commonalities of the different solution concepts are extracted to a supertype concept, which can be extended in order to provide alternative solutions for specific fragments. This can be seen as a 1-to-1 binding from the general concept to its extensions. Fig. 4 shows our example expressed in this way. The parent concept C only includes the class and its name, and children concepts $C1$ and $C2$ provide two alternatives to express the inheritance. This solution implies a fragmentation of the transformation template as well, and relies on a composition/extension mechanism in the transformation language. In the figure, both concepts $C1$ and $C2$ extend the template defined in C. Hence, this way of reuse has the drawback that the developer has to foresee all possible extensions, and the template has to be built in such a way that can be extended, which sometimes can be difficult or undesired. Moreover, not all transformation languages support rule extension.

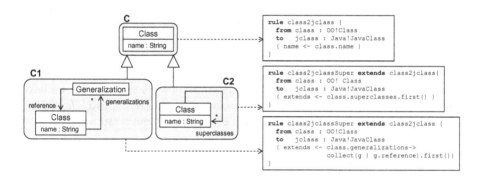

Fig. 4. Binding concepts to concepts, seen as a subtyping relation between concepts

For this reason, we have devised a more flexible mechanism that does not impose restrictions on the way concepts and templates are built. In this case, one of the possible concepts is chosen, and only one template is defined accordingly. When the template is instantiated for a particular meta-model, if the structure of the concept and the meta-model differ, it is possible to build an *adapter* to fix the heterogeneity. An adapter is an expression evaluated in the context of a bound meta-model type, returning a value (a primitive type or a reference type) that is assigned as binding for some attribute or association in the concept.

Fig. 5 illustrates this solution. It shows the binding of our concept to a UML meta-model where inheritance is represented by an intermediate class. To solve this heterogeneity, the binding of the superclasses association is given by an OCL expression that returns a suitable value. In this way, the adapter induces a modification in the transformation template so that each reference to superclasses is replaced by the adapter expression. Note how this solution is non-intrusive as it does not require modifying the bound concrete meta-models, which in some cases may not be possible.

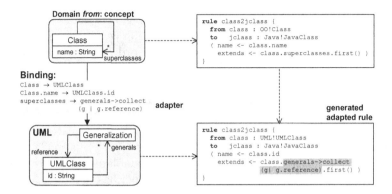

Fig. 5. A binding adapter (left). Semantics of adapter as template modification (right).

A side benefit of adopting adapters to solve heterogeneities is that, as many adaptations are recurrent, we can build libraries of reusable common adapters. These can be implemented using genericity as well, defining them atop generic types that are bound to the concept and meta-model of the binding that needs to be adapted. We are currently creating a categorization of adapters to resolve commonly occurring heterogeneities. For instance, one generic adapter we have identified in this categorization is called *association to intermediate class association*, which permits mapping directly superclasses to Generalization in Fig. 5.

5 Implementing Genericity over ATL

We have implemented a prototype, available at [9], to support our approach to generic model transformations. It currently targets ATL.

In our tool, a concept is defined as an Ecore meta-model, and its elements can be annotated with the allowed cardinality. A binding between a concept and a meta-model is represented as a model. We have created a textual concrete syntax to describe such bindings, and use OCL to define adapters. As an example, Listing 1 shows the binding presented in Fig. 2 expressed with our concrete syntax. Class is mapped to Component (line 2), and Attribute is mapped to both Property and Port (line 3). The superclasses property is naturally mapped to parents (line 5). However, mapping the Attribute.isPublic and Attribute.owner properties requires specifying a context, as Attribute is bound to two classes. In the listing, the property is mapped to public in the case of Property (line 6), and to an OCL expression (i.e. an adapter) in the case of Port (line 7). Our tool also allows some mappings to be implicit. For instance, it is not needed to map Class.name to Component.name. Finally, the None keyword allows a concept element to be unbound whenever its minimum cardinality is 0.

```
 1   binding Components for OO {
 2      class Class       to Component
 3      class Attribute to Property, Port
 4
 5      feature Class. superclasses is parents
 6      feature Attribute [Property]. isPublic is public
 7      feature Attribute [Port]. isPublic = true
 8      feature Attribute [Property]. owner is cprop
 9      feature Attribute [Port]. owner is cport
10   }
```

Listing 1. Binding a concept to a meta-model.

Templates are written in ATL. Given a template and a binding from the participating concepts to some meta-models, a HOT is in charge of instantiating the template, replacing generic types by those in the meta-models. So far we support the declarative part of ATL. The modifications to the original template depend on whether the concept is for the source or target domains, and on the chosen cardinality for each particular concept element. The following rules are applied in the case of binding elements of a source concept:

– *Class with cardinality 1.* Each usage of the concept class is renamed to its bound class.
– *Class with a binding cardinality >1.* We have identified several cases where it is possible to safely instantiate the original template. Each ATL construct requires a different strategy:
  • *Matched rule.* Currently, it is restricted to rules with one *from* element. A new copy of the rule is created for each bound class, where the name of the latter replaces the one of the original concept class.
  • *Helper.* A new copy is created for each bound class. The context is replaced accordingly to the bound class.
  • *Lazy rule.* A new copy is created for each bound class. Explicit calls to the original lazy rule are replaced with an OCL expression that checks the type of the source element in order to call one of the new lazy rules. For instance, the expression thisModule.myLazyRule(obj) is replaced by the expression in Listing 2, if the type of obj has been mapped twice.

```
1   if obj. ocIIsKindOf(ConcreteMetaclass1) then
2       thisModule.myLazyRule_for_ConcreteMetaclass1(obj)
3   else
4       if obj. ocIIsKindOf(ConcreteMetaclass2) then
5           thisModule.myLazyRule_for_ConcreteMetaclass2(obj)
6       endif
7   endif
```

Listing 2. OCL expression that replaces an invocation to a lazy rule.

  • *allInstances.* Each occurrence of ConceptMetaclass.allInstances is replaced by ConcreteMetaclass1.allInstances.union(ConcreteMetaClass2.allInstances).union(...).
  • *oclIsKindOf.* Each occurrence of obj.oclIsKindOf(ConceptMetaclass) is replaced by obj.oclIsKindOf(ConcreteMetaclass1) or obj.oclIsKindOf (ConcreteMetaclass2). The same applies to oclIsTypeOf.
– *Class with cardinality 0.* If a class is mapped to none, the following rewritings are applied:

- *Matched rule.* It is restricted to rules with one *from* element. The rule is safely deleted, because ATL does not fail with unresolved bindings.
  - *Helper.* Every helper for that class is deleted.
  - *Lazy rule.* It is deleted. Every call to the rule is replaced by OclUndefined.
  - *allInstances.* Each occurrence of ConceptMetaclass.allInstances is replaced by an empty collection.
  - *oclIsKindOf.* Each occurrence of obj.oclIsKindOf(ConceptMetaclass) is replaced by false.
- *Feature and binding adapter.* Each usage of a concept feature is renamed to the bound feature, or in case a binding adapter is used, replaced by the adapter's OCL expression. Since this requires typing information that is not provided by the ATL compiler, we rely on ATL/OCL attribute helpers. Thus, for each concept feature, a new attribute helper with its name is attached to the bound class. If several bindings are specified for a class, then several helpers are created. The helper's body is either the name of the concrete feature or the OCL expression of the adapter. In this way, the rules in the instantiated template use the name of concept features, and the ATL engine selects the appropriate attribute helper dynamically.

For target concepts, we apply the following rewriting rules to the templates:

- *Class.* Each usage of the concept class is renamed to the bound class. The cardinality of target classes must be always 1.
- *Feature with cardinality 1.* The feature in the left part of an ATL binding is renamed to the bound feature.
- *Feature with cardinality >1.* The ATL binding is replicated as many times as the cardinality indicates, and then the features are renamed as before.
- *Feature with cardinality 0.* The ATL binding is removed.

Please note that binding adapters are only possible for source concepts.

6   Case Study

This section illustrates the applicability of our approach in a non-trivial scenario, namely a generic transformation to compute the *flow graph* for a family of languages with imperative constructs. Flow graphs are widely used in program analysis to describe the control flow of imperative programs. Given the flow graph of a procedure, several analysis and further transformations are possible, such as visualizing the structure of the algorithm implemented by the procedure, detecting unreachable code or invalid "configurations" (e.g. jumping within a loop), computing the cyclomatic complexity of a procedure, or performing some program profile analysis [2].

A naive approach to tackle this scenario would be to build specific transformations from each particular procedural language into flow graphs. Instead, since all these languages share common features that can be included in a concept, we choose to build just a unique transformation template defined over such a concept. In this way, the template will be applicable to every procedural language once we bind their meta-model to the concept.

Fig. 6 shows to the left the concept used by our generic transformation as source domain. It includes standard control statements commonly found in many imperative languages. The class procedure is used to model both functions and procedures, and hence it has been labelled with "1..*" cardinality to accommodate the specific modularity notions of different languages. A procedure is made of a sequence of statements. Statements may be annotated with a label, and are refined into typical control instructions: *if*, *while* and *goto*. No further statements are needed, as the flow graph transformation only deals with control statements.

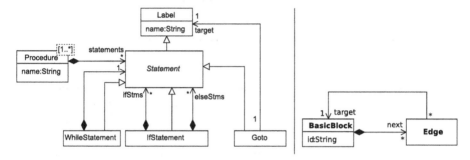

Fig. 6. Concept for imperative languages (left). Meta-model for control flows (right).

Our transformation template implements a variation of the algorithm proposed in [1], based on partitioning a piece of code into basic blocks. A *basic block* is "*a sequence of consecutive statements where the execution flow can only enter the basic block through the first instruction in the block and leave the block without halting or branching*". We omit the details of the implementation for space limitations, but it is worth noting that this is not a straightforward ATL transformation, comprising 7 rules and 13 helpers.

The right side of Fig. 6 shows the *flow graph* meta-model used by the transformation template as target domain. It represents a directed graph, where the nodes are basic blocks and the edges are jumps to other basic blocks.

We have instantiated our template to transform programs written in NQC (Not Quite C), a C-like language used to program Lego Mindstorms. We have used a meta-model defined by a third party [18] in order to assess to what extent our approach is flexible enough to adapt meta-models not foreseen by the generic transformation developer. Fig. 7 shows an excerpt of the NQC meta-model.

There are several mismatches between the source concept and the NQC meta-model. Listing 3 shows the binding that solves these mismatches, namely:

– *Renamings.* For instance, Goto is mapped to GoToStatement (line 2), and the target reference of Goto is mapped to JumpLabel of GoToStatement (line 5).

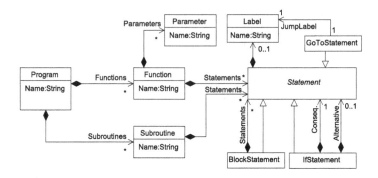

Fig. 7. Excerpt of the meta-model for NQC

- *Class with binding cardinality >1.* This is the case of Procedure that is bound to both Function and Subroutine (line 3).
- *Association to intermediate class association.* Statement in the concept and the meta-model can be mapped naturally, except when the statement is a BlockStatement, which from the partitioning algorithm point of view behaves as an association represented with an intermediate class. We use a binding adapter to tackle this issue (lines 9-11).
- *Monovalued association to multivalued association.* The IfStatement concept class has two multivalued associations, ifStms and elseStms, while the counterparts in the concrete class are monovalued (Consequence and Alternative). Moreover, the else clause is optional. In order to solve this heterogeneity, we define a binding adapter for each association (lines 13 and 15-17). These adapters make use of helpers factoring common code, which are also specified with our concrete syntax (flattened helpers in lines 19-20).

```
1   binding nqc {
2      class Goto to GoToStatement
3      class Procedure to Function, Subroutine
4
5      feature Goto.target     is JumpLabel
6
7      feature Procedure.name is Name
8
9      feature Procedure.statements = self.Statements->collect(s |
10        if   s.oclIsKindOf(BlockStatement) then s.Statements
11       else s endif )->flatten();
12
13     feature IfStatement.ifStms = self.Consequence.flattened;
14
15     feature IfStatement.elseStms =
16        if    self.Alternative.oclIsUndefined() then Sequence { }
17       else self.Alternative.flattened  endif;
18
19     helper      Statement.flattened  : Sequence(Statement) = Sequence { self };
20     helper BlockStatement.flattened  : Sequence(Statement) = self.Statements;
21       ...
22   }
```

Listing 3. Binding between the source concept and the NQC meta-model

Altogether this case study shows the feasibility of our approach, but two issues are worth noting. First, computing the flow graph of an imperative program is a non-trivial transformation, and therefore we do not want to implement it for each possible procedural language. Here we were able to follow the motto *"write once, reuse everywhere"* by designing a suitable concept and defining the transformation over the concept. Second, our binding proved to be flexible enough to adapt the concept to an unforeseen third-party meta-model.

7   Related Work

Meta-model concepts were first proposed in [6], with an application to the definition of generic in-place transformations using EOL [13]. The architecture in [6] uses an interpreted approach for the instantiation of templates which does not generate new transformations, but it uses the binding to resolve the concrete types at run-time. In the present paper, we use a compiled approach on top of ATL, where a HOT creates a specific transformation according to the binding. Moreover, the binding function in [6] is 1-to-1, whereas here we propose two mechanisms to enhance flexibility: adapters and replication of concept elements.

The term transformation template has also been used in previous works, although with a different purpose. For instance, in [12] the authors build transformation templates for a family of languages defined by a unique meta-model. Variations in this meta-model induce modifications in the template. However, it is not possible to apply a template to unrelated meta-models as we do here.

Other approaches to reusability are not based on concepts. For instance, in [15], reuse is achieved by adapting the meta-models to which an existing transformation is to be applied. The aim of adapting the meta-model is to make it a subtype of the expected input meta-model of the transformation [16], so that the transformation can be applied without changing it. In contrast, our approach is less intrusive because we do not need to modify the meta-models which sometimes can be unfeasible. Moreover, once a template is instantiated, we can extend the generated transformation with rules using concrete types. Nonetheless, our binding is similar to the notion of model subtyping [16], as one can see a concept as a supertype of the bound meta-model. However, our cardinality and adapters makes this relation more flexible than pure subtyping.

Another approach to reuse are the mapping operators (MOps) [19]. These are similar to our adapters, but oriented to the declarative construction of transformations by composing transformation primitives. Reusable transformations must be completely developed using MOPs, while we permit using a regular transformation language. The same authors present in [20] a categorization of common heterogeneities, which we solve through adapters and cardinality in concepts.

8   Conclusions and Future Work

In this paper we have brought elements of generic programming to model-to-model transformations in order to promote reusability. In our approach, it is possible to define transformation templates that use generic types defined on a concept. Concepts can be bound to a range of specific meta-models satisfying the concept requirements. In this way, transformation templates can be instantiated for different meta-models and applied to the meta-model instances. We have proposed two mechanisms to provide flexibility to the binding function and resolve heterogeneities between concepts and meta-models: cardinality annotations and binding adapters. We have implemented this approach atop ATL, and illustrated its use through a non-trivial example. The tool is available at [9].

In the future, we plan to extend our categorization of binding adapters, and to implement libraries of reusable adapters and reusable transformation templates. We would also like to apply our approach to other transformation languages.

Acknowledgements. Work funded by the Spanish Ministry of Science (projects TIN2008-02081 and TIN2009-11555), and the R&D programme of the Madrid Region (project S2009 /TIC-1650).

References

1. Aho, A.V., Sethi, R., Ullman, J.D.: Compilers: principles, techniques, and tools. Addison-Wesley Longman Publishing Co., Inc., Amsterdam (1986)
2. Ball, T., Larus, J.R.: Branch prediction for free. SIGPLAN 28, 300–313 (1993)
3. Bézivin, J., Jouault, F., Palies, J.: Towards model transformation design patterns. In: EWMT 2005 (2005)
4. Bottoni, P., Guerra, E., de Lara, J.: A language-independent and formal approach to pattern-based modelling with support for composition and analysis. IST 52(8), 821–844 (2010)
5. de Lara, J., Bardohl, R., Ehrig, H., Ehrig, K., Prange, U., Taentzer, G.: Attributed graph transformation with node type inheritance. TCS 376(3), 139–163 (2007)
6. de Lara, J., Guerra, E.: Generic meta-modelling with concepts, templates and mixin layers. In: Petriu, D.C., Rouquette, N., Haugen, Ø. (eds.) MODELS 2010. LNCS, vol. 6394, pp. 16–30. Springer, Heidelberg (2010)
7. Durán, F., Meseguer, J.: Parameterized theories and views in full maude 2.0. ENTCS 36 (2000)
8. García, R., Jarvi, J., Lumsdaine, A., Siek, J., Willcock, J.: A comparative study of language support for generic programming. SIGPLAN 38(11), 115–134 (2003)
9. Generic model transformations, http://www.modelum.es/projects/genericity
10. Gregor, D., Järvi, J., Siek, J., Stroustrup, B., dos Reis, G., Lumsdaine, A.: Concepts: linguistic support for generic programming in C++. SIGPLAN Not. 41(10), 291–310 (2006)
11. Jouault, F., Allilaire, F., Bézivin, J., Kurtev, I.: ATL: A model transformation tool. Science of Computer Programming 72(1-2), 31–39 (2008), http://www.emn.fr/z-info/atlanmod/index.php/Main_Page (last accessed November 2010)
12. Kavimandan, A., Gokhale, A.: A parameterized model transformations approach for automating middleware QoS configurations in distributed real-time and embedded systems. In: WRASQ 2007 (2007)
13. Kolovos, D.S., Paige, R.F., Polack, F.A.C.: The Epsilon Object Language (EOL). In: Rensink, A., Warmer, J. (eds.) ECMDA-FA 2006. LNCS, vol. 4066, pp. 128–142. Springer, Heidelberg (2006)

14. OMG. UML 2.3 specification, http://www.omg.org/spec/UML/2.3/
15. Sen, S., Moha, N., Mahé, V., Barais, O., Baudry, B., Jézéquel, J.-M.: Reusable model transformations. Software and System Modeling (2010) (in press)
16. Steel, J., Jézéquel, J.-M.: On model typing. SoSyM 6(4), 401–413 (2007)
17. Stepanov, A., McJones, P.: Elements of Programming. Addison-Wesley, Reading (2009)
18. van Amstel, M., van den Brand, M., Engelen, L.: An exercise in iterative domain-specific language design. In: IWPSE-EVOL 2010, pp. 48–57. ACM, New York (2010)
19. Wimmer, M., Kappel, G., Kusel, A., Retschitzegger, W., Schönböck, J., Schwinger, W.: Plug & play model transformations - a DSL for resolving structural metamodel heterogeneities. In: DSM 2010 (2010) (online Publication)
20. Wimmer, M., Kappel, G., Kusel, A., Retschitzegger, W., Schönböck, J., Schwinger, W.: Towards an expressivity benchmark for mappings based on a systematic classification of heterogeneities. In: MDI 2010, pp. 32–41. ACM, New York (2010)

Combining Specification-Based and Code-Based Coverage for Model Transformation Chains

Eduard Bauer and Jochen M. Küster

IBM Research Zurich, Säumerstr. 4, 8803 Rüschlikon, Switzerland
{edb,jku}@zurich.ibm.com

Abstract. For testing model transformations or model transformation chains, a software engineer usually designs a test suite consisting of test cases where each test case consists of one or several models. In order to ensure a high quality of such a test suite, coverage achieved by test cases with regards to the system under test must be systematically measured. Specification-based or code-based coverage can be measured, which leads to the question of how these two approaches are related. In this paper, we investigate the relation between specification- and code-based coverage analysis for model transformation chains and show how such a relation can be established. Based on this, we propose several usage scenarios of such a relation which include identification of code relevant for parts of a given specification and vice versa.

1 Introduction

Model transformations are nowadays used in model-driven engineering for model refinement, model abstraction, and for code generation. Model transformations can either be implemented directly in programming languages (such as Java) or using one of the available model transformation languages that have been developed in recent years (e.g. [6,13]). For complex model transformation problems, several model transformations can be concatenated to a model transformation chain [20]. This enables reuse and distributed development of individual model transformations. One example for such a model transformation chain is a solution for difference detection of process models in the IBM WebSphere Business Modeler [1].

For developing model transformations or model transformation chains, systematic software testing has to be applied in order to ensure a high quality of the model transformation chain and its test suite. For this, a software engineer usually designs a test suite consisting of test cases where each test case consists of one or more models. One important aspect of testing is to determine how thoroughly the test suite tests the model transformation chain, which is based on coverage analysis and the resulting coverage information. Ensuring thorough testing means achieving high coverage levels.

Two quite different approaches exist for coverage analysis: On the one hand, traditional code-based coverage analysis techniques can be used that derive test requirements from the code of the System Under Test (SUT). On the other hand, coverage can be analyzed using a specification-based coverage analysis approach [5] which uses the specification of the SUT to derive test requirements. Given these two different

J. Cabot and E. Visser (Eds.): ICMT 2011, LNCS 6707, pp. 78–92, 2011.

approaches, it raises the question whether there exists a relation between these two kinds of coverage information and how such a relation can be computed.

Such a relation can be beneficial for numerous reasons: If there is a strong correlation between the coverage levels for code-based coverage and specification-based coverage, then a high coverage level with regards to specification-based coverage would also imply a high code coverage level and vice versa. In addition, relating code-based coverage information and specification-based coverage information can be used during the development of model transformations. For example, one could analyze which test cases execute specific lines of code and thereafter identify commonalities of these test cases with regards to the specification.

In this paper, we investigate the relation between code-based coverage criteria and specification-based coverage criteria [5] for model transformation chains. We show how such a relation can be established. In addition, we show several applications of this relation and describe how a tester can benefit from it.

The paper is structured as follows. We first introduce fundamentals for model transformation chains, testing, and coverage analysis in Section 2. Section 3 introduces a specification-based and a code-based coverage analysis approach for model transformation chains. In Section 4 we establish a relation between the coverage information resulting from the two coverage analysis approaches. We apply the theoretical concepts to a model transformation chain for difference detection of process models in Section 5. Finally, we discuss related work in Section 6 and conclude.

2 Background and Motivation

A model transformation chain is composed of several individual model transformations. Each model transformation itself transforms one or more source models into one or more target models. For one model transformation one can distinguish between the specification and the implementation (source code) of the transformation.

The input and output domain, i.e. the possible source and target models, of a model transformation are specified by metamodels, see Figure 1. Metamodels can be used by relying on an input/output

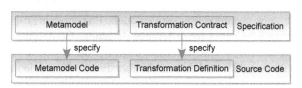

Fig. 1. Specification and Code of Model Transformation

language that is defined by a standard (i.e. the UML language definition) or can be specified by the software engineer on his own. The logic for transforming the source models to target models is specified declaratively by transformation contracts [8]. Transformation contracts are inspired by the design-by-contract approach [17], adapted for model transformations. They consist of preconditions of the model transformation that have to be fulfilled by the source models and postconditions that have to be fulfilled by target models and possibly their relation to the source models. Transformation contracts are also part of the specification of model transformations, as illustrated in Figure 1.

The logic specified by transformation contracts is implemented by so-called transformation definitions [7]. Transformation definitions can be expressed using one of the numerous model transformation languages (e.g. Query View Transformation (QVT) [10] or ATLAS Transformation Language (ATL) [13]) or using general purpose programming languages such as Java. For transforming source models to target models, some transformation definitions use code to represent the models by objects and references. Such code, called metamodel code, is usually automatically derived from the metamodels. The transformation definition and the metamodel code belong to the implementation of the model transformation, as shown in Figure 1. Besides these two kinds of code, glue code implementing functionalities such as logging, exception handling, initializers, controllers, etc might exist. In the following we do not pay attention to these pieces of code.

For a model transformation chain, model transformations are combined in such a way that models produced by one model transformation can be used as input for a consecutive model transformation. One example for such a model transformation chain is a solution for version management of process models in the IBM WebSphere Business Modeler [1]. We call this model transformation chain Compare/Merge Model Transformation Chain (CMTC) and use it as a case study. Given two business process models expressed in Business Process Modeling Notation (BPMN) [18], this model transformation chain computes the differences between them in the form of a Difference Model.

The models that are used and created during the execution of the CMTC are shown in Figure 2. They are illustrated by the rounded rectangles, the arrows represent which models are transformed to which other models. The two BPMN models $bpmn_1$ and $bpmn_2$ are trans-

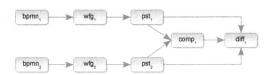

Fig. 2. Models of the CMTC

formed to the Workflow Graph (WFG) models wfg_1 and wfg_2. These are models that can be seen as a normal form for process models. WFG models are then transformed to models that are called Process Structure Trees (PSTs) (pst_1 and pst_2) which conform to the same metamodel as WFG models. PST models [19] have different properties which are more suitable for difference detection. Comparing and matching the PST models pst_1 and pst_2 yields the model $comp_1$, which maps the model elements that are similar in the two PST models to each other. Finally, based on these PST models and the $comp_1$ model, the Difference model $diff_1$ is computed which represents the differences between the two initial BPMN models. For a detailed overview of how differences are computed the reader is referred to Küster et al. [14]. In addition to specifying the domains of the model transformations by metamodels, the CMTC makes use of transformation contracts to specify what the different model transformations have to do.

A complex model transformation chain, such as the CMTC, has to be thoroughly tested in order to achieve a high quality. Software testing is usually done by creating a number of test cases, consisting of input values and expected results, which test the correct behavior of a SUT on given input [3]. For a model transformation chain, a test case consists of input models and expected output models. The input models of two sample test cases for the CMTC are shown in Figure 3.

To determine the quality of a test suite, coverage analysis is applied. In this context, the concept of a test requirement [3] is used in order to represent a particular element of the SUT that has to be tested. The elements that are used to derive test requirements from the SUT are defined by coverage

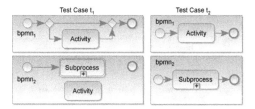

Fig. 3. Test Case 1 and Test Case 2

criteria. One very common coverage criterion is statement coverage, which derives a test requirement from each statement of the SUT. As this coverage criterion derives test requirements from the source code it is a so-called code-based coverage criterion. An example of a so-called specification-based coverage criterion is class coverage [9], which derives test requirements from the specification of model transformations. Class coverage derives test requirements from classes of metamodels.

A test requirement is covered, if the according element is executed/used by a test case during execution. A test requirement derived by statement coverage is covered, if the statement is executed. A test requirement derived from a class of a metamodel is covered if the class is instantiated. The information about covered and non-covered test requirements is collectively called coverage information.

For model transformation chains, specification-based coverage criteria as well as code-based coverage criteria can be used, which both yield different kinds of coverage information. Given these kinds of coverage information, the question arises whether a relation between them can be established. This can be beneficial for several reasons: If the coverage levels for test requirements derived by code-based and specification-based coverage criteria differ significantly for a test case, then this can be an indication that the test case should be manually inspected. A relation between test requirements derived by code-based and specification-based coverage criteria can also be used to better understand how parts of the specification are implemented. If a number of test cases fail, code-based and specification-based coverage information can be used to analyze the reason for the failure and provide additional insights. In the following, we first describe coverage analysis approaches in detail then show how a relation can be established.

3   Coverage Analysis Approaches

In this section, we introduce two different kinds of coverage analysis approaches for model transformation chains.

3.1   Specification-Based Coverage

The combined coverage approach [5] is an approach that derives test requirements by different specification-based coverage criteria from metamodels and transformation contracts of a model transformation chain. In the following, we briefly summarize the combined coverage approach. For a detailed introduction, the reader is referred to [5]. The examples used for illustration make use of the BPMN metamodel shown in Figure 4 and a simple instance is illustrated in Figure 5.

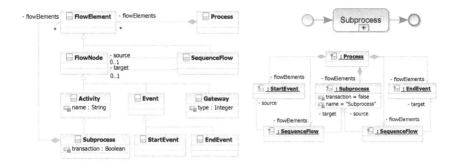

Fig. 4. BPMN Metamodel   **Fig. 5.** Exemplary BPMN Model

The coverage criterion *class coverage* [9] uses the classes of a metamodel to derive test requirements: For each class in a metamodel, a test requirement is derived. For the metamodel shown in Figure 4, one test requirement is, for example, derived for the class StartEvent. This test requirement is covered by the instance of the class StartEvent shown in Figure 5. The coverage criterion *attribute coverage* [9] derives test requirements from the attributes of the classes of a metamodel. For this, the common software testing technique equivalence partitioning [3] is used to partition the domain of an attribute into blocks. For the BPMN metamodel, a test requirement is e.g. derived from the block {*false*} for the attribute Subprocess.transaction. This test requirement is covered by the instance of the class Subprocess in Figure 5, which is no transaction. The coverage criterion *association coverage* [9] uses associations of a metamodel to derive test requirements. For this, equivalence partitioning is used for the multiplicity of the association. For example, a test requirement is derived from the block {0} for the association Subprocess.flowElements, which is covered by the instance of the class Subprocess as it does not contain any other FlowElements.

In addition to these coverage criteria, the combined coverage approach uses features to derive test requirements. A feature can be seen as a particular characteristic of a model. Since models consists of model elements, a feature is a particular combination of several model elements of that model. Features are defined by the tester of a model transformation chain. The coverage criterion *feature coverage* uses the features defined in the context of a metamodel to derive test requirements: A test requirement is created that requires instances of the metamodel to have the particular combination of model elements defined by the feature. An exemplary feature for the BPMN metamodel is defined by the Object Constraint Language (OCL) expression self.flowElements->exists(x | x.oclIsTypeOf(Subprocess)) (defined in the context of the class Subprocess). This feature describes nested subprocesses. The resulting test requirement is not covered by the exemplary BPMN model as it does not contain a Subprocess that itself contains another Subprocess. Currently, features in the combined coverage approach must be defined manually.

The combined coverage approach also derives test requirements from the transformation contracts. A transformation contract consists of contract rules specifying the preconditions and postconditions. *Transformation contract coverage* uses the contract rules of a transformation contract to derive test requirements. For each contract rule of a transformation contract, a separate test requirement is created. An exemplary contract rule based on the exemplary BPMN model is that each `Subprocess` without outgoing edges is transformed to a node in the WFG that is connected to the end of the WFG model.

The result of the evaluation of a transformation contract for a sequence of models is called contract result. The contract result contains the evaluation of each contract rule which is called contract rule result. A contract rule result is a number which counts how often the condition stated by the contract rule is fulfilled. The derived test requirement is satisfied if the contract rule result is positive. As the exemplary BPMN model does not contain any `Subprocess`es that are unconnected, the contract rule result is zero and thus the derived test requirement is not covered.

3.2 Code-Based Coverage

In contrast to specification-based coverage criteria, code-based coverage criteria derive test requirements from source code of a SUT.

One of the most common approaches is to use coverage criteria that derive test requirements from the control flow graph of the source code [2]. The control flow graph for a SUT is an abstraction of the source code, with nodes representing non-interruptible sequences of statements and edges representing possible consecutive executions of these sequences of statements. A coverage criterion that is based on the control flow graph is statement coverage: For each statement or sequence of non-interruptible statements a test requirement is derived that is satisfied if a test case executes the according statement or sequence of statements, respectively.

```
1   void doActivity(Activity a) {
2       Node result;
3       if (a instanceof Subprocess) {
4           result = new StructuredNode();
5       } else {
6           result = new Node();
7       }
8       result.setName(a.getName());
9   }
```

Listing 1.1. Code Example for Code Coverage

Listing 1.1 contains an extract of the transformation definition expressed in Java that transforms BPMN models to WFG models (part of the CMTC). The control flow graph is shown on the right. The numbers in the vertices are the lines of code that contain the statements. For example, line 4 yields a vertex in the control flow graph and thus results in a test requirement that is covered by test models that contain instances of the class `Subprocess`.

4 Relating Specification-Based and Code-Based Coverage Information

Following the techniques described in the previous section, both specification-based as well as code-based test requirements can be derived for a model transformation chain and coverage information can be computed. In this section, we investigate the relation between these two types of coverage information.

Figure 6 describes how a relation between test requirements obtained from specification-based and code-based coverage criteria can be established. The idea is to use test cases as binding elements to establish a relation between the two kinds of test requirements. For example, test case t_1 satisfies test requirements r_2 and also r_1' and, as a consequence, a relation between r_2 and r_1' can be derived. In the following, we will discuss different techniques to use the relation between test requirements in the context of model transformation chains.

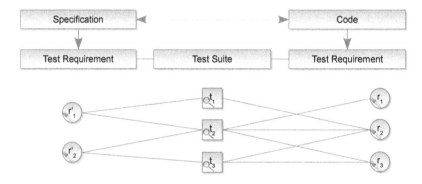

Fig. 6. Relation of Coverage Information.

4.1   Identifying Relevant Specification Parts for Code

Our technique results from using coverage information for the two different kinds of coverage criteria to establish a relation between the code and the specification. The goal of this technique is to find out which parts of the specification are relevant for a given piece of code. Such parts of the specification might be contract rules (cf. Section 3) that are implemented by this piece of code or parts of the metamodels that specify parts of models that are transformed by this piece of code. To find these parts of the specification, our technique first determines with the help of statement coverage which test cases of the test suite execute a particular piece of the code (shown on the right-hand side of Figure 6). Let us call this set of test cases T'. Then the commonalities of the test cases in terms of commonly covered test requirements derived from the specification are computed. These test requirements are covered by each of the test cases in T'. As these test requirements are derived from the specification, we get a link from a piece of code to a piece of the specification.

Exemplary test requirements and test cases are shown in Figure 6. We might be interested in the part of the specification that is relevant for the lines of code yielding the test requirements r_2 and r_3. The test cases t_2 and t_3 both execute this part of the code and thus both cover these two test requirements. The commonly covered test requirement of these test cases is the test requirement r_2', which is derived from a particular part of the specification. Accordingly, we can infer that for the lines of code that yield r_2 and r_3 the part of the specification that yields the test requirement r_2' is relevant.

For computing relevant specification parts for a given piece of code, we use Algorithm 1 which can be used to obtain, for a given set of test requirements derived from the code, an associated set of test requirements derived from the specification. In the following, we briefly describe this algorithm: T is an arbitrary test suite. Let R and R' be the two sets of test requirements. Let T_R and $T_{R'}$ be the sets containing the associated test sets [11] of all test requirements in R and R'. The associated test set T_{r_i} of a test requirement r_i contains all test cases that cover the test requirement r_i. Given a set of test requirements $S \subseteq R$, we first determine the test cases $t \in T$ that satisfy these test requirements–this is computed in line 2. These are test cases that belong to the associated test set of each test requirement $r \in S$. In a second step, we compute the commonalities of these test cases in terms of commonly covered test requirements $S' \subseteq R'$. This is done in line 5. To reduce the resulting test requirements to the most relevant ones, one can substract from the result those test requirements that are covered by all test cases.

Algorithm 1: Compute Associated Test Requirements

Input : $T = \{t_1, ..., t_k\}$ test suite
Input : $R = \{r_1, ..., r_n\}$ set of test requirements
Input : $T_R = \{T_{r_1}, ..., T_{r_n}\}$ associated test sets of requirements $R = \{r_1, ..., r_n\}$
Input : $R' = \{r'_1, ..., r'_m\}$ set of test requirements
Input : $T_{R'} = \{T_{r'_1}, ..., T_{r'_m}\}$ associated test sets of requirements $R' = \{r'_1, ..., r'_m\}$
Input : $S \subseteq R$ subset of test requirements
Output: $S' \subseteq R'$ subset of related test requirements

1: relate $(T, R, T_R, R', T_{R'}, S)$
2: $\quad$ $T' \longleftarrow \{t \in T \mid \forall r \in S : t \in T_r\}$
3: $\quad$ $S' \longleftarrow \emptyset$
4: $\quad$ **if** $T' \neq \emptyset$ **then**
5: $\quad\quad$ $S' \longleftarrow \{r' \mid r' \in R' \wedge T' \subseteq T_{r'}\}$
6: $\quad$ **end**
7: $\quad$ **return** S'
8: **end**

4.2 Identifying Relevant Code for Specification Parts

To identify relevant pieces of code for a given part of a specification, we use a technique that is similar to the technique presented in the previous section. Instead of starting with a piece of code, we start with a given part of the specification. We compute the set of test cases that cover a given set of test requirements derived by combined coverage. Then we compute their commonalities in terms of commonly covered test requirements derived by statement coverage. As these test requirements are derived from lines of code, we can then relate parts of the specification to pieces of code. Similar to the previous section, we use the Algorithm 1, but pass test requirements derived from parts of the specification to the algorithm.

To limit the resulting executed pieces of code to the most relevant code, one can subtract from the result the pieces of code that are executed by each test case, such as initializers, loaders, setup-methods and other glue code.

4.3 Relevant Code and Specification Parts for Test Cases

The coverage information resulting from statement coverage and combined coverage can also be used to identify relevant code and specification parts for a given test case or a given set of test cases. One possible use case for identifying relevant code and specification parts is the investigation of failing test cases: For these, the coverage information resulting from the specification and from the code can provide additional information about the reason for the failure. This information can be used to locate the fault within the model transformation chain.

The technique works as follows: For a given set of failing test cases T', we can determine the commonly covered test requirements derived by statement coverage. These requirements indicate the statements that are executed by all failing test cases in T'. In addition, we can determine the commonly covered test requirements derived by specification-based coverage, providing us with parts of the specification that the failing test cases in T' have in common.

As an example, assume that the two test cases t_1 and t_2 might yield to a failure during their execution (see Figure 6). As both test cases cover the test requirement r_2, they both execute the statement from which r_2 is derived. In addition, they cover the test requirement r_1', which is derived from a particular part of the specification. This information can then be used to locate the fault that is found by these test cases.

4.4 Relating Coverage Levels

A relation between all test requirements can also be used to analyze how coverage levels of test cases relate to each other. For this purpose, we use coverage information such as the one illustrated in Figure 6 about the number of covered test requirements derived by the two coverage criteria: For each test case, the coverage levels for test requirements derived by each of the two coverage criteria are computed and related to each other.

Using a scatter plot, the values of the two coverage levels for the test cases can be visualized. The scatter plot indicates the relation between the coverage information for the two coverage criteria. The correlation coefficient for the coverage levels indicates to what extent the coverage levels behave similarly for the different test cases.

Analyzing the relation of coverage levels for a test suite can be beneficial for several reasons. In the following, we discuss different outcomes. Let us assume that the coverage levels for test requirements derived by combined coverage is plotted along the horizontal axis, the coverage levels for test requirements derived by statement coverage is plotted along the vertical axis.

A positive linear correlation is indicated by dots being distributed from lower left to the upper right of the scatter plot. In this case, the correlation coefficient is close to one. This means, the coverage levels for test requirements derived by combined coverage and statement coverage behave similarly.

In the case when the two kinds of coverage information for the coverage criteria are independent, the correlation coefficient is close to 0. In such a case, the covered test requirements derived by statement coverage are independent from the covered test requirements derived by combined coverage. Probably, the code does not implement the specified behavior, since the achieved coverage level for test requirements derived from the specification does not influence the covered test requirements derived from the code. Thus the covered specification does not influence the executed code. For example, instances of classes might belong to models which do not have any influence on the execution. It can be seen that an investigation of how coverage levels are related can be used to validate the overall setup of the test suite.

5   Validation and Tool Support

The techniques presented in Section 4 have been implemented in the Test Suite Analyzer [5] which consists of a set of Eclipse plug-ins that can be used to support testing of model transformation chains. A screenshot of this tool support is shown in Figure 7: The view on the left-hand side contains information about the metamodels, transformation contracts, test cases and test management data. The coverage view at the bottom contains an overview of the test cases and the coverage levels achieved by them. The views at the top and the right hand side show an exemplary use of the technique presented in Section 4.1. The lines of code related to the selected test requirement in the top view are shown in the console to the right. In the following, we summarize the results of applying the techniques to the exemplary model transformation chain CMTC.

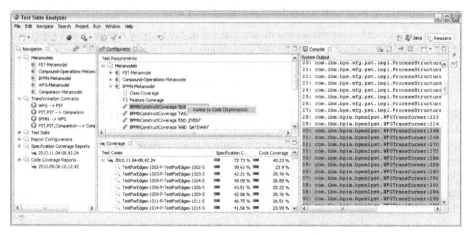

Fig. 7. Screenshot of Test Suite Analyzer

5.1   Identifying Relevant Specification Parts for Code

We applied the technique for identifying relevant specification parts for code (cf. Section 4.2) to the exemplary model transformation chain CMTC. Using this technique, we identified different pieces of code, as for example whole methods or separate if-branches, that are responsible for transforming instances of particular subparts of metamodels.

One example is the different pieces of code that are in charge of handling subprocess transformations, activity transformations, as well as edge transformations. This is illustrated in Figure 8: The shown piece of code is responsible for transforming instances the class `Activity`. The highlighted statement belonging to the if-branch transforms objects of the class `Subprocess`. If we compute the commonly covered test requirements derived from the specification for test cases that execute this statement, we find out that all of them contain instances of the type `Subprocess`. This shows that we can find out properties of this piece of code–without manually inspecting the preceding code and conditions.

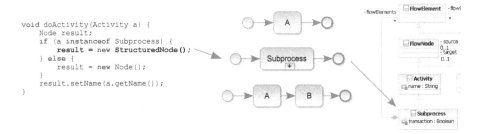

Fig. 8. Identifying Relevant Specification Parts for Code for the CMTC

5.2   Identifying Relevant Code for Specification Parts

We applied the technique presented in Section 4.2 to the sample model transformation chain CMTC. We selected parts of the specification and then computed the pieces of code following our technique. The result was that the relevant pieces of code implemented functionality for these particular parts of the specification.

In the following we give four different code extracts that are relevant to the class `Subprocess` belonging to the BPMN metamodel. This metamodel specifies the input domain of the BPMN to WFG transformation. For the sake of clarity, we removed the test requirements derived by statement coverage that are covered by all test cases in the test suite. Thus, the resulting covered statement is specific to handling instances of the class `Subprocess`. In the code extracts we print the lines of code in bold that have only been executed by test cases that cover the test requirement that is derived from the class `Subprocess`. We call this test requirement r_{sub}.

The first code extract in Figure 9 is the same example as shown in Figure 8. As expected, we find out that the separate if-branch is executed by test cases that cover r_{sub}. In addition to if-branches, whole blocks, like for example the while-block in the second code extract, might be relevant for instances of the class `Subprocess`. The shown statements are only executed if at least one BPMN model of the test case contains a subprocess. Similarly, whole methods and constructors might be relevant for the test requirement r_{sub}, as shown in the third and the fourth code extract. In case of the CMTC, prefixes only exist if subprocesses are used. They identify a particular element within the subprocess. Accordingly, this method and this constructor is only invoked, if r_{sub} is covered.

5.3   Relating Coverage Levels

We applied the technique described in Section 4.4 to the test cases belonging to the test suite of the CMTC. For each test case, we compute the coverage levels for test

```
void doActivity(Activity a) {                    List subprocesses = getEP().getSubprocesses();
    Node result;                                 while (subprocesses.size() > 0) {
    if (a instanceof Subprocess) {                   Subprocess s = subprocesses.remove(0);
        result = new StructuredNode();               ElementsProvider ep = getEP(s.getPrefix());
    }                                                [...]
    [...]                                        }
}                                        ①                                               ②
```

```
private void setupPrefix(String prefix) {        public ElementsProvider(Object doc, String prefix) {
    if (prefix.startsWith(this.prefix)) {            this.prefix = prefix;
        this.prefix = prefix;                        initialize((Document)doc, prefix);
        [...]                                    }
    }
}                                        ③                                               ④
```

Fig. 9. Identifying Relevant Code for Specification Parts for the CMTC

requirements derived by statement coverage and combined coverage. To visualize these two coverage levels achieved by each test case in the test suite we use a scatter plot, as described in Section 4.4. This scatter plot is shown in Figure 10. The coverage level for test requirements derived by combined coverage is plotted along the horizontal axis, the coverage level for test requirements derived by statement coverage is plotted along the vertical axis. Each dot represents one test case. The solid line is the trend line, resulting from linear regression analysis.

The first observation is the general tendency of the coverage levels to be positively linearly correlated. In general, a higher coverage level for test requirements derived by combined coverage yields a higher coverage level for test requirements derived by statement coverage, and vice versa. This result is not surprising for the CMTC which is used for difference detection between two process models (cf. Section 2). For a given test case consisting of two process models the coverage levels achieved by this test case depends on two factors: The first factor is the size and diversity–in terms of different model elements–of the process models. The second factor is the number of differences

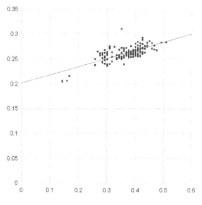

Fig. 10. Scatter Plot for the CMTC

between these process models. Large models with a lot of differences yield a high coverage level for test requirements derived by combined coverage. To transform these models to the derived models (WFG models and PST models) and to detect the differences between the models, a lot of different computations are necessary, which require a lot of code to be executed. This yields a high coverage level for test requirements derived by statement coverage.

The correlation coefficient for the correlation between the coverage levels for test requirements derived by combined coverage and statement coverage is $\varrho = 0.747$. Since $\varrho \geq 0.7$, we have a strong positive linear correlation between the two coverage criteria. We see that the coverage levels behave similarly, although the coverage artifacts–the specification and the code–from which the test requirements are derived are different.

5.4 Limitations

While applying the techniques mentioned in Section 4 to the CMTC, we encountered some limitations. In general, all techniques suffer from the drawback that they can only make statements about covered test requirements: For example, identifying relevant parts of the specification for pieces of code that are not executed is not possible with the described techniques.

Secondly, all approaches strongly depend on characteristics of the test suite. In particular, the size of the test suite influences the results. The calculation of the correlation coefficient is more meaningful if a large test suite is used. Another example is applying the technique given in Figure 8. If only one test case exists that executes the highlighted statement, several non-relevant parts of the specification–the ones covered by this test case–are marked relevant. Similarly, if only one failing test case exists, the presented technique simply outputs the whole code that is executed and all parts of the specification that are relevant for this test case.

The two techniques to relate pieces of code with parts of the specification and vice versa suffered from the existence of test requirements that are covered by all test cases. For example, test requirements derived from container classes in metamodels (like e.g. the class Process of the BPMN metamodel shown in Figure 4) are covered by each test case. This yields commonly covered test requirements that are not very expressive. For more relevant pieces of information concerning relevant pieces of code and relevant parts of the specification, such test requirements have to be excluded during the analysis.

6 Related Work

In the domain of software testing, several coverage criteria exist that are used for coverage analysis. McQuillan et al. [16] introduce a code-based coverage criterion for model transformations to derive test requirements from transformation definitions composed in ATL. This coverage criterion can be used instead of statement coverage in our approach to relate coverage information.

Specification-based coverage analysis for models has been studied by Andrews et al. [4]. They define coverage criteria for models composed in Unified Modeling Language (UML), including coverage criteria for UML class diagrams. Andrews et al. define three coverage criteria, which are called association-end multiplicity criterion, generalization criterion, and class attribute criterion. Fleurey et al. [9] adapt the approach of Andrews et al. for deriving test requirements from the source metamodel of a model transformation. Based on this, Bauer et al. [5] define the combined coverage approach that in addition uses feature coverage and transformation contract coverage. We use this approach to derive test requirements from the specification of model transformation chains. In contrast to [5], we investigate in this paper the relation between specification-based coverage and code-based coverage and show how such a relation can be established and used.

Relating specification-based coverage to code-based coverage information has in parts been analyzed by Hennessy et al. [12]. They use rule coverage as a specification-based coverage criterion for grammars and relate the resulting coverage information to coverage information for statement coverage. They obtain a positive linear correlation between the resulting coverage information. In contrast to their approach, we focus on the domain of model transformation chains and use the combined coverage approach as a possibility to derive test requirements from the specification of a model transformation chain.

Another approach to analyze the relation between the different kinds of coverage information is given by Mathur et al. [15]. To find out whether one coverage criterion (e.g. a specification-based coverage criterion) subsumes another coverage criterion (e.g. a code-based coverage criterion), they propose the ProbSubsumes technique. Using this technique, one has to measure the coverage level for test requirements derived by one coverage criterion achieved by a test suite that is created to satisfy another coverage criterion. In this paper, we have not analyzed the subsumption relation between combined coverage and statement coverage but instead we have proposed an approach to relate test requirements via the test cases in a test suite.

7 Conclusion

Coverage analysis of test cases for a model transformation chain is important for ensuring the quality of a test suite. In this paper, we have investigated the relation between specification-based and code-based coverage analysis. Our approach is based on establishing a relation between test requirements and test cases.

Establishing such a relation is beneficial for several use cases: It can be used for identifying relevant specification parts for code and for identifying relevant code for specification parts. In addition, the relation can be exploited for relating coverage levels of code-based and specification-based coverage analysis which can yield insights into the status of the test suite and test requirements. We have validated the different use cases of our approach on a large model transformation chain.

There are several directions for future work: The application of the approach to other transformation chains can provide additional insights on the applicability in practice. Future work also includes the automatic generation of missing test cases based on the results of coverage analysis. Here, the relation between code- and specification-based coverage could potentially be used for generating a test case particularly for a given part of the code or given part of the specification.

References

1. IBM WebSphere Business Modeler,
   http://www.ibm.com/software/integration/wbimodeler/
2. Allen, F.E.: Control flow analysis. SIGPLAN Not. 5, 1–19 (1970)
3. Ammann, P., Offutt, J.: Introduction to Software Testing. Cambridge University Press, New York (2008)
4. Andrews, A., France, R., Ghosh, S., Craig, G.: Test Adequacy Criteria for UML Design Models. Software Testing, Verification and Reliability 13(2), 95–127 (2003)
5. Bauer, E., Küster, J.M., Engels, G.: Test Suite Quality for Model Transformation Chains. IBM Research Report RZ 3797, IBM Zurich Research Laboratory (Feburary 2011)
6. Csertán, G., Huszerl, G., Majzik, I., Pap, Z., Pataricza, A., Varró, D.: VIATRA: Visual Automated Transformations for Formal Verification and Validation of UML Models. In: ASE 2002: 17th IEEE International Conference on Automated Software Engineering, pp. 267–270. IEEE Computer Society, Los Alamitos (2002)

7. Czarnecki, K., Helsen, S.: Feature-based Survey of Model Transformation Approaches. IBM Systems Journal 45(3), 621–645 (2006)
8. Cariou, E., Marvie, R., Seinturier, L., Duchien, L.: OCL for the Specification of Model Transformation Contracts. In: Workshop OCL and Model Driven Engineering of the Seventh International Conference on UML Modeling Language and Applications (UML 2004) (2004)
9. Fleurey, F., Baudry, B., Le Muller, Y., Traon, P.: Qualifying Input Test Data for Model Transformations. Software and Systems Modeling 8(2), 185–203 (2009)
10. Object Management Group. MOF 2.0 Query / Views / Transformations RFP (December 2009)
11. Harrold, M.J., Gupta, R., Soffa, M.L.: A Methodology for Controlling the Size of a Test Suite. ACM Transactions on Software Engineering and Methodology 2(3), 270–285 (1993)
12. Hennessy, M., Power, J.: An Analysis of Rule Coverage as a Criterion in Generating Minimal Test Suites for Grammar-based Software. In: ASE 2005: Proceedings of the 20th IEEE/ACM International Conference on Automated Software Engineering, pp. 104–113. ACM Press, New York (2005)
13. Jouault, F., Allilaire, F., Bézivin, J., Kurtev, I.: ATL: A Model Transformation Tool. Science of Computer Programming 72(1-2), 31–39 (2008)
14. Küster, J.M., Gerth, C., Förster, A., Engels, G.: Detecting and Resolving Process Model Differences in the Absence of a Change Log. In: Dumas, M., Reichert, M., Shan, M.-C. (eds.) BPM 2008. LNCS, vol. 5240, pp. 244–260. Springer, Heidelberg (2008)
15. Mathur, A., Wong, E.: An Empirical Comparison of Data Flow and Mutation-based Test Adequacy Criteria. Software Testing, Verification and Reliability 4(1), 9–31 (1994)
16. McQuillan, J., Power, J.: White-Box Coverage Criteria for Model Transformations. In: Proceedings 1st International Workshop on Model Transformation with ATL, Nantes, France (2009)
17. Meyer, B.: Applying "Design by Contract". Computer 25(10), 40–51 (1992)
18. Object Management Group (OMG). Business Process Modeling Notation, V1.1 (January 2008)
19. Vanhatalo, J., Völzer, H., Leymann, F.: Faster and More Focused Control-Flow Analysis for Business Process Models Through SESE Decomposition. In: Krämer, B.J., Lin, K.-J., Narasimhan, P. (eds.) ICSOC 2007. LNCS, vol. 4749, pp. 43–55. Springer, Heidelberg (2007)
20. von Pilgrim, J., Vanhooff, B., Schulz-Gerlach, I., Berbers, Y.: Constructing and Visualizing Transformation Chains. In: Schieferdecker, I., Hartman, A. (eds.) ECMDA-FA 2008. LNCS, vol. 5095, pp. 17–32. Springer, Heidelberg (2008)

A Transformation Workbench for Building Information Models

Jim Steel, Keith Duddy, and Robin Drogemuller

Queensland University of Technology, Australia
{james.steel,keith.duddy,robin.drogemuller}@qut.edu.au

Abstract. The building industry is undergoing a significant evolution, with increasing use of digital models during the design process and subsequent lifecycle of a building. These models, which span multiple design disciplines, multiple stakeholders, and many phases of the building's life, represent an interesting study for the application of ideas from model-driven engineering, being large, complex, and highly interrelated. Building models are typically represented using the Industry Foundation Classes (IFC), an industry standard supported by many of the popular CAD tools, defined in the STEP/Express technical space. Because the majority of research in MDE has focussed on the Eclipse Modeling Framework (EMF) technical space, it has previously been difficult to experiment with IFC models using model-driven engineering tools and techniques. In this paper we describe a workbench which provides for the integration of the STEP and EMF technical spaces. We also describe a number of initial experiments in bringing model transformation techniques and tools to bear on the domain of building models, and propose some future work.

1 Introduction

The building industry is undergoing a significant evolution, with increasing use of digital models during the design process and throughout the life of a building. There is a rapid transition underway from 2-dimensional, paper-based drawings towards rich 3-dimensional digital models, known as Building Information Models (BIMs), which incorporate detailed geometries as well as metadata related to materials, processes and construction lifecycle. There is, however, a wide variety of different models in use, corresponding to different stakeholders (architects, engineers, owners, regulators, etc), as well as different purposes (as a guide to construction, for performance simulation, for facilities maintenance, etc). The next stage of the change process will be the increasing use of these digital models to perform automated checking, analysis and optimisation of models, and this will require transformations for managing the mappings between the different models in use.

As well as diversity in the kinds of models, there is also diversity in the modelling languages being used, which poses challenges to interoperability [22]. The closest thing to a standardised modelling language is the Industry Foundation

J. Cabot and E. Visser (Eds.): ICMT 2011, LNCS 6707, pp. 93–107, 2011.

Classes, or IFC [6]. IFC offers a broad set of modelling constructs covering a wide variety of disciplines, and is supported (to varying extents) by all the major CAD tool vendors. The IFC specifications are based on the STEP (ISO-10303) suite of modelling standards, and most significantly the Express schema language, ISO 10303-11, and its textual expression, ISO 10303-21.

The Eclipse Modeling Framework (EMF), is the predominant modelling framework being used in the emerging field of model-driven engineering, or MDE. MDE is based on representing artifacts as models, and expressing the mappings between these models using model transformations. EMF provides a metamodelling language, Ecore, and a set of frameworks for managing modelling languages and models, as well as for the generation of serialisation and editing tools. Many of the model transformation languages and tools that have emerged over the past decade have targeted EMF as a platform for representing the models they wish to transform. These include ATL[13], Tefkat [16], and Kermeta [17].

The use of emerging model transformation languages will assist the building industry to leverage its models and open up new possibilities for analysis and optimisation. Simultaneously, the transformations required for managing the relationships between models in the building industry will pose interesting challenges to these languages and tools in terms of scalability, modularity and reusability, and hopefully this will stimulate continuing research into model transformation techniques.

In order to bring the benefits of MDE to bear on the problems of BIM, this paper presents a workbench for experimentation and tool development using model transformation tools on building models. The workbench is achieved using a bridge between the technical spaces of STEP and EMF, in the style of [15]. This is based on a model transformation between the respective metametamodels of the two spaces, in order to map between STEP and EMF metamodels, as well as a mapping of STEP's textual syntax into the EMF framework in order to support integration at the model level. The resultant workbench allows us not only to support the use of STEP models (and especially IFC models) transparently within the EMF environment, but to experiment with evolutions of the these languages in their STEP representation, and to have these variations flow through to be used in transformations.

This paper is structured as follows. The following section provides a brief introduction to the STEP and EMF technical spaces. Section 3 presents the details of the architecture of the technical bridge between the two, including an explanation of the use of transformation technologies in its construction. Section 4 describes early experiments with transformations on building models, as well as a number of future avenues for explorations. Section 5 discusses related work, and is followed by conclusions.

2   Introduction to the Two Technical Spaces

The idea of technical spaces (or technological spaces) was introduced in [15], and elaborated in [3] as a means for reasoning about integration of different technologies. Essentially, a technical space represents a coherent modelling space, with concepts for the construction and management of models, as well as tools for their manipulation, transformation, etc. In this paper, we are interested in the technical spaces of the Eclipse Modeling Framework (EMF), and the Standard for the Exchange of Product model data (STEP).

These technical spaces are well suited for bridging. Much like the spaces used in previous works describing technical space bridges [4,2], the EMF and STEP spaces both have a distinct 3-layer (metametamodel, metamodel, model) architecture (as shown in Figure 2). In addition, the formalisms used in the respective metametamodels are fairly similar, which simplifies (although does not trivialize) the task of mapping between them.

In the remainder of this section, we give brief descriptions of the EMF and STEP technical spaces.

2.1 The EMF Technical Space

The Eclipse Modeling Framework (EMF) [5] is a framework for the definition and management of modelling languages and models within the Eclipse environment. The core of EMF is the Ecore language, which provides a set of constructs for defining a modeling language, playing the "M3" or metametamodel role of the typical 3-layer modelling hierarchy. The Ecore language is based on simple object-oriented modelling structures including packages, classes, attributes and references, and is a very close match to the EMOF variant of the MOF 2.0 specification from the OMG [18].

This language is supported by a number of code generation facilities that allow for the generation of various artifacts from an Ecore modeling language definition. The most significant of these is a set of Java interfaces (and default implementations) for the definition and access of models conforming to it.

Another significant artifact that can be generated from an Ecore model is an XML-based syntax corresponding to the XMI standard, including a reader and writer, which EMF bundles as a "Resource Implementation". However, it is important to note, especially for the purposes of this paper, that although it is the default, XMI is not the only serialization accepted by EMF. The Resource Implementation facility allows for the definition of arbitrary Resource Implementations by implementing *load* and *save* methods for mapping between a URI and a set of Java objects conforming to the generated interfaces.

In addition to the API and XMI generators, there are myriad tools available for the manipulation of EMF models, including frameworks for the checking and enforcement of OCL constraints, for serializing to/from relational databases, for generating reports, and for the construction of graphical editors. Also, and crucially for our interests, EMF is also a common underlying platform for model transformation languages and tools, including ATL, Tefkat, Kermeta, and others.

2.2 The STEP Technical Space

The engineering disciplines in general, and the building construction industry in particular, have long presented interesting technical challenges to software

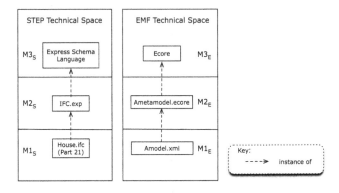

Fig. 1. The three layer architectures of STEP and EMF

developers. The information captured when representing a building design includes a wide variety of considerations, from 2- and 3-dimensional geometry, material information, information about the technical specifications of equipment being used, and information about the organisations and processes involved in assembly. Also, different stakeholders have different viewpoints on the information. For example, a simple concrete column with a marble finish can have information about its size before the finish is applied, its size after it is applied, about its load-bearing characteristics, and about its appearance. Depending whether it is being modelled by architects, structural engineers, mechanical engineers or furniture installation personnel, only a few of these characteristics are of interest.

The most significant activity in the representation of building designs, and their exchange between different CAD/CAM (computer-aided design/manufacturing) systems, has been based on the use of the STEP (Standard for the Exchange of Product model data) ISO standard [10]. The goal of this standard, whose definition began in 1984, is to support the exchange of information about engineering products throughout their lifecycle – from design, through to manufacture and maintenance in use. The STEP standards are intended, as an object-based interoperability specification, to support a virtual representation of physical objects and their constituent parts.

The STEP suite [10] defines a data definition language (or schema language), Express, (Part 1) and methods of encoding files in ASCII text (Part 21), database interfaces (Part 22), using XML (Part 28), and various bindings to programming languages (Parts 23 – 27). The two areas of relevance to this paper are the Express language [12] and the Part 21 exchange file [11]. The Ecore concepts of classes and objects have very similar counterparts in Express, called "entity types" and "instances" respectively. A simplified entity definition for a column, and a Part 21 encoding of a 300 mm square concrete column, 3 m high, are given in Listing 1.1.

Listing 1.1. Sample of Express Schema and Part 21 serialisation

```
ENTITY Column;
    Material: STRING;
    Depth: LengthMeasure;
    Width: LengthMeasure;
    Height: LengthMeasure;
END_ENTITY;

TYPE LengthMeasure = REAL;
    WHERE
        WR1: SELF > 0;
END_Type;

#345= COLUMN("concrete", 300.0, 300.0, 3000.0);
```

There was some building-related activity under the STEP standards, but software vendors became impatient with the speed of the ISO processes and disliked some of the techniques they used in their modelling. In 1995, the International Alliance for Interoperability (now buildingSMART) was formed. The goal was to develop a new standard, the IFCs (Industry Foundation Classes), based on the previous STEP work, but without the overheads of formal ISO standardisation. Express was used as the data modelling language and relevant aspects of STEP were used as the starting point for the IFC development. Most of the STEP geometry model was used, with modifications due to the use of single inheritance. The major modelling effort in the IFCs has been to define the most useful range of object definitions (walls, doors, windows, etc), while retaining a reasonable model size (still over 600 entity definitions) and supporting model extensibility.

3   The STEP-EMF Bridge

The motivating example for building the bridge to mediate between the STEP and EMF technical spaces, which has been used throughout the development of the different pieces of the bridge, is the Express schema definition for version 2x3 of the Industry Foundation Classes (IFC). This is a very large schema, including 653 entity types and 327 data types. This makes it a reasonable test of scalability for the bridge, but the main interest in using it is that the STEP models upon which we are most interested in writing transformations are IFC models.

The process of constructing the bridge consists of 3 main stages. These are depicted in Figure 2 and will be explained in detail in the following subsections. The parts of the figure which are shaded are models which were available to us from various sources and required some minor preparation. The first stage (a) results in a means of reading an Express schema and making it available for processing by a model transformation. The figure shows that an EMF Resource Implementation for the Express metamodel enables the IFC schema to be used as a valid instance of the Express metamodel, and therefore as an input to the second stage. Details of stage (a) of development are given in Section 3.1.

The second stage (b) involves a model transformation that transforms Express schemata (with some limitations, as explained in 3.4) into Ecore models, storing the traceability links between the two as a model. The diagram shows the IFC schema, used as an EMF model via the Express Resource Implementation, being used as an input to the Express2Ecore Tefkat transformation. The Express2Ecore metamodel is the trace model for the transformation, and is used as another input to the transformation. The result is an IFC Ecore model, and an instance of the trace model which will be used in the third stage. This is what we refer to as the "promotion transformation", as the resulting model is an instance of Ecore, and therefore a metamodel in its own right. Details of this stage are explained in Section 3.2.

The third stage (c) is the development of another Resource Implementation which is a means of reading a STEP model in from a part-21 format file and, using the traceability information that has been stored, making the model accessible as an instance of the previously generated Ecore model. The figure shows this process being applied to the trace model of IFC, which allows IFC format files to now be used as valid instances of the IFC Ecore model, and therefore to apply transformations in the workbench to building models, and then write them back out into their CAD-tool-readable format. This stage is explained in detail in Section 3.3.

3.1   Reading Express Schemas

In order to build the transformation from an Express schema to an Ecore model, it was first necessary to be able to access an Express schema as a model under EMF. This was done by defining an Express metamodel using Ecore, then building a parser that could then expose an Express schema file as an instance of this Express Ecore model using EMF's Resource Implementation mechanism.

In defining an Ecore model for the Express schema definition language we cleaned up a copy of a metamodel from the Atlantic Ecore Zoo[1] which is taken from the OMG's reference model for express schemas [20], based on original work by Krause et al[14].

We then build a parser in JavaCC for the Express schema textual format using a grammar from the JavaCC repository of grammars[2] as input. The parser is bundled as an EMF resource implementation registered with the .exp file extension, so that any reference to an express schema file is available within Eclipse as an EMF model with its contents accessible through the EMF interfaces.

3.2   The Express2Ecore Mapping

The second major component of our architecture is the Express2Ecore mapping. This mapping allows for an Express schema file to be transformed into an

---

[1] Atlantic Ecore Model Zoo, http://www.emn.fr/z-info/atlanmod/index.php/Ecore. Initially retrieved October 2009.

[2] JavaCC project site, https://javacc.dev.java.net. Initially retrieved October 2009.

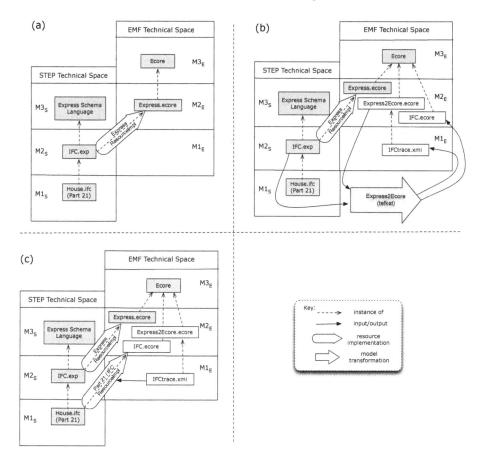

Fig. 2. The architecture of the STEP-EMF technical space bridge

Ecore model. We chose to implement this mapping using a model transformation defined with the Tefkat model transformation language and tool.

The Tefkat language [16] is a logic-based declarative transformation language in which transformations are defined in terms of rules and patterns. It is very similar in its concepts to the QVT Relations language [19] (having originated as a proof of concept for a submission to the QVT standardisation process). The language is implemented by an open-source tool[3] which executes Tefkat transformations on models expressed in the EMF framework.

In addition to its declarative rule underpinnings, one of the advantages of Tefkat for this project was its central use of traceability. Tefkat makes significant use of many-to-many traceability relationships in order to control the production of models during transformation, and these traceability links are persisted as a model for later use. This is significant, as these traceability relationships are used by the Part 21 Resource Implementation described in the next section. Figure 2

---

[3] Tefkat, http://tefkat.net

shows the metamodel used for the traceability links between the Express schema and the generated Ecore model.

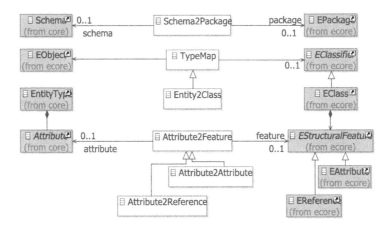

Fig. 3. Model for traceability links

The Express2Ecore transformation expressed in Tefkat currently consists of 29 transformation rules and 8 patterns. For the sake of brevity, the entire transformation is not included in this paper, but an extract - the rule for transforming schemas to packages - can be seen in Listing 1.2.

Listing 1.2. The schema2package rule written in Tefkat

```
RULE schema2package
FORALL Schema s
MAKE EPackage pkg {
    name: s.name;
    nsURI: append("http://",s.name,".ecore");
    nsPrefix: s.name;
}
LINKING Schema2Package WITH schema=s, package=pkg;
```

On the whole, the express2ecore transformation is of moderate size and complexity. There is a reasonable degree of similarity in the high-level structures of the Express and Ecore languages, notably between packages and schemas, classes and entity types, and data types, which exhibit fairly simple one-to-one correspondences. The more complex parts of the transformation involve the transformation of collection types, of Express Select Types, and the potential for "asymmetric" references. In these cases, it is important to maintain a record (as a trace model) of which Express model objects are mapped to which Ecore model objects.

3.3 Part 21 Implementation

The final component of the bridge is an implementation of the Part 21 representation format for models defined in terms of an Express schema. Listing 1.3 shows an extract of a Part 21 file for an IFC 2x3 model that has been exported out of a CAD tool.

Listing 1.3. Extract from a .ifc file using part 21 representation

```
#78=IFCPRODUCTDEFINITIONSHAPE($,$,(#71));
#79=IFCCARTESIANPOINT((1465.63,-476.77,0.));
#80=IFCAXIS2PLACEMENT3D(#79,$,$);
#81=IFCLOCALPLACEMENT(#38,#80);
#82=IFCFURNISHINGELEMENT('323WDY8ln2uPVVI1iuJUG_',#33,'
    table:117565',$,'table',#81,#78,'117565');
```

The file is a flat list of objects, each consisting of an object ID, a type name, and a list of attribute values. The attribute values include basic values (strings, numbers, etc), object references (#1), enumeration literals (delimited by decimal points) as well as symbols for "not defined" ($), and "not needed" (∗). As can perhaps be seen from this example, the file cannot be parsed into a useful EMF model without awareness of the Express schema defining its elements, and the Ecore model to which it has been transformed.

To deal with this, the parser is constructed as an abstract Part 21 parser, which is extended by a helper class to produce a specific EMF Resource Implementation for each schema.

The abstract Part 21 parser and loader is built similarly to the Express parser described in section 3.1. The parser is built on a JavaCC grammar retrieved from the JavaCC repository of grammars[4].

The language-specific aspects of the load process are encapsulated behind an abstract helper class, which provides these methods for each schema/metamodel, mostly by querying the stored trace model. This helper class provides the parser with language-specific information, e.g. finding the right class to instantiate, finding the correct order of attributes, and populating derived attribute values.

The reverse process, of converting an in-memory STEP model into a Part-21 file, is performed by a Visitor pattern, using the same helper to manage the metamodel-specific elements.

3.4 Limitations

The bridge in its current state has a number of limitations.

Expressions, used for attribute derivations and well-formedness rules, are not supported. In order to fully support these, it would be necessary first to extend the Express schema parser to parse these and populate the model appropriately. They would then need to be transformed into some representation attached to the generated Ecore model. One possibility would be to map the expressions to

---

[4] JavaCC project site, https://javacc.dev.java.net. Initially Retrieved October 2009.

OCL, and use the OCL module from the Eclipse MDT project to generate code, in the style of [7].

Although we have covered a substantial portion of the Express schema language (enough to support the mapping of IFC), there are some features that are not handled, such as attribute overriding and schema subsetting, which are not used in IFC.

At present, the bridge allows an Express schema and its instances to be brought into the EMF space, but the reverse, bringing an arbitrary Ecore model and its instances into the STEP space, is not supported. This would require defining an Ecore2Express transformation, and finding some way of bridging Ecore model instances. However, for models migrated from Express, due to the use of EMF Resource Implementations, we do create models from the workbench as files that are usable directly by CAD tools.

4   Using the BIM Workbench

In this section we discuss some of the ways we are using the workbench to write transformations on building models. The first of these is a transformation from IFC to the GDL language used within the ArchiCAD CAD tool family.

4.1   Transforming between IFC and GDL

The first transformation that we have investigated is the transformation from IFC models into GDL programs, used within the ArchiCAD tool family. Although ArchiCAD does include an IFC import feature, our intention in the long term is to explore evolutions of the IFC language to include features such as treatment of parametric models (in the style of [21]), and to validate these evolutions, we need to be able to explore how they integrate into commercial tools.

GDL (Geometric Description Language) is a procedural scripting language for describing and manipulating geometric objects in the ArchiCAD tool family from Graphisoft [9]. Its syntax and control statements resemble BASIC. It contains a large number of statements for drawing three dimensional objects at a location and orientation in a space determined by a small number of coordinate transformation primitives. It also has two dimensional constructs for drawing shapes in plan or elevation views. Each shape or object command has a set of named parameters with some repeating groups. The parameters include textual information about materials, as well as numeric parameters for determining heights, lengths, relative positions of boundary points, angles of extrusion, etc. The objects may also be volumetrically unified, intersected and cut.

GDL uses a stack of geometric coordinate transformations in order to manage repeated and relative placement of multiple objects. For example, a number of floors of a building can be placed at regular intervals in the vertical axis, or a set of wheel spokes can be placed at an angle relative to one another, calculated from a variable containing the number of spokes around a hub.

A Metamodel and Resource Implementation for GDL. For the purpose of importing tool-independent library object descriptions into the ArchiCAD tool family, we have created an Ecore metamodel of the coordinate transformations and object creation primitives in GDL. This was a fairly straightforward translation of each GDL language primitive of interest, representing it as a class, and its parameters as a set of attributes. This model is used as a target metamodel for transformations from IFC objects. In the same way as we deal with the concrete syntax of IFC, we have created an EMF Resource Implementation of the GDL metamodel which saves model instances directly into the GDL language syntax. This was done with the Xtext tools by manipulating the default grammar generated from the metamodel to match the language syntax described in the GDL Reference Manual [9]. The grammar is partial, and the Resource Implementation is intended only to parse the generated GDL from an ArchiCAD composite object export, rather than an arbitrary GDL program.

Transforming IFC to GDL. Our first GDL metamodel use case is the import of an object into ArchiCAD from a tool-independent library of IFC models provided by building product manufacturers. For this purpose we define a Tefkat transformation from IFC to GDL, using our Ecore metamodels as source and target model types, respectively.

One of the main challenges in using a declarative transformation language such as Tefkat, where there is no explicit control of the order in which transformation rules are evaluated, is ensuring that the target GDL statements are placed in the correct order. Ordering of GDL statements in the target model is achieved using Tefkat's traceability features, and constraining the order of collections in the target model using the BEFORE constraint.

Another challenge in the transformation was dealing with relative coordinate systems. Both IFC and GDL allow the user to define objects and the shapes that make them up using relative coordinate systems (as opposed to using a single coordinate system). This is essential in order to allow the replication or transposition of a hierarchy of shapes within a design while preserving their relative position. So, as well as mapping between IFC's geometry concepts and appropriate statements in GDL, it is important to handle the coordinate system conversions. However, the two languages represent these coordinate systems in different ways, with IFC attaching a coordinate system, in the form of a location and two reference axes, to any geometric object, while GDL uses a stack of matrix transforms. The generation of an appropriate matrix transform, and the appropriate placement of push and pop operations within the GDL program, are handled, once again, using Tefkat's traceability features.

Currently, the IFC to GDL transformation supports the most commonly used IFC geometric shape representations, which has been sufficient to demonstrate the viability of using Tefkat to manage the transformation between the two languages. Early indications are that large IFC models do not pose a problem, although this may change as the transformations also become more complex.

The next steps will be to expand the coverage of geometric representations, and to begin exploring modifications to the IFC Express schema to support new features such as parametric geometry and object families.

Transforming GDL to IFC. Our second use case, not yet underway, for the GDL metamodel and its Resource Implementation is the export of library objects from ArchiCAD to the tool-independent IFC object model library. However, at this point it is unlikely that we will use a declarative language such as Tefkat, for this transformation. The transformation from an imperative language like GDL to a more declarative, like IFC, resembles the definition of an interpreter, and this style of transformation may be better supported by an imperative language like Kermeta[17], or using Java and the generated EMF interfaces.

4.2   Future Uses of the Workbench

There are a number of other applications that we are beginning to explore using the workbench.

The first of these is a transformation to convert our IFC-based library objects to Revit. Rather than providing a file-based format for importing models like ArchiCAD, Revit provides a programmatic API. One possibility for this is to build an XML-based representation based on the factory methods provided as part of this API.

Another interesting potential application is the use of model merging tools such as those in the ATL, Kermeta and Epsilon suites, to support the integration of different discipline models. It is quite common for architects, structural engineers, mechanical engineers, etc to build separate models during a design project. In order to perform even simple analyses such as clash detection, these models must be merged, ensuring that objects are placed correctly relative to each other, and that objects are not duplicated. Most current tools rely on shared object identifiers in order to merge correctly, and it would be interesting to see whether approaches to model merging might offer more flexibility.

A third area of exploration is that of domain-specific languages. IFC is a generalist language, in that it covers a wide variety of design disciplines, and at a fine level of detail. However, as discussed in [8], there is also a good case to be made for the definition of smaller languages, specific to a certain discipline, or at a higher level of abstraction.

A final application is the use of aspect-oriented modelling techniques. On a large project, rather than explicitly modelling all the aspects of a building's objects, it is common to express details such as paints, finishes, and wall constructions in a building specification. The building specification uses predicates to describe which objects should have which finishes applied, e.g. "all walls of bathrooms on floors 3 through 7 will have marble tiles". This is very similar to the way aspect-orientation works, and we are beginning to investigate these techniques in order to either add or check detail in a building information model.

5   Related Work

This is our second attempt at bringing IFC models in the Eclipse/EMF technical space. The previous attempt was the DesignView platform, which formed the basis for the LCADesign[5] and Automated Estimator design analysis tools. DesignView took a different approach to integrating IFC models, based on the programmatic conversion of IFC models into a much simpler Ecore model for representing buildings called the Intelligent Building Model. This model used a more ad-hoc notion of building element and material types, and a simple geometric representation using triangles. This simplified the development of applications to analyse designs, but made it difficult to modify objects' geometry, to build transformations involving geometry, and to take models back into the CAD tools from which they had come.

The use of the technical (or technological) spaces metaphor for describing the kind of meta-hierarchical integration that we describe here dates from an initial paper by Kurtev, Bézivin and Aksit [15]. Bézivin et al developed the theoretical framework for bridging technical spaces in [3], and they present two practical applications of the approach in [2] and [4], describing bridges between GME and EMF, and MS/DSL and EMF respectively.

The approach we have taken with our bridge is very similar philosophically to that used by Bézivin et al, in that both their and our approaches involve a concept mapping at the M3 level, the representation of the M3 model of one space in the M2 level of the other, and a "promotion" transformation for bridging at M2. There are differences in method, however. Bézivin et al use transformations in order to bring non-EMF concrete representations into and out of the EMF space as new artifacts, whereas we use handwritten Java parsers and printers, wrapped in the EMF Resource Implementation mechanism. We hope that this will make for a more transparent import/export of STEP models, but the difference is small. Also, at the M1 level, [2] uses a higher order model transformation as a generative approach to customising an M1 translation, whereas our approach uses a generalised Resource Implementation customised using the trace model.

As was discussed in section 3.1, our Express metamodel was sourced from work originating with [14] and continuing with [20], on mapping Express schemata to UML models. Given the commonalities between UML class diagrams and Ecore, there is obviously crossover between our work and the ongoing work within the OMG. However, there are significant differences between the range of constructs available in UML and Ecore. Because of the increased scope of UML, a transformation from Express to UML would probably be simpler, although this would limit our choice of transformation technologies, most of which do not operate on CMOF models.

Agostinho et al, in [1], also discuss bridging the STEP technical space, albeit not using that terminology. They present a framework for using model morphisms in order to map an Express schema and models into the ontologies technical space.

---

[5] http://www.ecquate.com

6   Conclusion and Future Work

We have presented a workbench in which building information models defined using IFC and related STEP languages, can be used in combination with model transformation languages and tools based in the EMF technical space. This is achieved through a bridge between the STEP and EMF technical spaces, that brings the Express schema definition and Part-21 file format languages into the EMF space (and writes them back out in their original format), and uses a transformation between Express schemas and Ecore models to expose STEP models as EMF models.

The workbench allows us to experiment both with writing model transformations using EMF-based model transformation languages and tools, but on models initially defined using STEP standards. Because of the way we bridge the technical spaces using EMF Resource Implementations, rather than using model-level transformations, these models work straight out of STEP-based tools without the need for the user to explicitly import them into EMF.

Using the Express2ecore mapping (and its resultant trace model) as the basis for the bridge allows us to experiment with alternative versions of the metamodels we are interested in (most significantly IFC). It also allows us to experiment (to some extent) with modifying the original IFC Express schemas to support new building modeling techniques (such as parametric geometry).

The workbench has been used in the definition of a Tefkat transformation for converting object definitions expressed in IFC into the GDL language used by ArchiCAD. We also outline a number of other transformations which are being explored, using a range of model transformation languages and associated tools.

References

1. Agostinho, C., Sarraipa, J., D'Antonio, F., Jardim-Gonçalves, R.: Enhancing STEP-based Interoperabity Using Model Morphisms. In: Proceedings, 3rd International Conference on Interoperability of Enterprise Software and Applications (I-ESA 2007), pp. 817–828. Springer, Heidelberg (2007)
2. Bézivin, J., Brunette, C., Chevrel, R., Jouault, F., Kurtev, I.: Bridging the Generic Modeling Environment (GME) and the Eclipse Modeling Framework (EMF). In: Proceedings, Best Practices for Model Driven Software Development at OOPSLA 2005, San Diego, California, USA (2005)
3. Bézivin, J., Devedzic, V., Djuric, D., Favreau, J.M., Gasevic, D., Jouault, F.: An M3-neutral infrastructure for bridging model engineering and ontology engineering. In: Proceedings. In: 1st International Conference on Interoperability of Enterprise Software and Applications (INTEROP-ESA 2005), pp. 159–171. Springer, Heidelberg (2005)
4. Bézivin, J., Hillairet, G., Jouault, F., Kurtev, I., Piers, W.: Bridging the MS/DSL Tools and the Eclipse Modeling Framework. In: Proceedings, International Workshop on Software Factories at OOPSLA 2005, San Diego, California, USA (2005)
5. Budinsky, F., Steinberg, D., Merks, E., Ellersick, R., Grose, T.J.: Eclipse Modeling Framework: A Developer's Guide. Addison-Wesley, Reading (2003)

6. BuildingSMART: Industry Foundation Classes, Edition 3, Technical Corrigendum 1 (July 2007), http://www.buildingsmart.com
7. Damus, C.: Implementing Model Integrity in EMF with MDT OCL. Eclipse Corner Articles (February 2007)
8. Fernando, R., Steel, J., Drogemuller, R.: Using domain-specific languages in the building information modeling workflow. In: Proceedings, 16th International Conference on Computer Aided Architectural Design Research in Asia (CAADRIA 2011) (2011) (to appear)
9. Graphisoft: GDL Reference Guide. Graphisoft (2004)
10. International Standards Organisation (ISO): Industrial automation systems and integration – product data representation and exchange – part 1: Overview and fundamental principles. ISO Standard 10303-1:1994 (1994)
11. International Standards Organisation (ISO): Industrial automation systems and integration – product data representation and exchange – part 21: Implementation methods: Clear text encoding of the exchange structure. ISO Standard 10303-21:2002 (2002)
12. International Standards Organisation (ISO): Industrial automation systems and integration – product data representation and exchange – part 11: Description methods: The express language reference manual. ISO Standard 10303-11:2004 (2004)
13. Jouault, F., Kurtev, I.: Transforming models with ATL. In: Bruel, J.-M. (ed.) MoDELS 2005. LNCS, vol. 3844, pp. 128–138. Springer, Heidelberg (2006)
14. Krause, F.L., Kaufmann, U.: Meta-modelling for interoperability in product design. CIRP Annals - Manufacturing Technology 56(1), 159–162 (2007)
15. Kurtev, I., Bézivin, J., Aksit, M.: Technological spaces: An initial appraisal. In: Chung, S., et al. (eds.) CoopIS 2002, DOA 2002, and ODBASE 2002. LNCS, vol. 2519, Springer, Heidelberg (2002)
16. Lawley, M., Steel, J.: Practical declarative model transformation with tefkat. In: Bruel, J.-M. (ed.) MoDELS 2005. LNCS, vol. 3844, pp. 139–150. Springer, Heidelberg (2006)
17. Muller, P.-A., Fleurey, F., Jézéquel, J.-M.: Weaving executability into object-oriented meta-languages. In: Briand, L.C., Williams, C. (eds.) MoDELS 2005. LNCS, vol. 3713, pp. 264–278. Springer, Heidelberg (2005)
18. Object Management Group: Meta Object Facility (MOF) Core Specification Version 2.0. OMG Document No. formal/2006-01-01 (March 2006)
19. Object Management Group: MOF 2.0 Query/View/Transformation. OMG Document No. formal/2008-04-03 (January 2006)
20. Object Management Group: Reference Metamodel for the EXPRESS Information Modeling Language Specification. OMG Document No. formal/2010-10-01 (October 2010)
21. Pratt, M.J.: Extension of the standard ISO10303 (STEP) for the exchange of parametric and variational CAD models. In: Proceedings of the Tenth International IFIP WG 5.2/5.3 Conference PROLAMAT98 (1998)
22. Steel, J., Drogemuller, R.: Model interoperability in building information modelling. In: Knowledge Industry Survival Strategy (KISS) Workshop at Australian Software Engineering Conference (ASWEC 2009) (April 2009)

Model Transformation Analysis:
Staying Ahead of the Maintenance Nightmare*

Marcel F. van Amstel and Mark G.J. van den Brand

Department of Mathematics and Computer Science
Eindhoven University of Technology
P.O. Box 513, 5600 MB, Eindhoven, The Netherlands
{M.F.v.Amstel,M.G.J.v.d.Brand}@tue.nl

Abstract. Model-driven engineering (MDE) is a software engineering discipline that is gaining popularity, both in academia and industry. One of the integral concepts of MDE is model transformation. The prominent role of model transformations in MDE requires them to be treated in a similar way as traditional software artifacts. Numerous analysis techniques supporting the maintenance process exist for traditional software artifacts. However, few techniques tailored towards analyzing model transformations currently exist. We present in this paper three complementary techniques for the analysis of model transformations. These techniques are mainly focused on increasing the understanding of model transformations. Two of the proposed techniques have already been employed for the analysis of different kinds of software artifacts, viz. metrics, and structure and trace analysis. The third analysis technique, i.e., metamodel coverage analysis is specific for model transformations and does therefore not exist for different kinds of software artifacts.

1 Introduction

Model-driven engineering (MDE) is a software engineering paradigm that aims at dealing with increasing software complexity and improving productivity [1]. MDE combines domain-specific languages [2] for modeling at a higher level of abstraction and model transformations for the automated generation of various artifacts from these models [3]. MDE is gradually being adopted by industry [4]. From collaborations with our industrial partners, we can conclude that this is a trend likely to continue. Since MDE is becoming increasingly important, so are model transformations. Model transformations are in many ways similar to traditional software artifacts, i.e., they have to be used by multiple developers, have to be changed according to changing requirements and should preferably be reused. Numerous analysis techniques supporting software maintenance exist for all kinds of software artifacts such as source code or models. However, few techniques currently exist for analyzing model transformations. A reason for this is

---

* This work has been carried out as part of the FALCON project under the responsibility of the Embedded Systems Institute with Vanderlande Industries as the industrial partner. This project is partially supported by the Netherlands Ministry of Economic Affairs under the Embedded Systems Institute (BSIK03021) program.

J. Cabot and E. Visser (Eds.): ICMT 2011, LNCS 6707, pp. 108–122, 2011.

that MDE and thereby model transformations is a relatively young research discipline and most effort is invested in applications and in improving model transformation techniques and tools[1]. To prevent model transformations from becoming the next *maintenance nightmare*, analysis techniques should be developed for them to assist in the maintenance process. Moreover, proper tool support is required for further adoption of MDE by the industry [5]. Therefore, we present in this paper three complementary techniques for analyzing model transformations. These techniques are mainly focused on facilitating model transformation comprehension since a significant proportion of the time required for maintenance, debugging, and reusing tasks is spent on understanding [6]. In this paper, we focus on model transformations created using a heterogeneous collection of EMF-based model transformation languages, viz., ATL [7], Xtend [8], and QVT Operational Mappings (QVTO) [9]. However, we expect that the techniques can be applied to different model transformation formalisms as well.

Two of the analysis techniques we propose have already been employed for analyzing different kinds of software artifacts. In this paper, we show that they can be used for model transformations as well. The first analysis technique is metrics collection. Metrics can give quick insights in a transformation and can also be used for quality assessment. The second analysis technique is structure and dependency analysis. This analysis technique can be used to explicate the relations between different parts of a model transformation. The last analysis technique is metamodel coverage visualization. It can be used to analyze the relation between a model transformation and the metamodels it is defined on. This analysis technique is specific for model transformations and does therefore not exist for different kinds of software artifacts. The analysis techniques we propose are not specific for a particular model transformation formalism. Some of the analysis techniques may however be less applicable for certain formalisms. For example, a formalism with only implicit invocations, such as typical graph transformation formalisms, has no need for the trace analysis technique.

The remainder of this paper is structured as follows. In Section 2, we discuss the three techniques for analyzing model transformations. Section 3 describes the toolset we use for automating the analysis. In Section 4, we demonstrate how the techniques can be applied in practice. Section 5 describes related work. Conclusions and directions for future work are given in Section 6.

2   Analysis Techniques

2.1   Metrics

Software metrics have been studied extensively over the last decades [10]. Metrics have been proposed for measuring various kinds of software artifacts, e.g., object-oriented software, functional programs, UML models, and process models. Although it has been recognized that metrics should be proposed for measuring model transformations [11], little research has been performed in this area.

---

[1] See the proceedings of the ICMT 2008, ICMT 2009, and ICMT 2010 conferences.

Metrics for Model Transformations. We have proposed four sets of metrics for measuring model transformations, viz., for ASF+SDF [12], ATL [13], Xtend [14], and QVTO [14]. All four of these formalisms have different characteristics. ASF+SDF is a term rewriting system in which transformations are implemented in a functional style using conditional rewrite rules [15]. ATL is a hybrid language, i.e., transformation rules can be written using both imperative and declarative constructs [7]. Xtend can best be characterized as an imperative language with some traits of a functional language [8]. QVTO is an imperative language [9]. Although the formalisms differ, there is still a lot of overlap. This should not be surprising, since they serve a common purpose, i.e., implementing model transformations. Therefore, similar metrics can be found for all four formalisms and probably for other model transformation formalisms as well. However, due to the different nature of the formalisms also a number of formalism-specific metrics have been defined.

Metrics as Quality Predictors. Metrics can be used for various purposes. They give quick insights into the characteristics of a transformation such as its size or the number of input models it requires. Metrics can also be used to detect bad smells in a transformation. Some of the traditional code smells [16] apply, maybe in a slightly adapted form, to model transformations as well. Examples of this are *long helper function, large module, long parameter list*, and *dead code*.

Since long, research has been performed to use metrics to evaluate the quality of software [17]. In a similar way, metrics can be used to assess the quality of model transformations. Quality attributes such as *understandability* and *modifiability* are important with respect to the maintenance process, since they directly affect the maintainability of a model transformation. For the maintenance process, the quality of the model transformation artifact itself is of relevance. This is referred to as the internal quality of a model transformation [18]. Measuring a model transformation using a set of metrics alone is not enough for assessing its (internal) quality. A relation between metrics and quality attributes [17,19] should be established. Therefore, empirical studies should be conducted. For ASF+SDF, we performed such an empirical study [12]. Metrics were extracted from a number of model transformations created using ASF+SDF. The same collection of model transformations was quantitatively evaluated by experts. We analyzed the correlations between the metrics data and the expert feedback. Significant correlations with metrics were found for a number of quality attributes. The main challenge with these empirical studies is to find enough participants to acquire significant results. Therefore, performing empirical studies for the other formalisms discussed in this paper is a point for future work.

2.2   Structure and Dependency Analysis

Structure Analysis. Most model transformation formalisms have support for structuring model transformations by packaging transformation rules into modules [20]. We propose to visualize the import graph of a model transformation, i.e., the modules comprising the model transformations and their import relations. A (small) example of this visualization is depicted in Figure 1. The arrows should be interpreted as *imports* relations. Such a high-level overview can act as a guide for navigating the model transformation, for instance during maintenance tasks. The visualization depicted in Figure 1 shows the import relation between a pair of modules only. In the remainder of this section, we will show another visualization where calls between modules are visualized as well.

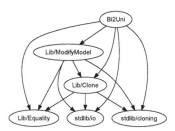

Fig. 1. Structure visualization

Dependency Analysis. In Section 2.1, we discussed a number of metrics that can be used to acquire insights into the dependency relation of modules and transformation functions comprising a model transformation. These metrics measure the fan-in and fan-out of modules and transformation functions. While these metrics provide quick insights, they are merely numbers. Therefore we propose another analysis technique that makes the call relation between transformation functions visible. For this purpose we use the tool ExtraVis [21]. A partial screen shot of the tool displaying the call relation of an, in this case Xtend, model transformation is depicted in Figure 2. The outer ring displays the modules that comprise the transformation. The second ring displays the different kinds of transformation function types per module. Note that in Xtend there is only one function type, i.e., *extension*, therefore only that is shown. The third ring displays the different kinds of transformation function subtypes per function type. The inner ring displays the transformation functions that comprise the transformation grouped per function subtype. The circle in the middle displays the calls that are being made between transformation functions. Callers and callees are connected to each other by an edge. The caller is on the green end of the edge, the callee is on the red end of the edge.

Visualization of dependency data has various useful applications in the development and maintenance process of a model transformation. By actually seeing in what way transformation functions depend on each other and interact, the understanding of a transformation may increase. Also, undesired calls between transformation functions can be identified just by looking at the visual representation of the call graph. Similarly, transformation functions that are never called, and which may therefore be obsolete, can easily be recognized. We will show an example of this in Section 4.1. Metrics data can indicate whether there are transformation functions with a high fan-in or fan-out value. Using the visualization, fan-in/fan-out analysis can be performed in more detail. Not only

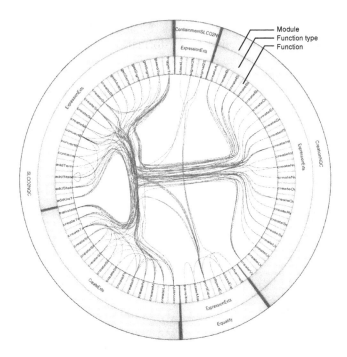

Fig. 2. Trace visualization

can it be observed that there are some transformation functions with high fan-in/fan-out, the exact functions that cause this can be pointed out. Since the visualization groups transformation functions per module, calls between modules can be examined as well. In this way, modules with low cohesion and high coupling [22] can be revealed.

Dynamic Dependency Analysis. ExtraVis has the option to provide additional detail with the call relation, such as for example the order and frequency of the calls. This feature could be exploited to analyze the dynamics of a model transformation by adding runtime data to the call relation. A declarative formalism like ATL or QVTR does not require explicit rule invocation, therefore this technique may be less applicable for these formalisms. However, for imperative transformation formalisms it can have similar additional benefits as for traditional programming languages, such as feature location and feature comprehension. Since runtime data is input dependent, in the case of model transformation input model dependent, feature location may be useful for deriving characteristics of a possibly huge input model.

2.3 Metamodel Coverage Analysis

A model transformation transforms models corresponding to a source metamodel to models corresponding to a target metamodel, i.e., it is defined on the metamodel level. For some transformations it is required to transform all elements of the source metamodel, e.g., in case of language migration, whereas for other transformations it suffices to transform only a subset of the elements of the source metamodel, e.g., in case of partial refinement. Similarly, some transformations generate model elements for every metamodel element in the target metamodel, whereas other transformations generate model elements for a subset of the metamodel elements only. To acquire insight in the parts of the source and target metamodel that are *covered* by a transformation, we propose two visualization techniques for coverage analysis.

Metamodel Coverage. Figure 3 shows an example of coverage visualization. The figure shows a metamodel, where the metaclasses and references that are

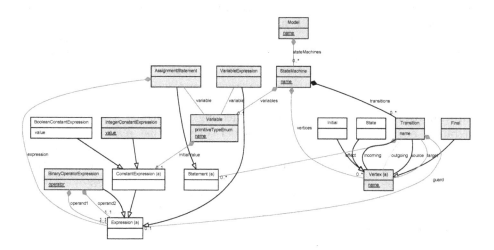

Fig. 3. Metamodel coverage visualization

covered by the transformation are colored grey. Attributes that are covered are underlined. An input metamodel element is covered if it serves as input for a transformation function in the transformation. An output metamodel element is covered if it is generated as output by a transformation function in the transformation. The metamodel elements that are considered in the coverage analysis are metaclasses, attributes, and references.

Coverage analysis can be used to analyze the completeness of a transformation. Using the visualization, it can be observed whether all the metamodel elements from the source model that should be transformed are in fact covered by the transformation. Conversely, it can be observed whether all metamodel elements from the target metamodel that should be generated are generated by the transformation. Of course the coverage visualization can also be used to detect metamodel elements that should *not* be covered by a transformation.

There may be several reasons why a particular metamodel element is not covered by a transformation. First, coverage of a metamodel element may not be required for the transformation task at hand. If the requirements of the transformation dictate that only part of the metamodel needs to be transformed, it is not necessary that the remainder of the metamodel is covered by transformation functions. Second, the transformation may be incomplete, e.g., a transformation function for the metamodel element that is not covered has not yet been implemented. Third, the metamodel element may be an abstract metaclass. Some model transformation formalisms do not allow an abstract metaclass to be the input of a transformation function since they cannot be instantiated. However, there are transformation formalisms that do allow this. For example, in ATL it is possible to use an abstract metaclass as input pattern of an abstract transformation rule that can be extended to transform the non-abstract children of the abstract metaclass. In this case, the abstract class is covered by the transformation, however, by a rule that will not be executed. Last, a bidirectional reference may have been used in one direction only. A bidirectional reference between two metaclasses is a reference that is navigable from both metaclasses. It may have a different name in both metaclasses. In our visualization, we treat a bidirectional reference as two distinct references. In this way it can be determined in which direction the reference is used in the transformation. Therefore, it is possible that the reference is not covered by the transformation in the other direction.

Metamodel Coverage Relation. Projecting coverage on a metamodel diagram is one way of visualizing metamodel coverage that may provide useful insights into a model transformation. It is however impossible to trace the coverage back to the transformation, i.e., the relation between a transformation element and the metamodel element it covers is invisible in the diagram. Therefore, we introduce another coverage visualization technique to overcome this matter. Figure 4 shows an example of a visualization where the relation between a transformation element and the metamodel elements it covers is made explicit. The visualization shown here is part of a screen shot from the tool TreeComparer [23]. TreeComparer has originally been designed for comparing hierarchically organized data sets. Therefore, the metamodels and transformation are structured hierarchically in the image. On the top of the image, the metamodels are shown. On the bottom of the image, the transformation is shown. There is a line between a module element and a metaclass if and only if the metaclass is covered by a transformation element. Note that in this visualization attributes and references are not considered.

TreeComparer has support for selecting a part of the metamodel elements, transformation elements, or relations. In Figure 4, for example, a selection is made of all the input and output metamodel elements covered by the lazy matched rules of an ATL model transformation. The tool also allows zooming in on a selection to get a more detailed view on that selection. This selection and zooming functionality enables detailed study of coverage of part of a transformation or the involved metamodels. Highlighting the transformation functions that cover a (group of) metamodel element(s) facilitates navigation of a transformation, which may increase the understanding of a transformation. Moreover, visualization of the coverage of certain parts of a transformation can be used

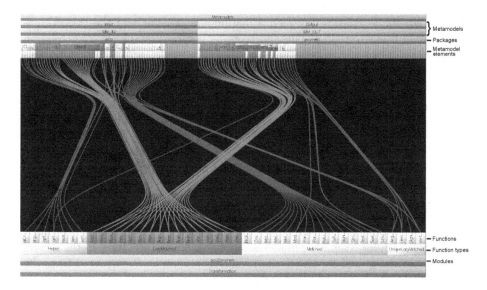

Fig. 4. Metamodel coverage relation visualization

by developers to determine whether the selected transformation functions cover the required parts of the involved metamodels. In this way, coverage relation visualization helps in finding errors during development.

Model transformations can be defined on multiple input or output metamodels. It may be the case that another transformation has to be developed for one of the involved metamodels. By selecting this metamodel, the transformation functions that cover this metamodel are highlighted. In this way, coverage relation visualization can be used to identify parts of a transformation eligible for reuse. Similarly, when a metamodel is developed based on an existing one, this analysis technique can be used to identify reusable transformation functions.

Coverage analysis can also be used to assist in the process of co-evolution of metamodel and transformation. It can be used to determine whether the changes to a metamodel affect the transformation. If the meta-classes that are covered by a transformation do not change, there is no problem and the transformation is still usable with the evolved metamodel. However, if there are meta-classes that are covered by a transformation that do change or are removed, then the transformation will have to evolve as well. The coverage relation analysis technique can be used to determine which transformation functions are affected by changed or removed meta-classes. In Section 4.2, we will elaborate a use case where coverage analysis is used in the process of co-evolution of metamodel and transformation.

The two coverage visualization techniques described in this section are complementary rather than competing alternatives. The first coverage visualization technique, i.e., where coverage is projected on a diagram representing an input or output metamodel of a transformation has a familiar layout. Besides the coverage of metaclasses, it also shows coverage of attributes and references. However, there is no visible relation between a metamodel element and the transformation element it is covered by. This shortcoming is solved by the coverage relation visualization technique, where these relations are made explicit. However, this visualization is less detailed. It only shows coverage of metaclasses.

3   Toolset

We have implemented a toolset such that the analysis techniques presented in Section 2 can be applied automatically. The transformation formalisms we have implemented the toolset for are ATL, QVTo and Xtend. Figure 5 depicts the extensible architecture of the toolset. In the first step, the code of a model transformation is parsed, resulting in a model that represents the abstract syntax tree (AST) of that transformation. This model can be represented in different formats depending on the transformation formalism. For ATL and QVTo this is an Ecore model, for Xtend the model is represented using POJO's. In the second step, the data required for the desired analysis technique is extracted from the model representing the AST and represented as another model. For ATL this extraction is implemented as an ATL transformation, for QVTo as a QVTo transformation, and for Xtend as a Java program. Note that for the coverage analysis techniques, the source and target metamodel of the transformation need to be provided as input as well. In the third and last step, the analysis model is transformed into the input format of the tool used for the analysis. Typically, this step is performed using some form of pretty-printing. We used a combination of Xpand templates and Java programs to perform the pretty printing.

Fig. 5. Tool set architecture

The advantage of this architecture is that it is extensible. To enable the analysis techniques for a new model transformation formalism, only the data extractors have to be implemented. The pretty-printers can be reused. In principal, also a parser need to be implemented. However, a parser is typically provided with the implementation of the formalism. When implementing a new analysis technique, extractors need to be implemented for each of the formalisms as well as a pretty-printer for that technique.

4   Case Studies

We describe our experiences with the analysis techniques in an ongoing MDE project. In [24], we have described our experiences with the iterative development of a domain-specific language. This language is accompanied with a set of model transformations, implemented using Xtend and ATL, that can be used to refine models created with the language. These model transformations are the subjects of our study.

4.1   Detecting Obsolete Transformation Elements

Metrics were extracted from one of the Xtend transformations using our toolset. Table 1 shows an excerpt of the generated metrics report.

Metric	Value
# Modules	4
# Extensions	94
# Uncalled Extensions	18
# Uncalled Modules	2

Metric	Min.	Max.	Mean	Median	Std. Dev.
# Extensions per Module	3	58	23,5	16,5	24,45
# Unique Extension Names per Module	2	40	17	13	17,17
Extension Fan In	0	14	2,63	1	3,44
Extension Fan Out	0	30	2,63	1	5,04
Module Fan In	0	48	12,25	0,5	23,84
Module Fan Out	0	49	12,25	0	24,5

Table 1. Excerpt of the metrics report

The metrics indicate that the transformation contains eighteen extensions (transformation functions) that are never called by other extensions. These extensions are divided over two modules, since the metrics indicate that there are two modules that contain extensions that are never called from other modules and that there are no modules that contain no extensions. From a maintenance perspective it is useful to determine which extensions and modules are uncalled, such that the transformation can be adapted if required. For this purpose, the dependency graph can be employed. The dependency graph of the transformation is depicted in Figure 6.

The eighteen extensions that are never called can easily be recognized using the ExtraVis tool. For illustratory purposes, they have been marked in the figure. Note that some of these extensions do have incoming calls. These are self calls that are excluded when determining uncalled extensions. From the graph can be concluded that the modules containing extensions that are never called by extensions from different modules are named MergeObjects (left) and Clone (top). From the import graph (not shown here) can be concluded that the transformation is built up hierarchically. The MergeObjects module is the top module that only calls functions lower in the import hierarchy. Since it does not receive calls from modules lower in the hierarchy, the module is considered uncalled. As for the other uncalled module and extensions, we presented our findings to the designer of the transformation. He indicated that the Clone module is a leftover from an earlier version of the transformation and that it can (and should) be removed. The CreationSLCO module (right) is a module that is used by six other transformations as well. We also analyzed these transformations. It turned out that four of the extensions in the CreationSLCO are never called by any of these transformations. Also these turned out to be obsolete and should be removed.

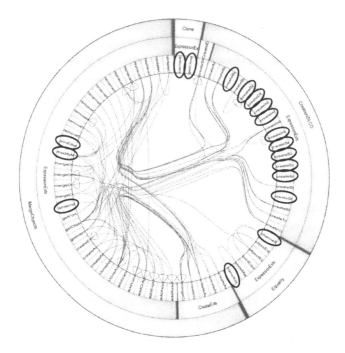

Fig. 6. Using dependency analysis to detect obsolete transformation elements

4.2 Metamodel and Transformation Co-evolution

During every iteration in the language development, the language has evolved. This is reflected in the metamodel. Since the refining model transformations are based on that metamodel, they have to evolve as well. To identify the transformation rules and helpers that are affected by the evolution, we employed the coverage relation visualization technique described in Section 2.3.

Figure 7 shows the relation between the evolved metamodel on top and a model transformation that needs to co-evolve on the bottom. On the top right, there are a number of metaclasses that have not outgoing edges. This means these metaclasses are not covered by any of the transformation functions or helpers in the transformation. These metaclasses are all the metaclasses that were added to the metamodel due to the evolution of the language. Since, in this case, all metaclasses need to be covered by the transformation, it is easily observed for which metaclasses transformation rules should be added. On the bottom of the figure there are ten matched rules that have no outgoing edges. Matched rules have to match on a metaclass. This implies that these matched rules match on metaclasses that are not present in the metamodel. Therefore they are obsolete and may be removed from the transformation. After inspection of the transformation it turned out that these rules all match on metaclasses that were removed from the metamodel due to the evolution of the language.

Already in this example with a relatively small metamodel and ditto model transformation, the coverage relation visualization turned out to be of great help.

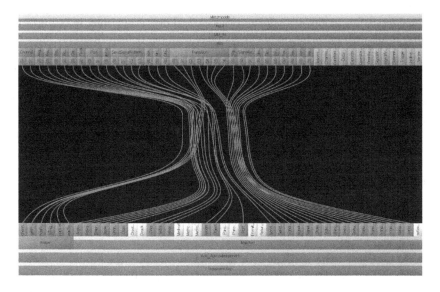

Fig. 7. Using coverage analysis for transformation co-evolution

Therefore we expect that it will prove even more beneficial in cases with larger metamodels and model transformations.

5   Related Work

Anastasakis et al. recognize that the quality of model transformations is crucial for the success of MDE [25]. Suitable validation and analysis techniques should therefore be applied to them. They consider model transformations as a special kind of models that can be subject to existing model analysis techniques. The authors use Alloy, a textual declarative modeling language based on first-order relational logic that is accompanied with a fully automated analysis tool. A model transformation and its source and target metamodel are transformed into an Alloy model and subsequently analyzed using the analysis tool. The analysis tool can among others be used to simulate the model transformation and to check whether certain assertions hold.

Kapová et al. have defined a set of metrics for evaluating maintainability of model transformations created with QVT Relations [26]. Most of the 24 metrics they defined are similar to the metrics we have defined. Their extraction process of 21 of their metrics has been automated by means of a tool in a similar way as we have done for ATL [13] and QVTO [14]. They have applied their tool to three different transformations to demonstrate how to judge the maintainability of a model transformation using their metrics. This judgement is based on expectations rather than empirical evidence. Performing empirical validation is also a point they indicate for future work.

Verification of metamodel coverage has been studied by others before. Wang et al. see metamodel coverage as an aspect of validation and verification that should be considered for model transformations [27]. They state that it is important because it allows identification of the scope of a model transformation. They base coverage on the core MOF structural constructs, viz., class, feature, inheritance, and association. The coverage analysis we propose does not consider inheritance coverage, although this can be derived from the coverage visualization. In the paper, they present a prototype implementation for the Tefkat transformation language. McQuillan and Power address metamodel coverage in the context of testing model transformations [28]. They base their coverage criteria on criteria for coverage of UML class diagrams. The main difference between our approach and the two aforementioned approaches is that we use visualization techniques to present coverage instead of listing the (un)covered metamodel elements.

6   Conclusions and Future Work

We have addressed the necessity for analysis techniques for model transformations to, among others, assist in the maintenance process. In this paper, we proposed three such techniques. First, we proposed the use of metrics to acquire quick insights into transformations and to assess their quality. Second, we proposed two different ways to visualize dependencies between the components of a transformation. Third, we proposed to analyze the coverage of the metamodels that a transformation is defined on by means of two different visualizations. The proposed techniques complement each other rather than being competing alternatives. A toolset has been implemented to automate the analysis techniques.

The metrics we defined for ASF+SDF have been validated by means of an empirical study. Also the metrics for ATL are currently being validated in a similar empirical study. We have actively used the dependency and coverage analysis techniques in an MDE project. They have shown to be of great assistance when dealing with evolution or maintenance of model transformations. To reap the full benefits of the techniques, they should be embedded in (existing) model transformation tools.

An obvious point for future work is to generalize the techniques even further. Currently, all three analysis techniques have been implemented for three model transformation formalisms. Metrics have even been implemented for two other formalisms as well, one by us for ASF+SDF [12] and one for QVTR by Kapová et al. [26]. We expect that our techniques can be applied to other model transformation formalisms as well, however research has to be performed to confirm this. We would also like to investigate the applicability of our techniques to graph transformation formalisms.

Two of the techniques discussed in this paper have already been employed for the analysis of traditional software artifacts. Of course this is just the tip of the iceberg. There are a lot more analysis techniques available that could be beneficial for model transformations as well. One such technique that could be considered is code clone detection. Code clone detection can be employed in two different ways. It is possible to compare a number of different model transformations to identify reused code. It is also possible to identify code clones within one model transformation. Both approaches can be used to indicate improvements for modularity and reusability of a transformation.

In the case studies we conducted, the analysis techniques proved useful for increasing the understanding of model transformations. While this is a promising perspective, experiments should be conducted to empirically validate the benefits of the proposed (and future) techniques.

References

1. Schmidt, D.C.: Model-Driven Engineering. Computer 39(2), 25–31 (2006)
2. van Deursen, A., Klint, P., Visser, J.: Domain-Specific Languages: An Annotated Bibliography. SIGPLAN Notices 35(6), 26–36 (2000)
3. Sendall, S., Kozaczynski, W.: Model Transformation: The Heart and Soul of Model-Driven Software Development. IEEE Software 20(5), 42–45 (2003)
4. Mohagheghi, P., Fernandez, M.A., Martell, J.A., Fritzsche, M., Gilani, W.: MDE Adoption in Industry: Challenges and Success Criteria. In: Schieferdecker, I., Hartman, A. (eds.) ECMDA-FA 2008. LNCS, vol. 5095, pp. 54–59. Springer, Heidelberg (2008)
5. Mohagheghi, P., Dehlen, V.: Where Is the Proof?–A Review of Experiences from Applying MDE in Industry. In: Schieferdecker, I., Hartman, A. (eds.) ECMDA-FA 2008. LNCS, vol. 5095, pp. 432–443. Springer, Heidelberg (2008)
6. Storey, M.A.D., Wong, K., Muller, H.A.: How do program understanding tools affect how programmers understand programs? Science of Computer Programming 36(2–3), 183–207 (2000)
7. Jouault, F., Kurtev, I.: Transforming Models with ATL. In: Bruel, J.-M. (ed.) MoDELS 2005. LNCS, vol. 3844, pp. 128–138. Springer, Heidelberg (2006)
8. Haase, A., Vlter, M., Efftinge, S., Kolb, B.: Introduction to openArchitectureWare 4.1.2. Model-Driven Development Tool Implementers Forum (2007)
9. OMG: Meta Object Facility (MOF) 2.0 Query/View/Transformation Specification. formal/ 2008-04-03, Object Management Group (2008)
10. Fenton, N.E., Pfleeger, S.L.: Software Metrics: A Rigorous & Practical Approach, 2nd edn. PWS Publishing Co. (1996)
11. Mohagheghi, P., Dehlen, V.: Developing a Quality Framework for Model-Driven Engineering. In: Giese, H. (ed.) MODELS 2008. LNCS, vol. 5002, pp. 275–286. Springer, Heidelberg (2008)
12. van Amstel, M.F., Lange, C.F.J., van den Brand, M.G.J.: Using Metrics for Assessing the Quality of ASF+SDF Model Transformations. In: Paige, R.F. (ed.) ICMT 2009. LNCS, vol. 5563, pp. 239–248. Springer, Heidelberg (2009)
13. van Amstel, M.F., van den Brand, M.G.J.: Quality Assessment of ATL Model Transformations using Metrics. In: Second International Workshop on Model Transformation with ATL (2010)
14. van Amstel, M.F., van den Brand, M.G.J., Nguyen, P.H.: Metrics for model transformations. In: Proceedings of the Ninth Belgian-Netherlands Software Evolution Workshop. (2010)
15. van Deursen, A., Heering, J., Klint, P. (eds.): Language Prototyping: An Algebraic Specification Approach. World Scientific, Singapore (1996)
16. Fowler, M.: Refactoring: Improving the Design of Existing Code. Addison-Wesley, Reading (1999)

17. Boehm, B.W., Brown, J.R., Kaspar, H., Lipow, M., Macleod, G.J., Merrit, M.J.: Characteristics of Software Quality. North-Holland, Amsterdam (1978)
18. van Amstel, M.F.: The Right Tool for the Right Job: Measuring Model Transformation Quality. In: Proceedings of the Fourth IEEE International Workshop on Quality Oriented Reuse of Software, pp. 69–74. IEEE Computer Society, Los Alamitos (2010)
19. ISO - International Organization for Standardization: International Standard ISO/IEC 25000 - Software engineering – Software product Quality Requirements and Evaluation, SQuaRE (2005)
20. Czarnecki, K., Helsen, S.: Feature-based survey of model transformation approaches. IBM Systems Journal 45(5), 621–645 (2006)
21. Cornelissen, B., Holten, D., Zaidman, A., Moonen, L., van Wijk, J.J., van Deursen, A.: Understanding Execution Traces Using Massive Sequence and Circular Bundle Views. In: Proceedings of the fifteenth IEEE International Conference on Program Comprehension, pp. 49–58. IEEE Computer Society, Los Alamitos (2007)
22. Stevens, W.P., Myers, G.J., Constantine, L.L.: Structured design. IBM Systems Journal 13(2), 115–139 (1974)
23. Holten, D., van Wijk, J.J.: Visual comparison of hierarchically organized data. Computer Graphics Forum 27(3), 759–766 (2008)
24. van Amstel, M.F., van den Brand, M.G.J., Engelen, L.J.P.: An Exercise in Iterative Domain-Specific Language Design. In: Proceedings of the Joint ERCIM Workshop on Software Evolution and International Workshop on Principles of Software Evolution, pp. 48–57. ACM, New York (2010)
25. Anastasakis, K., Bordbar, B., Kster, J.M.: Analysis of Model Transformations via Alloy. In: Proceedings of the Fourth Workshop on Model-Driven Engineering, Verification and Validation, pp. 47–56 (2007)
26. Kapová, L., Goldschmidt, T., Becker, S., Henss, J.: Evaluating Maintainability with Code Metrics for Model-to-Model Transformations. In: Heineman, G.T., Kofron, J., Plasil, F. (eds.) QoSA 2010. LNCS, vol. 6093, pp. 151–166. Springer, Heidelberg (2010)
27. Wang, J., Kim, S.K., Carrington, D.: Verifying metamodel coverage of model transformations. In: Proceedings of the Australian Software Engineering Conference, pp. 270–282. IEEE Computer Society, Los Alamitos (2006)
28. McQuillan, J.A., Power, J.F.: White-Box Coverage Criteria for Model Transformations. In: First International Workshop on Model Transformation with ATL (2009)

Iterative Development of Consistency-Preserving Rule-Based Refactorings*

Basil Becker, Leen Lambers, Johannes Dyck, Stefanie Birth, and Holger Giese

Hasso Plattner Institute at the University of Potsdam
Prof.-Dr.-Helmert-Straße 2-3
14482 Potsdam, Germany
{basil.becker,leen.lambers,holger.giese}@hpi.uni-potsdam.de,
{johannes.dyck,stefanie.birth}@student.hpi.uni-potsdam.de

Abstract. A model refactoring does not only need to ensure behavior preservation. First of all, it needs to ensure that specific well-formedness constraints of the modeling language under consideration are preserved (consistency preservation). The consistency of model refactorings can be ensured by runtime checks. However, this means that not the developer of the refactorings but the user is confronted with the problem.

In this paper we present an approach to statically check for consistency preservation of rule-based refactorings at design time. Thereby, refactoring rules describe which side-effects may take place on the model to be refactored. We formalize rule-based refactorings using graph transformation and consistency using graph constraints. We extend a verification technique capable of proving statically that refactoring rule applications preserve consistency. By automatically computing meaningful counterexamples, this technique allows for the iterative development of refactoring rules guaranteeing consistency preservation. We demonstrate the approach for common Java refactorings applied to a fine grained EMF model and can show that bugs that were present in refactorings of former Eclipse versions could have been avoided using our approach.

Keywords: model refactoring, model-driven development, Java, verification, graph transformation.

1 Introduction and Motivation

Refactorings are widely accepted as a technique to restructure a program or model in order to improve its readability, extensibility, or reduce its complexity. An important property of refactorings is that they should be behavior-preserving. Therefore, during refactoring development this is one of the main aspects developers are concerned with. However, another property that refactorings should

---

* This work was partially developed in the course of the project - Correct Model Transformations - Hasso Plattner Institut, Universität Potsdam and was published on its behalf and funded by the Deutsche Forschungsgemeinschaft. See http://www.hpi.uni-potsdam.de/giese/projekte/kormoran.html?L=1.

J. Cabot and E. Visser (Eds.): ICMT 2011, LNCS 6707, pp. 123–137, 2011.

demonstrate is consistency preservation, in the sense that specific direct or indirect well-formedness constraints of the language should be preserved.

Indeed, when browsing, for example, through the Eclipse bug database a significant number of bugs are concerned with consistency preservation, instead of behavior preservation. For example, consider the following well-formedness constraint for an object-oriented language like Java: "An interface only contains method signatures". Suppose that a refactoring like, for example, Encapsulate Field [9] would allow to encapsulate a field belonging to an interface. This would lead to a violation of the aforementioned well-formedness constraint, since a setter and getter method with corresponding method bodies would be generated in the interface (see Sect. 6). The objective of our approach is to avoid these kind of violations by statically analyzing the refactoring specification. Checking behavior preservation in a static way is very difficult (see Sect. 2), but we show with our approach that it is feasible for consistency preservation. Note that our static analysis technique clearly goes beyond checking of type consistency.

We specify refactorings in a rule-based manner and rely on a formalization using graph transformation [5] allowing for the development and application of static analysis techniques. In general, rules consist of pre- and post-conditions describing under which pre-condition particular local side-effects may be performed on the model. Side-effects may be deletion or creation of model elements. Preconditions specify what kind of pattern should be present, but also what kind of pattern should not be present in the model before applying the rule. Postconditions specify how the detected pattern should be modified by the rule. In [1] – an approach originally introduced in order to analyze systems with dynamic structural adaptation – it was shown already that preservation of specific direct well-formedness constraints for graph transformation systems can be analyzed statically. We will extend the technique presented in [1] to also be applicable to indirect well-formedness constraints.

To show the applicability and relevance of our approach we use a realistically complex model namely the fine grained meta-model of the Java programming language, that is provided by the JaMoPP (Java Model Parser and Printer) project. This model and its consistency rules are well understood and are more complex than most DSLs and related refactorings in MDE. Using the Java meta-model allows us to explain our approach with widely known and well understood refactorings and having an agreed upon understanding of what makes a valid model. The fact that we were able to detect some real bugs that were present in some former Eclipse version shows the relevance of our result.

JaMoPP [12](http://www.jamopp.org) is an approach with the prospective of bridging the gap between models and source code. For a complete in depth description of JaMoPP and its Java meta-model we refer to [12]. Our case study consists of several refactorings but we will only show two of them in detail. We use one of the most common refactorings "Pull Up Method" as a running example. The "Pull Up Method" refactoring is a special variant of the "Move Method" refactoring and moves a method from a sub- to a super-class. According to Fowler [9] this refactoring is used to remove duplicate behavior, which occurs in all sub-classes of a common super-class. In Section 6, we illustrate on the refactoring "Encapsulate Field" that our approach is applicable also to more complex Java refactorings.

Our paper is structured as follows: First, we give an overview of the state of the art of verifying model refactorings (see Section 2). In Section 3, we present informally what we mean by consistency-preserving refactorings and how our approach can be used for their iterative development. Then, we explain how to specify and formalize rule-based refactorings and consistency based on graph transformation in Section 4. Section 5 explains our verification technique being able to analyze statically consistency preservation. In Section 6, we illustrate the applicability of our approach on a Java refactoring more complex than our running example refactoring Pull Up Method. The paper ends with a conclusion and an outlook on future work.

2   State of the Art

The idea to specify model refactorings by graph transformation has been followed by several authors [3,8,14,15,16,2]. In [14] graph transformations are used to formally specify refactorings. However, the paper focuses on verifying behavior preservation. Nevertheless, the authors identify and formalize some, as they call it, well-formedness constraints that have to be met by the refactored models, to be considered correct Java programs. It is mentioned that a refactoring should ensure preservation of these well-formedness constraints, but it does not provide a static and automatic analysis technique guaranteeing consistency preservation as we do in this paper. In [8] graph transformations have been facilitated to refactor UML models using the tool AGG, but no verification is performed. Also here, well-formedness constraints are formalized using graph constraints, but no static analysis technique is proposed ensuring consistency preservation. In [15] rule-based refactorings are formalized by graph transformation in order to apply static conflict and dependency analysis on refactorings. It is used to find out more about how different refactorings to the same model may influence each other. In [16,3], graph transformation is used as a formalism to specify model refactorings in order to develop static analysis techniques verifying behavior preservation. In [2] a graph transformation based refactoring of EMF models is presented. The notion of consistency used in this work is very specific to EMF and not suited to express the more complex notion of consistency we used throughout our paper.

Note that, in principle, it would be possible to tackle the problem of consistency preservation by translating constraints into application conditions for refactoring rules guaranteeing consistency by definition when added to the rules.[1] Doing this for a large number of constraints would not only blow up the refactoring specification making it illegible, it would also render the rule application inefficient because preconditions become unnecessarily complex. A number of

---

[1] This translation is presented formally in [6] for nested graph constraints, being expressively equivalent to first order formulas on graphs.

application conditions would be added although the rule in question merely violates the constraint in case that it would have been violated already before rule application. Therefore, our static verification technique [1] aims at finding out which rules may allow transitions from consistent into inconsistent states.

Concerning the verification of refactorings using other techniques than graph transformation most work concentrates on behavior preservation as well. In [4], an equational semantics based approach to Java refactorings is proposed and detailed proofs of behavior preservation are given. Also in [10], it is shown how to prove behavior preservation using a refinement language inspired on Java allowing for reasoning on object-oriented programs and specifications. In [7], an incremental technique is proposed to check consistency-preservation during model evolution. Also here, consistency properties regard model behavior.

In [17], a model refactoring approach is presented relying on detection and (user-guided) rule-based resolution of inconsistencies (formalized by Description Logics) in or between models. It is argued that during a non-trivial model refactoring inconsistencies can not be avoided and therefore, inconsistency resolution is considered as a key artifact during refactoring. The disadvantage of this approach is that the user of the refactoring might be confronted with consistency problems more than the refactoring designer.

In [13], it is described theoretically how constraint preservation can be analyzed statically based on implication checks for constraints and based on the translation of constraints [6] into left application conditions. Basically, this theory follows the idea that rules are safe as long as the constraint to be checked for preservation already implies the left rule application conditions derived by this translation. Since implication checking for nested constraints is, in general, undecidable, implementations verifying consistency preservation as [1] need to restrict to a suitable subclass of constraints in order to obtain verification results.

On the contrary to all discussed approaches and the current state of the art, we demonstrate in this paper that it is possible to specify complex refactorings and verify them automatically for consistency preservation at design time. Our invariant checker [1] restricts to graph constraints of a specific kind as described in detail in Section 4.

3   Iterative Development of Consistency-Preserving Refactorings

Figure 1(a) depicts how *consistency-preserving refactorings* can be *developed iteratively* using our approach. Given a modeling language with well-formedness constraints and a refactoring specification, our invariant checker is able to detect well-formedness constraint violations for refactorings following this specification. Our invariant checker reports violations by returning as counterexamples all minimal problematic situations. The developer is then able to inspect these counterexamples and change the refactoring specification accordingly. This step can be iterated up until the invariant checker does not find any refactoring rule anymore violating one of the well-formedness constraints. In this way, it is guaranteed that the specified refactorings are consistency-preserving. In the following,

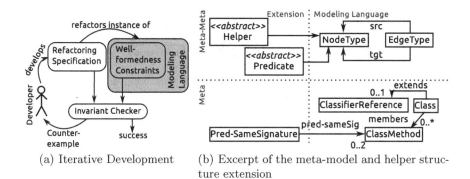

(a) Iterative Development

(b) Excerpt of the meta-model and helper structure extension

Fig. 1. Specifying rule based refactorings and iterative development

we explain informally which kind of well-formedness constraints can be handled by our approach. Moreover, we explain our notion of refactoring specification that can be verified for consistency preservation using our approach.

We assume that a modeling language, i.e. the language that is to be refactored, is defined by a meta-model and a set of *well-formedness constraints*, consisting of direct or indirect constraints. The well-formedness constraints that we consider are of the following kind: "A specific pattern should not occur in the model. (*forbidden pattern*)" or "A specific pattern should not occur without some other specific pattern. (*conditional forbidden patterns*)". A *direct* well-formedness constraint can be expressed either as a forbidden or a conditional forbidden pattern of the modeling language's meta-model. However, certain well-formedness constraints are not expressible as direct well-formedness constraints. For example, the well-formedness constraint "Two methods with the same signature should not be contained in the same class." is not expressible as a direct well-formedness constraint. Consequently, it is impossible to encode such a forbidden situation by a (conditional) forbidden pattern directly. Alternatively, we can build a set of so-called *maintenance* rules to compute if two methods have a different signature. They mark the result of this check with specific Predicate nodes or edges, describing either that the property holds or that it does not hold. We extend the meta-model with predicate nodes (prefixed with "Pred-", see Figure 1(b)) and predicate edges (prefixed with "pred-"). *Indirect* well-formedness constraints can then be expressed by (conditional) forbidden patterns making use of these predicate elements. In Example 1, we describe an indirect constraint and maintenance rules that are important for the refactoring Pull Up Method.

Example 1 (indirect constraint and maintenance rules). Concerning the consistency of the refactoring Pull Up Method, it is important that afterwards "no two Methods sharing the same signature are contained in one Class". This indirect constraint is depicted as a forbidden pattern in Fig. 2. We use the Predicate types Pred-SameSignature and Pred-NotSameSignature marking that two Methods have the same or a different signature, respectively. The decision which of the two node types we need between two Methods is left to a set of maintenance rules. If two

Fig. 2. A forbidden pattern (with predicate elements) specifying that no two methods with the same signature are members of the same class

Methods have Parameters, the rules iterate through them and only advance if the Parameters are of the same Type and both Methods have either at least one more Parameter or none. If the rules have successfully iterated through the Parameters, a node of type Pred-SameSignature is created that points to both Methods. A node of type Pred-NotSameSignature is added if the Method names are different or the Parameters differ in number or Type. We can now use this information to express the "same signature" well-formedness constraint as a forbidden pattern (cf. Figure 2).

The language's meta-model, the set of well-formedness constraints and maintenance rules are language-specific. They have to be defined only once and can be reused for all refactorings specified for this language. Given a modeling language with maintenance rules and a set of well-formedness constraints, a model is *consistent* if no maintenance rule is applicable to it and if it satisfies each well-formedness constraint. We require that no maintenance rule is applicable, since the predicates used by the indirect constraints need to be up-to-date.

Usually, a refactoring holds a list of *parameters*, expressing which model elements are to be refactored, where model elements should be moved to by the refactoring, and which new elements need to be added to the model during refactoring. For example, for the refactoring Encapsulate Field (described in detail in Sect. 6) we mark which field is to be encapsulated and how the new getter and setter methods are to be named. For the first case, we allow to extend the meta-model with so-called Helper nodes (prefixed with "Help-") and edges (prefixed with "help-") that may point to model elements (see Figure 1(b)). For the latter case, we allow so-called helperMember edges connecting a Helper node with a model element specifying that it is still *implicit* (outgoing model edges of implicit model nodes are to be considered also as *implicit*). We say that an *extended model* is a model containing helper structures. A *refactoring specification* holds *add-helper rules*, describing manipulations of these kind of helper structures, as well as *refactoring rules*, describing local changes on the model to be refactored. A rule-based *refactoring* consists of a preprocessing phase in which helper structures according to the add-helper rules are constructed, a refactoring phase in which the actual refactoring according to the refactoring rules is performed and a cleanup phase, where helper structures are deleted again. Each implementation of the refactoring specification S has to provide proper undo mechanisms in case that any of the above-mentioned phases can not be completed successfully.

Example 2 (rule-based refactoring). The "Pull Up Method" refactoring specification contains, for example, the refactoring rule depicted in Figure 3. We use

Fig. 3. Refactoring rule for the "Pull Up Method" refactoring

the following notation: rules delete all elements that are augmented with a -- (double minus), elements augmented with a ++ (double plus) are created by the rule and elements without any annotation are preserved by the rule. The depicted rule deletes a members edge from the Class sub to the refactored ClassMethod and creates a members edge from the Class super to the ClassMethod. The complete specification of the refactoring Pull Up Method contains the above mentioned refactoring rule and an add-helper rule that marks the method to move.

A refactoring is *consistency-preserving* if it transforms each *consistent model* into a consistent model. Our *invariant checker* [1] statically analyzes, given a refactoring specification, if each corresponding refactoring preserves the well-formedness constraints (details of the verification are described in Section 5). In Section 4, we formalize well-formedness constraints and refactorings using graph transformation.

4   Formalizing Well-Formedness Constraints and Rule-Based Refactorings

Since our formalization relies on graph transformation, we briefly introduce the necessary elements of this specification technique and refer to [5] for more details.

4.1   Preliminaries

Graphs are often used to describe the abstract syntax of visual models. When formalizing object-oriented modeling, graphs occur at two levels: the type level (defined based on class diagrams) and the instance level (given by all valid object diagrams). This idea is described by the concept of *typed graphs*, where a fixed *type graph* TG serves as an abstract representation of the class diagram and moreover, types can be structured by an inheritance relation[2]. Instance graphs of a type graph have a structure-preserving mapping (i.e. a graph morphism) to the type graph. We encode attributes as in the fundamental theory for attributed graph transformation [5] by edges to data nodes.

Graph transformation is the rule-based modification of graphs. Rules are expressed by two graphs (L, R), where L is the left-hand side of the rule and R is the right-hand side, and a mapping between nodes and edges in L and R. Rule graphs may contain variables for attributes. The left-hand side L represents the pre-conditions of the rule, while the right-hand side R describes the

---

[2] We flatten rules and patterns before verifying them, since our invariant checker does not support inheritance yet.

post-conditions. $L \cap R$ (the graph part that is not changed) and the union $L \cup R$ should form a graph again, i.e., they must be compatible with edge source and target settings as well as type settings. Graph $L \setminus (L \cap R)$ defines the part that is to be deleted, and graph $R \setminus (L \cap R)$ defines the part to be created when applying the rule. The application of a graph rule may be restricted by so-called *negative application conditions* (NACs) which prohibit the existence of certain graph patterns in the current instance graph. The sets $read_r$ and $write_r$ define the types that are read (match, forbid) or written (create, delete) by a graph transformation rule r, respectively. A *graph transformation step* $G \Rightarrow_r H$ via rule r from an instance graph G to graph H is defined by first finding a match m of the left-hand side L of rule r in the current instance graph G such that m is structure-preserving and type-compatible and satisfies the NACs (none of the forbidden graph patterns is found in G). The resulting graph H is constructed by (1) deleting all graph items from G that are in $L \setminus (L \cap R)$; (2) adding all those new graph items that are in $R \setminus (L \cap R)$. Non-determinism due to several applicable rules can be explicitly reduced by *priorities* (in case that more than one rule is applicable to the same graph, the rule with the highest priority is applied first) or by defining some more specific control flow over the rules.

4.2   Formalizing Well-Formedness Constraints

We formalize the *meta-model* of the modeling language to be refactored L by a *type graph* TG_L.

Each *direct well-formedness constraint* is formalized by a so-called *graph constraint* [6] typed over TG_L. The absence of a *forbidden pattern* is formalized as follows: $\neg \exists P$, expressing that no pattern of the form P should occur. Formally, a graph G satisfies $\neg \exists P$ if no injective graph morphism $q : P \to G$ can be found. The absence of a *conditional forbidden pattern* is formalized as follows: $\neg \exists (P, \neg \exists n)$ with $n : P \to N$, expressing that there should not occur a pattern of the form P without some occurrence of N. Formally, a graph G satisfies $\neg \exists (P, \neg \exists n)$ if there does not exist an injective morphism $m : P \to G$ such that there does not exist an injective morphism $q : N \to G$ with $q \circ n = m$. We write $G \models P$ if the graph G satisfies the (conditional) forbidden pattern P.

For the meta-model of L extended with Predicate-elements we use a type-graph TG_{Pred} that contains all elements of TG_L and the additional Predicate nodes and edges.

A *maintenance* rule m is formalized as a graph transformation rule with $write_m \subseteq TG_{Pred} \setminus TG_L$ and $read_m \subseteq TG_{Pred}$. For each predicate occurring in $TG_{Pred} \setminus TG_L$ a set of maintenance rules needs to be given responsible for computing the predicate. Finally, we can formalize *indirect well-formedness constraints* as graph constraints expressing a (conditional) forbidden pattern typed over TG_{Pred}.

4.3   Formalizing Rule-Based Refactorings

We extend the type-graph TG_L with the additional Helper elements to a type-graph TG_{Help} to capture the Helper elements formally. The union of the type-graphs TG_L, TG_{Pred} and TG_{Help} is TG. We formalize *extended models* as graphs typed over TG and *models* as graphs typed over TG_{Pred}.

A *refactoring specification* S consists of a set of rules, formalized by graph rules typed over TG, with priorities, where rules may be refactoring rules or add-helper rules characterized as follows:

refactoring rule r is a graph transformation rule with $read_r \subseteq TG$ and $write_r \subseteq TG_L$. Moreover, it may delete helperMember edges, expressing that implicit model elements are mounted into the model.

add-helper rule h is a graph transformation rule, with $read_h \subseteq TG_{Help}$ and $write_h \subseteq TG_{Help}$ with the restriction that added nodes typed over TG_L (with outgoing edges typed over TG_L) have to be connected with a helper-Member edge to some node typed over $TG_{Help} \backslash TG_L$, expressing that implicit model elements are created.

A *refactoring step* or *helper step* corresponds to a refactoring rule or helper rule application, respectively.[3] *Maintenance steps* are maintenance rule applications, where maintenance rules have a higher priority than add-helper rules as well as refactoring rules. Given a refactoring specification S, a *successful preprocessing* of the model M to be refactored corresponds to a sequence of add-helper steps and maintenance steps starting from M ending up with a consistent extended model M_{pre}. Given a refactoring specification S, a *refactoring* of the model M corresponds to a successful preprocessing of M into a consistent extended model M_{pre} (preprocessing phase), followed by a sequence of at least one refactoring step and maintenance steps ending up with an extended model M_{ref} without implicit model elements (refactoring phase) and is completed by restriction of the extended model M_{ref} to all elements of a type in TG_{Pred} obtaining the result model M_{res} (cleanup phase).

5   Verifying Consistency Preservation

A graph transformation rule r is said to be *constraint-preserving* in the set of rules R (with $r \in R$) for a set of well-formedness constraints C if no two graphs G, H with $G \models C$ and $H \not\models C$ exist such that $G \Rightarrow_r H$ w.r.t. to the priorities in R. $G \models C$ is a shorthand notation that G satisfies each graph constraint in C. Given a set of graph constraints, stemming from (conditional) forbidden patterns, and a set of graph transformation rules with priorities, our invariant checker [1] automatically computes as *counterexamples* all minimal situations indicating why rules might be applied to a *constraint-satisfying graph leading to a violating one*.

The invariant checker proceeds as follows for verifying statically that the absence of *forbidden patterns* is preserved by a set of graph transformation rules with priorities: it is analyzed statically which kind of graph elements may be

---

[3] We assume injective matching and rule applications without dangling edge deletion, i.e. DPO with injective matching [5].

produced by a rule and then, it is checked how these created graph elements may be overlapped with the forbidden pattern P. In case that overlappings are present, counterexamples can be constructed (by inverse rule application to the overlapping), expressing that if the rule is applied to a graph holding the remaining part of the forbidden pattern (*source pattern*), then after rule application the complete forbidden pattern P will be present (*target pattern*). Thereby, counterexamples may be rejected because of three reasons: (1) the source pattern comprises the precondition for a rule with a higher priority to be applicable (2) the source pattern comprises forbidden elements of one of the NACs of the rule (3) the source pattern comprises a forbidden pattern. In the first case, the rule with the higher priority ensures that the rule with lower priority under verification would not be applicable anyway. In the second case, similarly, the rule under verification would not be applicable because the source pattern comprises one of its NACs. In the latter case, the rule under verification would lead to a state comprising the forbidden pattern, if it is applied to a state which comprises the forbidden pattern already. If no counterexamples exist, it is ensured that a set of rules with priorities cannot be applied in such a way that they allow for transitions from states holding no forbidden pattern to states holding some forbidden pattern. For an explanation of invariant checking for *conditional forbidden patterns*, we refer to [1].

In order to have a consistency-preserving refactoring we can use the invariant checker to show that the refactoring rules do not produce any forbidden patterns. In Theorem 1, we show that in addition we need to check that no maintenance rule is provoked during the refactoring phase. Otherwise, the addition of some predicate by a maintenance rule could lead to a violation of some forbidden pattern during the refactoring phase as well. Given two graphs G, G' and two graph transformation rules p, r such that $G \Rightarrow_r G'$ and p is not applicable to G. We say that r *provokes* p if p is applicable to G'.

Theorem 1 (consistency-preserving refactoring). *Given a modeling language L with maintenance rules, a set of well-formedness constraints C_L and a refactoring specification S typed over TG, then each refactoring is consistency-preserving if each refactoring rule in S is constraint-preserving and if no refactoring rule provokes any of the maintenance rules.*

Proof. Given the consistent extended model M_{pre} as result of the preprocessing phase, we need to show that after the refactoring phase and after cleanup we end up with a consistent model M_{res}. First, let us consider the refactoring phase. Since each refactoring rule is constraint-preserving, we know that after the first refactoring step we end up with an extended model M' satisfying the well-formedness constraints. Thus, M' is consistent if no maintenance rule is applicable. This is the case because no maintenance rule is applicable to M_{res} and because no refactoring rule provokes any of the maintenance rules. We can repeat this argumentation for each following refactoring step such that we can conclude that the refactoring phase consists of refactoring steps only. Therefore, the refactoring phase ends up with a consistent extended model M_{ref} without implicit model elements (cf. Section 4.3).

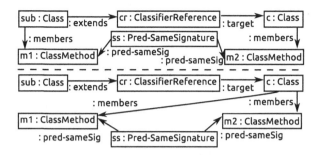

Fig. 4. The counterexample showing the wrong implementation of the refactoring rule in Figure 3

Given the consistent extended model M_{ref} without implicit model elements, we need to show that M_{res}, the restriction of M_{ref} to elements of a type in TG_{Pred} (cleanup phase), is a consistent model. M_{res} satisfies each well-formedness constraint in C_L, since M_{ref} satisfies them and the constraints do not contain elements of a type in $TG_{Help} \setminus TG_L$. No maintenance rule is applicable to M_{res}, since no rule is applicable to M_{ref} and maintenance rules do not read elements typed over $TG_{Help} \setminus TG_L$.

Lemma 1 (rule provocation). *Given two graph transformation rules r and p. Rule r does not provoke the rule p if $read_p \cap write_r = \emptyset$.*

Proof. We prove this lemma by contradiction. Let G, G' be two graphs and $G \Rightarrow_r G'$. We assume that p is not applicable to G, i.e. some elements that have to exist in G are missing or some elements that are forbidden in G exist, but that p is applicable to G'. Since r does not write any elements that are read by p ($write_r \cap read_p = \emptyset$) the match for p in G' can not be created by r. Consequently, there must exist a match for p in G. This contradicts our assumption.

As shown in Lemma 1 it can be checked that rules don't provoke each other using a simple type check as sufficient condition. In case this fails, we can still use the invariant checker to verify that p is not provoked by r: The non-applicability of p, expressed as a (conditional) forbidden pattern, should be invariant w.r.t. r.

Example 3 (Verifying the Pull Up Method specification).
Running the invariant checking tool on our refactoring specification for Pull Up Method (see Example 2) results in the report of a violation. The counterexample provided by our tool is shown in Figure 4. The figure's upper part shows the situation before the rule is applied (source pattern) and the lower part the situation after the rule application (target pattern) demonstrating the violation of the constraint. It can be easily identified that the refactoring rule does not check the existence of the Pred-SameSignature nodes and edges. Consequently we change the refactoring rule to forbid their existence and the verification finally succeeds. The maintenance rules for Pred-SameSignature read only Method, Parameter, TypeReference and Type elements but not the members edge between

Class and Method. Hence the refactoring rule does not provoke any of the maintenance rules.

6   Complex Java Refactoring "Encapsulate Field"

The refactoring *Encapsulate Field* is an example of a more complex Java refactoring that can be checked using our approach. Fowler [9] sketches the Encapsulate Field refactoring as: "There is a public field. Make it private and provide accessors." We specified the Encapsulate Field refactoring in our approach with a set of rules, which also comprise some *helper-rules*. The general idea behind our set of rules is that we first identify the field to refactor. Then we create the necessary access methods (i.e. a getter-method for read access and a setter-method for write access, respectively) as part of the helper-structure. If the created access methods do not have the same signature as any method already contained in the refactored field's class, we mount the access methods into the Java model. Before we can safely change the field's visibility to *private* it is required that any access to the field (except from within the newly created access methods) is redirected to use the access methods instead. We therefore gave the refactoring rules dealing with the redirection of the Field access a higher priority than the refactoring rule that sets the Field's visibility to private.

In order to check whether or not two methods have the same signature we reused the set of maintenance rules, that has already been used for the Pull Up Method refactoring. Beside the information which field will be refactored the Help-Marker also contains information about the added access methods (marked through the associations help-get and help-set). Instances of the type Pred-Read mark a pair of a ClassMethod and a IdentifierReference if and only if the IdentifierReference occurs within the ClassMethod. The type Pred-Write is analogously defined for each write access contained in the ClassMethod, but also marks the AssignmentExpression.

The refactoring has been verified to satisfy the following well-formedness constraints: not two methods with the same signature are contained in the same class (see Figure 2), no private member is accessed from a class other than its containing one (see Figure 5(b)), and interfaces contain only method signatures (see Figure 5(a)). Beside these well-formedness constraints, we have some other ones, expressing that the multiplicities, specified in the Java meta-model and our helper-model extension, are fulfilled. Thus, it is forbidden that one Field is marked by two or more Help-Marker instances. Further we forbid two refactorings to be concurrently executed in one Class. However, two refactorings of Fields in two different Classes is allowed and shown to be safe. We also successfully checked that no refactoring rule provokes any maintenance rule.

The refactoring specification consists of: Two add-helper rules that create the required getter and setter methods for the encapsulated field, refactoring rules that mount the getter and setter methods into the model and rules that redirect accesses to the field and finally a rule that declares the field as private. Figure 6 depicts the add-helper rule that adds the setter to the helper structure.

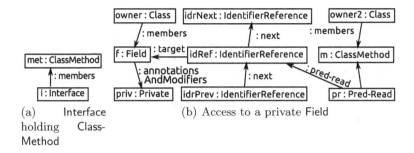

(a)   Interface
holding   Class-
Method

(b) Access to a private Field

Fig. 5. Constraints that have been checked for the Encapsulate Field refactoring

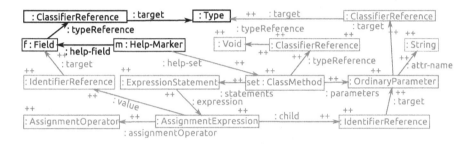

Fig. 6. The add-helper rule that adds a setter method to the helper structure

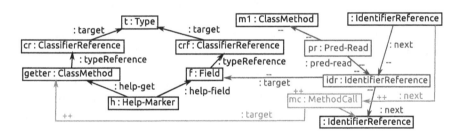

Fig. 7. Refactoring rule to redirect a read access from the field to an invocation of the getter method

The helperMembers edges (cf. Sect. 4.3) were ommitted for readability reasons. All created nodes should be marked by a helperMembers edge originating at the Help-Marker. In the Java meta-model IdentifierReferences can be composed to a linked list. Depending on the position (start, middle or end) of the IdentifierReference, targeting the refactored Field, we have different refactoring rules. The rule shown in Figure 7 specifies one replacement of a read-access to the field with an invocation of the new getter method.

We found a bug in this refactoring specification. The rules to mount the new ClassMethods were specified using the abstract type Classifier. In the JaMoPP meta-model a Classifier can be either an Interface or a Class and hence

the invariant checker created a counterexample where a ClassMethod has been
added to an Interface clearly violating the well-formedness constraint that a
ClassMethod must not be contained in a Interface. This bug in our specification
has also been present in the Eclipse IDE (cf. Eclipse Bug with ID 34310[4]). Although the entry in the Eclipse bug database is several years old, we were still
able to reproduce this wrong behavior up to the Galileo release of Eclipse. In the
most recent release Helios the bug is fixed. A further bug of Eclipse is concerned
with the handling of references to the encapsulated Field[5]. We do note describe
it in detail here, but the bug clearly violates the well-formedness constraint in
Figure 5(b) and thus would have also been avoided using our approach.

7   Conclusion and Outlook

We have presented our approach to develop in an iterative way rule-based refactorings preserving consistency. Models are consistent when they do not violate
a given set of well-formedness constraints for the modeling language under consideration. Moreover, we have shown how predicates and maintenance rules can
be used to augment the expressiveness of well-formedness constraints. We have
illustrated our approach on some most common Java refactorings applied to a
fine-grained model of the Java language. We have explained how a bug in the
Eclipse implementation of the Encapsulate Field refactoring could have been
avoided using our approach to refactoring development.

   We plan to couple our invariant checker in which refactoring specifications
can be checked for consistency with the StoryDiagramInterpreter [11] in order to be able to also execute the specified refactorings. Basically, this involves
translating the refactoring specifications in to a common exchange format. With
regard to our case study, we could moreover integrate JaMoPP [12] with the StoryDiagramInterpreter to be able to execute consistency-preserving refactorings
on Java source code, instead of on the fine grained Java model. Our invariant
checker verifies sets of rules with priorities and forbidden patterns (formalized
by graph constraints) defined over a type structure without inheritance. Consequently, the refactoring rules of our specification need to be flattened before
verifying them. It is part of current work to adapt the invariant checker such
that it copes with inheritance directly. Moreover, it is part of current work to
investigate how our invariant checker is to be extended in order to be able to
handle refactoring specifications holding more explicit control structures like the
ones provided by the Story Diagram language [11]. Finally, we plan to investigate which extensions and adaptions to our approach would be necessary to
support also consistency preservation verification of relational and operational
model transformation specifications.

Acknowledgement. We thank the anonymous reviewers for their valuable
comments.

---

[4] https://bugs.eclipse.org/bugs/show_bug.cgi?id=34310
[5] https://bugs.eclipse.org/bugs/show_bug.cgi?id=273190

References

1. Becker, B., Beyer, D., Giese, H., Klein, F., Schilling, D.: Symbolic Invariant Verification for Systems with Dynamic Structural Adaptation. In: Proc. of the 28th International Conference on Software Engineering (ICSE). ACM Press, New York (2006)
2. Biermann, E., Ehrig, K., Köhler, C., Kuhns, G., Taentzer, G., Weiss, E.: EMF Model Refactoring based on Graph Transformation Concepts. Electronic Communication of the EASST 3 (2006)
3. Bisztray, D., Heckel, R., Ehrig, H.: Compositional verification of architectural refactorings. In: de Lemos, R., Fabre, J.-C., Gacek, C., Gadducci, F., ter Beek, M. (eds.) Architecting Dependable Systems VI. LNCS, vol. 5835, pp. 308–333. Springer, Heidelberg (2009)
4. Cornélio, M., Cavalcanti, A., Sampaio, A.: Sound refactorings. Science of Computer Programming 75(3), 106–133 (2010)
5. Ehrig, H., Ehrig, K., Prange, U., Taentzer, G.: Fundamentals of Algebraic Graph Transformation. Springer, Heidelberg (2006)
6. Ehrig, H., Habel, A., Lambers, L.: Parallelism and Concurrency Theorems for Rules with Nested Application Conditions. In: Festschrift dedicated to Hans-Jorg Kreowski at the Occasion of his 60th Birthday, EC-EASST, vol. 26 (2010)
7. Engels, G., Heckel, R., Küster, J., Groenewegen, L.: Consistency-Preserving Model Evolution through Transformations. In: Jézéquel, J.-M., Hussmann, H., Cook, S. (eds.) UML 2002. LNCS, vol. 2460, pp. 212–226. Springer, Heidelberg (2002)
8. Folli, A., Mens, T.: Refactoring of UML models using AGG. Electronic Communication of the EASST 8 (2007)
9. Fowler, M.: Refactoring: Improving the Design of Existing Code. Object Technology Series. Addison-Wesley, Reading (1999)
10. Garrido, A., Meseguer, J.: Formal Specification and Verification of Java Refactorings. In: Proc. of 6th IEEE Intl. Workshop on Source Code Analysis and Manipulation SCAM 2006, pp. 165–174. IEEE Computer Society, Los Alamitos (2006)
11. Giese, H., Hildebrandt, S., Seibel, A.: Improved flexibility and scalability by interpreting story diagrams. In: Proceedings of the Eighth International Workshop on Graph Transformation and Visual Modeling Techniques (GT-VMT 2009), vol. 18. Electronic Communications of the EASST (2009)
12. Heidenreich, F., Johannes, J., Seifert, M., Wende, C.: Closing the Gap between Modelling and Java. In: van den Brand, M., Gašević, D., Gray, J. (eds.) SLE 2009. LNCS, vol. 5969, pp. 374–383. Springer, Heidelberg (2010)
13. Lambers, L.: Certifying Rule-Based Models using Graph Transformation. Ph.D. thesis, Technische Universität Berlin (2010)
14. Mens, T., Eetvelde, N.V., Demeyer, S., Janssens, D.: Formalizing refactorings with graph transformations. Journal of Software Maintenance and Evolution: Research and Practice 17(4), 247–276 (2005)
15. Mens, T., Taentzer, G., Runge, O.: Analysing refactoring dependencies using graph transformation. Software and Systems Modeling 6(3), 269–285 (2007)
16. Rangel, G., Lambers, L., König, B., Ehrig, H., Baldan, P.: Behavior Preservation in Model Refactoring using DPO Transformations with Borrowed Contexts. In: Ehrig, H., Heckel, R., Rozenberg, G., Taentzer, G. (eds.) ICGT 2008. LNCS, vol. 5214, pp. 242–256. Springer, Heidelberg (2008)
17. Van Der Straeten, R., D'Hondt, M.: Model refactorings through rule-based inconsistency resolution. In: Proc. of the ACM Symposium on Applied Computing, pp. 1210–1217. ACM, New York (2006)

Toward Bidirectionalization of ATL with GRoundTram

Isao Sasano[1], Zhenjiang Hu[2], Soichiro Hidaka[2], Kazuhiro Inaba[2], Hiroyuki Kato[2], and Keisuke Nakano[3]

[1] Shibaura Institute of Technology, Japan
sasano@sic.shibaura-it.ac.jp
[2] National Institute of Informatics, Japan
{hu,hidaka,kinaba,kato}@nii.ac.jp
[3] The University of Electro-Communications, Japan
ksk@cs.uec.ac.jp

Abstract. ATL is a language for describing model transformations currently in uni-direction. In our previous work we have shown that transformations of graph structures given in some form can be bidirectionalized and have implemented a system called GRoundTram system for bidirectional graph transformations. We say a transformation t is bidirectionalized when we obtain a backward transformation t' so that the pair (t, t') of transformations satisfies certain well-behavedness properties. Bidirectional model transformation is used to reflect the changes in the target model back to the source model, and vice versa. In this paper, as a first step toward realizing practical bidirectional model transformations, we present bidirectionalization of core part of the ATL by encoding it in the UnQL language, which is used as a transformation language in the GRoundTram system. We give the algorithm for the encoding, based on which we have implemented the system for bidirectionalizing the core ATL in OCaml language.

1 Introduction

ATL [16,15,1] is a widely used language for describing model transformation, and its environment is provided as an easy-to-use plug-in of the Eclipse framework. An ATL program consists of rules which specify how to transform components of a source model into components of a target model. A rule can describe computations like integer arithmetic or string manipulations and check various conditions in OCL expressions, and can change the structure between components when producing the target model. This rule-based mechanism enables us to declaratively describe a wide variety of model transformations.

Despite its practical and wide uses, ATL lacks the important *bidirectional* feature in that it can only describe unidirectional mapping from the source model to the target model. Bidirectionality, as being seen in many other model transformation languages such as QVT and TGG [18], plays an important role in model synchronization, consistency maintenance, and reverse engineering [9]. One attempt to bidirectionalize ATL was made in the level of byte code of the virtual machine of ATL system [21], but it imposes many restrictions on the ATL byte code, and this restrictions on the lower byte code is somehow difficult to be understood and controlled by the users who write ATL programs.

J. Cabot and E. Visser (Eds.): ICMT 2011, LNCS 6707, pp. 138–151, 2011.

As an alternative, by contrast to the low level attempt, we shall take an *incremental* approach to bidirectionalizing ATL in a high level. Our idea is to show that a small core of ATL can be bidirectionalized, while making use of the fact that this core part can coexist well with other parts that cannot be bidirectionalized. This coexistence is possible because of modular execution of ATL programs; each rule specifies direct mapping from some elements in the input model to those in the output model. This core part could be extended and generalized in the future to deal with more of bidirectional computation in an ATL program. Now the problem is how to bidirectionalize ATL transformation rule, the basic unit of model transformation. Can we use the existing bidirectional languages to interpret ATL?

Bidirectional transformations, originated from the view update problem in the databases [4], have received much attention from the programming language community, and several *well-behaved* bidirectional transformation languages have been proposed [7,17,14,19,5,20], where the round-trip properties like put-get or get-put, which characterizes the bidirectional transformations, are guaranteed to be satisfied. However, most of these well-behaved bidirectional transformation languages manipulate trees or strings, which are not suitable for bidirectionalizing ATL, because models are essentially graphs. Recently, in our previous work [11] it is shown that the UnQL language [8], a well-known graph query language, can be used as a well-behaved bidirectional graph transformation language. In addition, a bidirectional graph transformation system called GRoundTram (Graph Roundtrip Transformation) [2] has been developed, where we can write bidirectional graph transformations in the UnQL language.

In this paper, as a first step toward realizing practical and well-behaved bidirectional model transformations, we present bidirectionalization of core part of the ATL by encoding it in the UnQL language. We give the algorithm for the encoding, based on which we have implemented the system for bidirectionalizing the core ATL in OCaml language. With representing the source model in a graph data structure, we can bidirectionally apply the encoded transformation in GRoundTram system. Throughout the paper we use a simple example to illustrate our algorithm.

The organization of this paper is as follows. Section 2 shows the overview of ATL, GRoundTram system, and UnQL language. Section 3 shows the encoding and decoding process between models and UnQL graph structures. Section 4 presents the algorithm for encoding ATL rules. Section 5 concludes the paper.

2   Preliminaries

Here we show the overview of the ATL, UnQL, and the GRoundTram system.

2.1   ATL

In this paper we use the following subset of the ATL language to show the essential part of the bidirectionalization. The subset does not cover imperative features of the ATL. We also exclude the most of the OCL expressions to avoid cluttering the essential part of the bidirectionalization. Although the subset may not have the same description power as the full set, it is enough for the purpose of showing the idea of our approach to bidirectionalization of model transformations.

$$ATL = \textbf{module } id; \textbf{ create } id : id; \textbf{ from } id : id; rule^{+}$$
$$rule = \textbf{rule } id \textbf{ from } inPat \textbf{ to } outPat^{+}$$
$$inPat = id : oclType$$
$$outPat = id : oclType \; binding^{*}$$
$$binding = id \leftarrow oclExp$$
$$oclExp = id$$
$$\mid id.id$$
$$\mid string$$
$$\mid oclExp + oclExp$$

```
rule Class2Table {
    from
        s : ClassDiagram!Class
    to
        t : Relational!Table (
            name <- s.name,
            col <- s.attr
        )
}

rule Attribute2Column {
    from
        s : ClassDiagram!Attribute
    to
        t : Relational!Column (
            name <- s.name
        )
}
```

Fig. 1. A model transformation in ATL

ATL consists of rules, each of which specifies a transformation that is applied to some components in the source model. A rule is described by the *rule* construct in the above syntax and the *inPat* construct *id*: *oclType* in each rule specifies to which component the rule is applied. For the details of ATL, refer to the documents in the ATL web page [1].

Here we illustrate the intuitive meaning of the ATL language by using an example in Fig. 1. It consists of two rules, Class2Table and Attribute2Column. The example is made by simplifying the class2RDBMS example provided as a non-trivial benchmark application for testing the power of model transformation languages in the announcement of the workshop MTiP 2005 [6].

In ATL we need to specify the metamodels for source models and target models. Let the metamodel of source models be the one in Fig. 2 and the metamodel of target models be the one in Fig. 3. In the ATL environment the metamodels are described by the ECore diagram or KM3 (kernel meta meta model) [3]. The metamodels in Fig. 2 and 3 are given in KM3.

```
package Class {
    abstract class NamedElt {
        attribute name : String;
    }

    class Class extends NamedElt {
        reference attr[*] : Attribute oppositeOf owner;
    }

    class Attribute extends NamedElt {
        reference type : Class;
        reference owner : Class oppositeOf attr;
    }
}

package PrimitiveTypes {
    datatype Boolean;
    datatype Integer;
    datatype String;
}
```

Fig. 2. The meta model in KM3 for the source models

```
package Relational {
    abstract class Named {
        attribute name : String;
    }

    class Table extends Named {
        reference col[*] : Column oppositeOf owner;
    }

    class Column extends Named {
        reference owner : Table oppositeOf col;
    }
}

package PrimitiveTypes {
    datatype Boolean;
    datatype Integer;
    datatype String;
}
```

Fig. 3. The meta model in KM3 for the target models

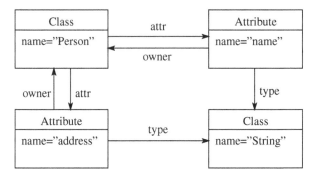

Fig. 4. A source model

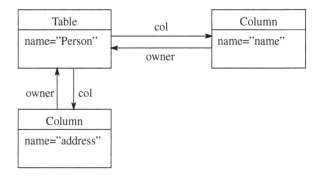

Fig. 5. The target model obtained by applying the rules to the source model

Let us use the model in Fig. 4 as an example of the source model. This model specifies that a Person class has two attributes (fields), name and address. This is transformed
into the target model in Fig. 5. In the next section we give the core idea of bidirectionalizing ATL by using the example given above.

2.2 UnQL

Let us briefly review the graph querying language, UnQL [8]. The language resembles
the SQL for relational databases in its **select-where** syntax, but is designed for manipulating graphs. In particular, it has a construct called structural recursion to traverse
over the given input graphs. We omit the formal definition of the language, which can
be found in [8]. We here informally present the basic concepts of UnQL starting with
its graph data model.

Graph Data Model. Graphs in UnQL are rooted and directed cyclic graphs with no
order between outgoing edges. They are edge-labeled in the sense that all information
is stored as labels on edges and the labels on nodes serve as a unique identifier and
have no particular meaning. The edge-labels can be either integers (e.g., 123, or 42),
strings (like "hello") for representing data-values, or bare-symbols (name, or attr)
for representing structures of graphs.

(query) Q ::= **select** T **where** $B, \ldots, B$
(template) T ::= Q | $\{L : T, \ldots, L : T\}$ | $T \cup T$ | $\$G$ | $f(\$G)$
             | **if** BC **then** T **else** T
             | **let sfun** $f \{Lp : Gp\} = T$
                | $f \{Lp : Gp\} = T$
                    $\ldots$
                sfun $f' \{Lp : Gp\} = T$
                  | $f' \{Lp : Gp\} = T$
                    $\ldots$
                 $\ldots$
             in T
(binding) B ::= Gp **in** $\$G$ | BC
(condition) BC ::= **not** BC | BC **and** BC | BC **or** BC
             | **isEmpty**$(\$G)$ | $L = L$ | $L \neq L$ | $L < L$ | $L \leq L$
(label) L ::= $\$l$ | a
(label pattern) Lp ::= $\$l$ | Rp
(graph pattern) Gp ::= $\$G$ | $\{Lp : Gp, \ldots, Lp : Gp\}$
(regular path pattern) Rp ::= a | _ | $Rp.Rp$ | $(Rp|Rp)$ | $Rp?$ | $Rp*$

Fig. 6. Syntax of UnQL

Two graphs in UnQL are considered to be equal if they are *bisimilar*. Intuitive understanding of bisimulation is that unfolding of cycles and duplication of equivalent subgraphs are not distinguished, and unreachable part from the root is ignored. Here is an examples of graphs that are bisimilar:

Every construct in UnQL respects bisimulation, i.e., if two bisimilar graphs are fed as inputs to a query, the results are always bisimilar again. This notion of equivalence plays an important role for query optimization [8] or bidirectionalization [12]. When the user does want to distinguish two bisimilar graphs as a different object, the user can add special *tag* edges labeled with unique identifiers to them, which breaks the bisimilarity and are dealt with separately.

Query Syntax. The syntax of UnQL query is summarized in Figure 6. The **select** T **where** $B, \ldots, B$ form is the entry point of the query. It selects the subgraphs satisfying the **where** B part and bind them to variables, and construct a result according to the template expression T. In T, the expression $\{L_1 : T_1, \ldots, L_n : T_n\}$ creates a new node having n outgoing edges labeled L_i and pointing to another node T_i. The union $G_1 \cup G_2$ constructs a graph with a root sharing the roots of G_1 and G_2. For example, $\{L_1 : g_1\} \cup \{L_2 : g_2\}$ equals to $\{L_1 : g_1, L_2 : g_2\}$. In the template, by using the keyword **sfun**, the programmer can also define a powerful *structural recursion*, which will be explained later. In the binding condition B part, comparison of label values and regular-expression based traversal on paths on graphs can be used.

Structural Recursion. A function f on graphs is called a structural recursion if it is defined by the following equations

$$
\begin{aligned}
f(\{\}) &= \{\} \\
f(\{\$l : \$g\}) &= e \\
f(\$g_1 \cup \$g_2) &= f(\$g_1) \cup f(\$g_2),
\end{aligned}
$$

where the expression e may contain references to variables $\$l$ and $\$g$, and recursive calls of the form $f(\$g)$, but no application of f to other graphs than $\$g$. Since the first and the third equations are common in all structural recursions, we omit them in UnQL. For the second line, since it is customary to dispatch the graph operation by labels, pattern-matching can be used instead of using long if-then-else sequence. For instance, we can write

$$
\begin{aligned}
\textbf{sfun } f\ (\{\texttt{class} : \$g\}) \quad &= e_1 \\
|\quad f\ (\{\texttt{interface} : \$g\}) &= e_2 \\
|\quad f\ (\{\texttt{int} : \$g\}) \quad &= e_3 \\
\vdots\ &
\end{aligned}
$$

instead of writing

$$
\begin{aligned}
\textbf{sfun } f\ (\{\$l : \$g\}) = \ &\textbf{if } \$l = \texttt{class} \textbf{ then } e_1 \\
&\textbf{else if } \$l = \texttt{interface} \textbf{ then } e_2 \\
&\textbf{else if } \$l = \texttt{int} \textbf{ then } e_3 \\
&\textbf{else} \ldots
\end{aligned}
$$

The following example shows a simple usage of structural recursion.

$$
\begin{aligned}
\textbf{sfun } a2d\_xc(\{\texttt{a} : \$g\}) \quad &= \{\texttt{d} : a2d\_xc(\$g)\} \\
|\quad a2d\_xc(\{\texttt{c} : \$g\}) \quad &= a2d\_xc(\$g) \\
|\quad a2d\_xc(\{\$l : \$g\}) &= \{\$l : a2d\_xc(\$g)\}
\end{aligned}
$$

It replaces all edges in the graph labeled a by d, contracts the edges labeled c, and keeps the other edges unchanged.

Despite its simplicity, structural recursion (and hence UnQL) is powerful enough to describe interesting nontrivial model transformations [13].

In this paper, for simplicity, we often write

$$
\textbf{sfun } f\ (\{\texttt{a} : \{\texttt{b} : \$v\}\}) = \ldots
$$

to denote

$$
\textbf{sfun } f'\ (\{\texttt{a} : \$g\}) = \textbf{let sfun } h\ (\{\texttt{b} : \$v\}) = \ldots \textbf{ in } h(\$g).
$$

Bidirectional Semantics. Usually, a query is run in one direction. That is, given an input environment (a mapping from variables to graphs) ρ, a query Q is evaluated and generated the result graph which we denote $\mathcal{F}[\![Q]\!]^\rho$. Now, let $G = \mathcal{F}[\![Q]\!]^\rho$ and consider the user has edited the result graph into G'. For example, he can add a new subgraph, or modify some label, or delete several edges, and so on. In our previous work [12], we have given a *backward semantics* that properly reflects back the editing to the original inputs. More formally speaking, given the modified result graph G' and the original input environments ρ, the modified environment $\rho' = \mathcal{B}[\![Q]\!]^\rho_{G'}$ can be computed.

By "properly reflecting back", we mean the following two properties to hold.

$$\mathcal{F}[\![Q]\!]^\rho = G \quad \text{implies} \quad \mathcal{B}[\![Q]\!]^\rho_G = \rho \qquad \text{(GETPUT)}$$
$$\mathcal{B}[\![Q]\!]^\rho_{G'} = \rho' \quad \text{implies} \quad \mathcal{B}[\![Q]\!]^\rho_{\mathcal{F}[\![Q]\!]^{\rho'}} = \rho' \qquad \text{(WPUTGET)}$$

The (GETPUT) property says that if no change is made on the output G, then there should occur no change on the input environment. The (WPUTGET) property is an unrestricted version of (PUTGET) property appeared in [10], which requires $G' \in$ Range($\mathcal{F}[\![Q]\!]$) and $\mathcal{B}[\![Q]\!]^\rho_{G'} = \rho'$ to imply $\mathcal{F}[\![Q]\!]^{\rho'} = G'$. The (PUTGET) property states that if a result graph is modified to G' which is in the range of the forward evaluation, then this modification can be reflected to the source such that a forward evaluation will produce the same result G'. In contrast to it, the (WPUTGET) property allows the modified result and the result obtained by backward evaluation followed by forward evaluation to differ, but require both to have the same effect on the original source if backward evaluation is applied.

2.3   GRoundTram system

In our previous work we have developed a system called GRoundTram system, which enables us to describe bidirectional transformations on graph data structures in the UnQL language. Note that we describe both the transformations and the graph data structures in UnQL language. We show the overview of the system in Fig. 7. Our system implements the bidirectional evaluator between source graphs and target graphs.

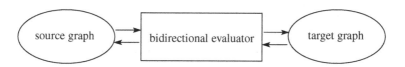

Fig. 7. GRoundTram system

Figure 8 shows a screenshot of our system. The user loads a source graph (displayed in the left pane) and a transformation written in UnQL. User can optionally specify the source metamodel and target metamodel in KM3. Once they are loaded, forward transformation can be conducted by pushing "forward" button (right arrow icon). The target graph appears on the right pane. User can graphically edit the target graph and apply backward transformation by pushing "backward" button (left arrow icon). Source graph can be edited as well, of course. Metamodel conformance of the source and the target can be checked any time by pushing check icon on both panes. The transformation itself can also be *statically* checked: given source/target metamodel and transformation, the system checks whether the target graph *always* conforms to given target metamodel. If not, a counterexample graph is displayed.

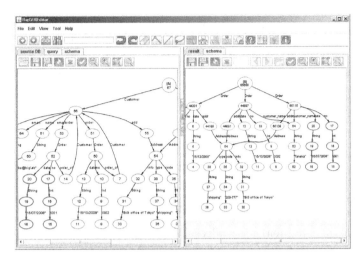

Fig. 8. Screenshot of GRoundTram System

Figure 8 also demonstrates the traceability between source and target (red part). If the user selects subgraphs on either pane, then corresponding subgraphs on other pane are also highlighted. This helps the user to predict modification on which part in the target will affect which part on the source, and vice versa.

3   Encoding and Decoding between Models and Graph Structures

In order to use the GRoundTram system we need to encode the models in UnQL language and decode the results back to models. Instead of giving algorithms for them, here we illustrate the encoding process using the model in Fig. 4.

Corresponding to the encoding of the rules in Section 4, we encode the models by using the constant pattern ClassName. For example, the component of the Class with name field "Person" is encoded into the following UnQL graph structure.

$$g_1 = \{\text{ClassName} : \{\text{Class} : \{\text{name} : \{''\text{Person}'' : \{\}\},$$
$$\text{attr} : g_2,$$
$$\text{attr} : g_3\}\}\}\}$$

The graphs g_2 and g_3 are obtained encoding of the components with Attribute class as follows.

$$g_2 = \{\text{ClassName} : \{\text{Attribute} : \{\text{name} : \{''\text{name}'' : \{\}\},$$
$$\text{owner} : g_1,$$
$$\text{type} : g_4\}\}\}$$
$$g_3 = \{\text{ClassName} : \{\text{Attribute} : \{\text{name} : \{''\text{address}'' : \{\}\},$$
$$\text{owner} : g_1,$$
$$\text{type} : g_4\}\}\}$$

The graph g_4, encoded as follows, is for the remaining component.

$$g_4 = \{\text{ClassName} : \{\text{Class} : \{\text{name} : \{''\text{String}'' : \{\}\}\}\}\}$$

The above representation is informal one for giving intuitive understanding. Formally, when encoding models with cycles as in Fig. 4, we use the cycle construct and markers in UnCAL language [8], which we omit for simplifying the presentation.

One thing we should note is we have to be able to get the original model representations from the graph structures. The overall figure of our approach is summarized in Fig. 9. The decoding process, which we omit, is performed naturally in the reverse way of the encoding process.

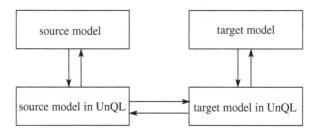

Fig. 9. Overview of our system

4   Encoding ATL Rules in UnQL

In this section we present the algorithm to encode a given ATL program into an UnQL expression. An ATL program consists of rules, as we have shown in Section 2.1. Our strategy for encoding is to transform each ATL rule into a function in the **sfun** construct in UnQL, by using the identifiers in the ATL rules when making an UnQL function.

We design the algorithm along the structure of the ATL language in the following. The top level transformation function is $atl2unql$.

$$atl2unql \ (\textbf{rule} \ r \ \textbf{from} \ inPat \ \textbf{to} \ outPatSeq) =$$
$$\textbf{sfun} \ r \ (inPat2arg \ inPat) = outPatSeq2unql \ outPatSeq$$

This function takes a rule in ATL and produces a function in UnQL language. This function is applied to rules in the ATL program, producing one function for each rule. We use the name of the rule as the name of the function. The $inPat$ is the pattern specifying to which components the rule is applied. We transform this part by applying $inPat2arg$, which produces a pattern that appears as the argument of the UnQL function. As we will mention in Section 3, each component in the model is encoded in UnQL graph structure so that the function can find the encoded components by pattern matching. For this purpose we encode each component using the constant pattern ClassName. So we define $inPat2arg$ to produce the pattern including the constant ClassName. The pattern $s : A$ in ATL is just encoded to the reversed pattern $\{A : \$s\}$ since we encode the model in the reverse order. The symbol $\$$ is just used for clarifying the variable pattern in the UnQL language.

$$inPat2arg \ (s : A) = \{\text{ClassName} : \{A : \$s\}\}$$

The transformation function $outPatSeq2unql$ is applied to $outPatSeq$ in the rule. The output pattern $outPat$ in ATL specifies each of the produced components. A rule may produce one or more components in the target model from a component in the source model, although the example in Fig. 1 produces just one component. The variables $t_1, t_2, \ldots$, each of which is bound to some component in the target model, may be used in the output patterns $outPatSeq$. We encode the rule into a mutually recursive functions in UnQL, where we use the name of the variables $t_1, t_2, \ldots$ in the encoded UnQL expression. Since in UnQL the value of the result of application of the function should be a graph, we just select one variable t_1 from the variables $t_1, t_2, \ldots$.

$$outPatSeq2unql\ (t1\ :\ ty1\ (binds_1),\ t2\ :\ ty2\ (binds_2),\ \ldots) =$$
$$\mathbf{letrec}\ t1 = outPat2unql\ (ty1\ (binds_1))$$
$$t2 = outPat2unql\ (ty2\ (binds_2))$$
$$\ldots$$
$$\mathbf{in}\ t1$$

The function $outPat2unql$ is applied to each output patterns. An output pattern consists of an identifier and a tuple of bindings. The identifier determines the class of the output pattern, so we attach the constant pattern ClassName.

$$outPat2unql\ (B\ (bind1,\ bind2,\ \ldots)) =$$
$$\{\text{ClassName}\ :\ \{B\ :\ (bind2unql\ bind_1)\ \cup\ (bind2unql\ bind_2)\ \cup \ldots\}\}$$
$$bind2unql(m \leftarrow oclExp) =$$
$$\mathbf{select}\ \{m\ :\ \$g\}$$
$$\mathbf{where}\ oclExp2unqlBinds\ \$g\ oclExp$$

The right-hand side of each binding is a subset of OCL expressions. The bindings are transformed and put in the where clause of the select-where construct in UnQL. We produce the bindings by applying the function $oclExp2unqlBinds$, defined as follows.

$$oclExp2unqlBinds\ p\ v = p\ \mathbf{in}\ \$v$$
$$oclExp2unqlBinds\ p\ (vs\ .\ v) = oclExp2unqlBinds\ \$g\ vs\ (\$g\ :\ \text{fresh})$$
$$\{v\ :\ p\}\ \mathbf{in}\ \$g$$
$$oclExp2unqlBinds\ p\ string = p\ \mathbf{in}\ \{string\ :\ \{\}\}$$
$$oclExp2unqlBinds\ p\ (e1 + e2) = oclExp2unqlBinds\ \{\$l1\ :\ \{\}\}\ e1$$
$$oclExp2unqlBinds\ \{\$l2\ :\ \{\}\}\ e2$$
$$p\ \mathbf{in}\ \{\$l1\ \text{++}\ \$l2\ :\ \{\}\}$$

One thing to note here is the sequence of ids separated by dot is encoded by sequence of bindings, where fresh variables are introduced for each binding. Another thing to note is that string concatenation is encoded in the string concatenation in UnQL, which is represented by ++ here.

By applying the algorithm above to the ATL example in Fig. 1, we obtain the UnQL functions in Fig. 10. Note that dummy is used as a dummy label for making mutually recursive functions. Note also that the actual UnQL does not allow patterns of general form in the argument part but here we used them for simplifying the presentation as we mentioned in Section 2.2. After obtained these functions, we apply these functions recursively to the encoded source model. We define the following functions to do this application.

```
sfun Class2Table ({ClassName:{Class:$s}}) =
    letrec
    sfun t ({_:{}}) =
        {ClassName:
            {Table:
                    select {name:$a}
                    where $b in $s,
                            {name:$a} in $b
                    U
                    select {col:$c}
                    where $d in $s,
                            {attr:$c} in $d
            }
        }
    in t({dummy:{}})
sfun Attribute2Column ({ClassName:{Attribute:$s}}) =
    letrec
    sfun t ({_:{}}) =
        {ClassName:
            {Column:
                    select {name:$a}
                    where $b in $s,
                            {name:$a} in $b
            }
        }
    in t({dummy:{}})
```

Fig. 10. UnQL functions obtained by encoding the example ATL

sfun $mapClass2Table$ $(\{\text{ClassName} : \$g\}) = f_1$ $\$g$
   | $mapClass2Table$ $\{\$l : \$g\} = \{\$l : mapClass2Table$ $\$g\}$
sfun f_1 $(\{\text{Class} : \$g\}) =$
   $Class2Table$ $(\{\text{ClassName} : \{\text{Class} : mapClass2Table$ $\$g\}\})$
   | f_1 $\{\$l : \$g\} = \{\$l : mapClass2Table$ $\$g\}$

sfun $mapAttribute2Column$ $(\text{ClassName} : \$g\}) = f_2$ $\$g$
   | $mapAttribute2Column$ $\{\$l : \$g\} = \{\$l : mapAttribute2Column$ $\$g\}$
sfun f_2 $(\{\text{Attribute} : \$g\}) =$
   $Attribute2Column$ $(\{\text{ClassName} : \{\text{Attribute} : mapAttribute2Column$ $\$g\}\})$
   | f_2 $\{\$l : \$g\} = \{\$l : mapAttribute2Column$ $\$g\}$

Then we apply these functions to the encoded source model as follows.

$$mapAttribute2Column \ (mapClass2Table \ \$db)$$

Here $\$db$ represents the encoded source model. We omit the algorithm for generating these functions since it is fairly straightforward.

We have implemented the algorithm in a functional language called OCaml. The complexity of the algorithm is linear in the size of the input model and the rule descriptions. For the examples given in this paper, the program in OCaml works well.

5   Conclusions

In this paper we presented an approach to bidirectionalizing a subset of ATL. Although small, the core part of the ATL is shown to be bidirectionalized. The prototype implementation in OCaml is available at `http://www.biglab.org/src/icmt11/index.html`. The program works by putting it in the src directory in the source code of the GRoundTram system. This work is a first step toward realizing a practical bidirectional model transformations. We believe this approach is promising and in the future we will further develop it on the settings with less restrictions on the ATL transformations.

Acknowledgments

We would like to thank Massimo Tisi and Frederic Jouault for valuable discussions and for providing us simple examples of ATL rules. The research was supported in part by the Grand-Challenging Project on "Linguistic Foundation for Bidirectional Model Transformation" from the National Institute of Informatics, Grant-in-Aid for Scientific Research (B) No. 22300012, Grant-in-Aid for Scientific Research (C) No. 20500043, and Encouragement of Young Scientists (B) of the Grant-in-Aid for Scientific Research No. 20700035.

References

1. The ATL web site, `http://www.eclipse.org/m2m/atl/`
2. The BiG project web site, `http://www.biglab.org/`
3. ATLAS group. KM3: Kernel MetaMetaModel manual, `http://www.eclipse.org/gmt/atl/doc/`
4. Bancilhon, F., Spyratos, N.: Update semantics of relational views. ACM Transactions on Database Systems 6(4), 557–575 (1981)
5. Barbosa, D.M.J., Cretin, J., Foster, N., Greenberg, M., Pierce, B.C.: Matching lenses: Alignment and view update. In: ACM SIGPLAN International Conference on Functional Programming, pp. 193–204. ACM, New York (2010)
6. Bézivin, J., Schürr, A., Tratt, L.: Model Transformations in Practice Workshop. In: Bruel, J.-M. (ed.) MoDELS 2005. LNCS, vol. 3844, pp. 120–127. Springer, Heidelberg (2006)
7. Bohannon, A., Pierce, B.C., Vaughan, J.A.: Relational lenses: a language for updatable views. In: Vansummeren, S. (ed.) PODS, pp. 338–347. ACM Press, New York (2006)
8. Buneman, P., Fernandez, M.F., Suciu, D.: UnQL: a query language and algebra for semistructured data based on structural recursion. VLDB Journal: Very Large Data Bases 9(1), 76–110 (2000)
9. Czarnecki, K., Nathan Foster, J., Hu, Z., Lämmel, R., Schürr, A., Terwilliger, J.F.: Bidirectional Transformations: A Cross-Discipline Perspective. In: Paige, R.F. (ed.) ICMT 2009. LNCS, vol. 5563, pp. 260–283. Springer, Heidelberg (2009)

10. Nathan Foster, J., Greenwald, M.B., Moore, J.T., Pierce, B.C., Schmitt, A.: Combinators for bi-directional tree transformations: a linguistic approach to the view update problem. In: POPL 2005: ACM SIGPLAN–SIGACT Symposium on Principles of Programming Languages, pp. 233–246 (2005)
11. Hidaka, S., Hu, Z., Inaba, K., Kato, H., Matsuda, K., Nakano, K.: Bidirectionalizing graph transformations. In: ICFP 2010, pp. 205–216. ACM Press, New York (2010)
12. Hidaka, S., Hu, Z., Inaba, K., Kato, H., Matsuda, K., Nakano, K.: Bidirectionalizing graph transformations. In: ACM SIGPLAN International Conference on Functional Programming, pp. 205–216. ACM, New York (2010)
13. Hidaka, S., Hu, Z., Kato, H., Nakano, K.: Towards a compositional approach to model transformation for software development. In: SAC 2009: Proceedings of the 2009 ACM symposium on Applied Computing pp. 468–475. ACM, New York (2009)
14. Hu, Z., Mu, S.-C., Takeichi, M.: A programmable editor for developing structured documents based on bidirectional transformations. Higher-Order and Symbolic Computation 21(1-2), 89–118 (2008)
15. Jouault, F., Allilaire, F., Bezivin, J., Kurtev, I.: Atl: A model transformation tool. Science of Computer Programming 72(1-2), 31–39 (2008)
16. Jouault, F., Kurtev, I.: Transforming models with ATL. In: Bruel, J.-M. (ed.) MoDELS 2005. LNCS, vol. 3844, pp. 128–138. Springer, Heidelberg (2006)
17. Matsuda, K., Hu, Z., Nakano, K., Hamana, M., Takeichi, M.: Bidirectionalization transformation based on automatic derivation of view complement functions. In: 12th ACM SIGPLAN International Conference on Functional Programming (ICFP 2007), pp. 47–58. ACM Press, New York (2007)
18. Stevens, P.: Bidirectional Model Transformations in QVT: Semantic Issues and Open Questions. In: Engels, G., Opdyke, B., Schmidt, D.C., Weil, F. (eds.) MODELS 2007. LNCS, vol. 4735, pp. 1–15. Springer, Heidelberg (2007)
19. Voigtländer, J.: Bidirectionalization for free (pearl). In: POPL 2009: ACM SIGPLAN–SIGACT Symposium on Principles of Programming Languages, pp. 165–176. ACM, New York (2009)
20. Voigtländer, J., Hu, Z., Matsuda, K., Wang, M.: Combining syntactic and semantic bidirectionalization. In: ACM SIGPLAN International Conference on Functional Programming, pp. 181–192. ACM, New York (2010)
21. Xiong, Y., Liu, D., Hu, Z., Zhao, H., Takeichi, M., Mei, H.: Towards automatic model synchronization from model transformations. In: 22nd IEEE/ACM International Conference on Automated Software Engineering (ASE 2007), pp. 164–173. ACM Press, New York (2007)

An Evaluation of the Graphical Modeling Framework (GMF) Based on the Development of the CORAS Tool

Fredrik Seehusen and Ketil Stølen

SINTEF Information and Communication Technology, Norway
{fredrik.seehusen,ketil.stolen}@sintef.no

Abstract. We present an evaluation of the Graphical Modeling Framework (GMF) based on our experiences in developing an editor for the risk modeling language CORAS using GMF. Our main hypothesis is that GMF shortens development time and results in more reliable and maintainable systems than alternative approaches which are not based on code generation. We conclude that the hypothesis is true, but that the answer is not as clear cut as we initially believed, and that there is still a large potential for improvement.

Keywords: Model-Driven Development, GMF, Domain Specific Languages, Evaluation.

1 Introduction

We present an evaluation of the Graphical Modeling Framework (GMF) [5] based on the experiences we got from developing a graphical editor for the risk modeling language CORAS [11]. GMF builds on the principles of Model-Driven Development (MDD) which advocate the use design time models as the basis for code generation. In the area of domain specific languages, the idea of generating code from specifications is not new; so-called parser generators have been in use for a long time. These tools usually take an EBNF-grammar as input, and produce parsers that transform concrete syntax (such as source code) into abstract syntax. The idea of GMF is similar, the main differences being that the language grammar is specified as an Ecore model (similar to a UML class diagram model) instead of EBNF, that the concrete syntax is graphical (not text-based as in the traditional case), and that GMF not only generates a parser, but also much of the language editor.

The language that we developed an editor for is called the CORAS language. The language is graphical and used for the purpose of documenting a risk analysis. The CORAS language editor was developed as part of a book release on the CORAS risk analysis method [11].

Software development in the industry is usually not based on code generation from models. We are therefore primarily interested in comparing the use of GMF to a development approach which is not based on code generation. Our main

J. Cabot and E. Visser (Eds.): ICMT 2011, LNCS 6707, pp. 152–166, 2011.

hypothesis is that GMF shortens the development time and results in more reliable and maintainable systems than alternative approaches which are not based on code generation.

Our evaluation suggests that GMF does shorten development time, but to a smaller degree than we initially expected. The main reason for this is that the code which is generated by GMF had to be modified, and this turned out to be very time consuming. Our evaluation furthermore suggests that GMF may result in more reliable systems, but that it does not result in more maintainable systems.

The main lesson learned during the development of the CORAS tool, was that there is a huge difference (in practice) between transformations that produce code that to little or no degree should be modified (like parser generators or compilers), and transformations that produce code that must be modified. In the former case, it is reasonable to hide the details of the transformation from the developer through configuration options, but in the latter case this is more problematic. In fact, we believe that in the latter case, the transformation should not only be visible to the developer, but that the developer should be expected (and accommodated) to modify the transformation much in the same way that the developer is expected to modify the generated source code.

The rest of the paper is structured as follows: in Sect. 2 we introduce basic concepts of GMF, in Sect. 3 we describe our research method and hypothesis, in Sect. 4 we describe relevant facts about the CORAS tool and its development process, in Sect. 5 and Sect. 6 we evaluate GMF w.r.t. our hypotheses and suggest improvements, respectively. Finally, in Sect. 7 we present related work, and in Sect. 8 we provide conclusions.

2   The Graphical Modeling Framework (GMF)

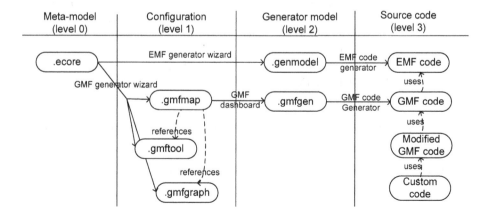

Fig. 1. Transformation in GMF

GMF is a framework for developing domain specific languages. GMF is built on the Eclipse Modeling Framework (EMF) [3] and the Graphical Editing Framework (GEF) [4]. In the context of GMF, EMF is used to define the meta model or abstract syntax of languages (expressed in Ecore), and for generating code for creating, editing, and accessing models. GEF is a framework that supports the development of graphical editors. In the context of GMF, GEF is used to implement the concrete graphical syntax of languages and for editing of concrete syntax.

The transformations of GMF are illustrated in Fig. 1. The top-most transformation consisting of the two arrows taking .*ecore* into EMF code will be referred to as the *EMF transformation* while the arrows taking .*ecore* into GMF code will be referred to as the *GMF transformation*.

As illustrated in Fig. 1, we distinguish between 4 different levels.

The meta model level (level 0). This level contains the meta model which is the basis of code generation. The meta model used by GMF must be stored in a format called Ecore.

The configuration level (level 1). This level contains the configuration model which is used by the GMF transformation (this is not used by the EMF transformation). The configuration model consists of three files: one file which is used to specify the shapes of the graphical constructs of the language (.*gmfgraph*), one file which specifies the language constructs which should appear in the tool palette of the language editor (.*gmftool*), and one file (.*gmfmap*) which maps the items of the tool palette (defined in .*gmftool*) to the graphical language constructs (defined in .*gmfgraph*) and to the meta model elements.

The default transformation from the meta model at level 0 to the configuration model at level 1 is based on a series of dialog windows where the user has to specify what elements of the meta model should be represented as arrows or nodes in the language editor.

The generator level (level 2). This level contains the code generator models for both the EMF and the GMF transformations. Both generator models contain a number of parameters that allows the user to customize the source code generated from the generator models.

The transformation from level 1 to level 2 (or from level 0 to level 2 in the case of the EMF transformation) is a one-button transformation as opposed to the dialog based transformation.

The source code level (level 3). This level contains the source code. Here we distinguish between:

- EMF code generated by the EMF transformation;
- GMF code generated by the GMF transformation, which makes use of the EMF code as well as the GEF framework;
- modified GMF code, i.e. generated GMF code which has been modified after generation;

– custom code which has not been generated from the meta model, but which makes use of the EMF-code and the GMF code.

Note that we do not distinguish between generated EMF code and modified EMF code. The reason is that we did not have to modify the generated EMF code (even though it is possible to do so).

The transformation from level 2 to level 3 is also a one-button transformation. However, the GMF transformation from level 2 to level 3 (which is written in a language called Xpand) can be customized. This was achieved by putting the files containing the transformation specification in a special folder with the same structure as the GMF transformation. When the transformation is executed, the transformation in the special folder will be used instead of the original transformation. The effect is essentially the same as modifying the original transformation directly.

In theory, all the modified GMF-code could have been specified in the transformation from level 2 to level 3, but GMF is not intended to be used in this way. Instead, GMF code which is modified after code generation can be tagged to ensure that modified code is not overwritten when code generation is executed at some later point in time.

3 Research Method and Hypotheses

According to [12], research evidence is gathered to maximize three things: the generalizability of the evidence over populations of actors; the precision of measurement of behavior; the realism of the situation or context. According the classification of research strategies of [12], our evaluation of GMF is a *field study*. Field studies are high on realism, but low on generalizability and precision.

The idea of evaluating GMF did not come about until after we had developed the CORAS tool. Therefore the development of the CORAS tool was not in any way biased by our evaluation.

We are primarily interested in comparing the use of GMF to a development approach which is not based on code generation. For us, a realistic alternative to using GMF, would have to use Eclipse and GEF. The main differences between the GMF approach and the alternative approach is that using the alternative approach, we would have to (1) write the code that uses GEF instead of generating it using GMF and (2) write the code with similar functionality as the EMF code, instead of generating it using the EMF transformation. Throughout the rest of this paper, whenever we write *the alternative development approach* (or alternative approach), we refer to the approach described above.

Note that we did not actually develop the CORAS tool using the alternative approach. Any judgment about the CORAS tool, for instance how long it would have taken to develop the CORAS tool had we used the alternative approach is therefore based on educated guesses rather than hard facts.

3.1   Hypotheses

The main reason why we chose to use GMF, was that we believed that it would shorten the development time. In fact, one of our colleagues claimed that it would only take 2 days to develop the editor using GMF; another colleague estimated that it would take about 2 weeks. Granted, our colleagues were not familiar with the requirements of the tool, but we were nevertheless given to believe that using GMF would shorten development time. Our first hypothesis is therefore:

H1: The time spent on developing the CORAS tool using GMF is shorter than the time spent on developing the tool had we followed the alternative approach.

The CORAS tool was intended to be used in industrial settings, often on the-fly during customer meetings. Consequently, the most important requirement of the CORAS tool (aside from the fact that it had to support the desired functionality) was its continuous delivery of correct service, also known as its *reliability* [2]. Our second hypothesis is therefore:

H2: The CORAS tool is more reliable when developed using GMF than it would have been if developed using the alternative approach.

From the start, it was anticipated that the CORAS tool would be extended into new prototype tools according the requirements of projects we were involved in. Already, we have made three such extensions, and further extensions are planned in the future. The situation can be described by an inheritance tree where the initial CORAS tool is the root of the tree, and each of the other tree nodes represent tool extensions that inherit functionality from their parent nodes in the tree. We are interested in evaluating how well GMF supports the maintainability of such an inheritance tree. For the purpose of our GMF evaluation, we therefore say that the *maintainability* of a tool is measure of how well it can be extended into an inheritance tree that satisfies the following requirements:

- The development of a tool in the tree should not affect any of the parents of that tool. This requirement is to make sure that the development of new tools does not cause the tools they inherit from to become unreliable.
- Updates made in a tool should automatically or semi- automatically be propagated to all its children in the inheritance tree. If we did not have this requirement, and made a change in the root node for instance, we would have to manually update all the other tools of the tree. This would be time-consuming, and it could potentially lead to reduced reliability.

Our third hypothesis is the following

H3: The CORAS tool is more maintainable when developed using GMF than it would have been if developed using the alternative approach.

4   Developing the CORAS Tool Using GMF

In this section, we present facts regarding the CORAS tool and the development setting.

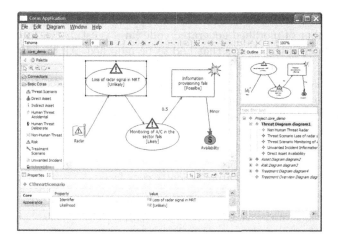

Fig. 2. Screenshot of the CORAS tool

4.1   Development Setting

Initial discussions about the CORAS tool started in September 2009. The tool requirements were completed in December 2009. The tool development was carried out by a single developer from the end of December 2009 until early May 2010. From February 2010 to May 2010, the developer worked close to full time on the CORAS tool development. The total time spent on the development was about 3.5 man months.

The developer is employed as a researcher and has a computer science background. His programming experience was mostly based on university graduate courses. The developer was somewhat familiar with Eclipse (the integrated development environment that supports GMF), but had no experience with GMF or the components that GMF builds on (EMF and GEF).

The developer was under pressure to finish the CORAS tool as quickly as possible. The development approach was based on trial and error; thereby learning exactly what was needed to get the job done. We do not argue that this is the best development approach, but merely give an account of what happened. Moreover, we believe that this situation is not uncommon in many industrial software projects.

4.2   The CORAS Tool

The CORAS tool is a graphical editor for the CORAS language which is used for the purpose of documenting risk analyses. CORAS diagrams are essentially graphs with arrows and nodes. The CORAS tool supports five kinds of diagrams, and it also supports a hierarchical structure in which one construct may be decomposed into other constructs to an arbitrary depth. A screenshot of the tool is shown in Fig. 2.

Table. 1 summarizes some statistics about the CORAS tool implementation. Here the number of modified generated code lines is estimated to be 10 percent of the code lines of the classes that had to be modified. All the other values are accurate facts (not estimations).

We have distinguished between code which has been generated by the EMF code generator, and code which has been generated by the GMF code generator. Notice that it is only the generated GMF code that had to be modified. Notice also that 18.5% of the generated GMF classes had to be modified, and that about 0.6% of the code lines had to be modified.

Table 1. Source code facts

	EMF	GMF	Total
Generated classes	131	465	595
Generated classes modified	0	86	86
Generated code lines	15220	78584	93804
Generated code lines modified	0	4767	4767
New classes	0	48	48
New code lines	0	4436	4436
Proportion of classes modified	0 %	18.50 %	14.45 %
Proportion of code lines modified	0 %	0.6 %	0.5 %

5   Evaluation of GMF

In this section, we evaluate GMF w.r.t. each of the hypotheses described in Sect. 3.

H1: The time spent on developing the CORAS tool using GMF is shorter than the time spent on developing the tool had we followed the alternative approach.

The development of the CORAS tool took about 3.5 man-months, which was more than we anticipated. Since we did have a stable meta model to begin with, it actually only took a couple of days to generate an initial version of the editor containing most of the required functionality. The problem was the huge amount of time required to modify the code that was generated.

Not much of the generated code had to be changed (see Table. 1), but finding the right places in the generated code to implement the modifications was very time consuming. It was not uncommon to spend days to search for the right place to edit, only to change a couple of lines here and there.

So, why did it take so long? One reason is that the developer had no prior experience with GMF, or the technologies used by GMF (GEF and EMF), and as it turned out, too little knowledge of Eclipse. Any of these technologies are challenging to learn on their own right; learning them all at the same time is even more challenging. Another aspect is poor documentation. In particular, the source code and the API contained very little documentation. Despite the fact that we had a book on GMF [7], this book did not address the very specific changes that we had to make to the generated code. Most of the answers we got were found browsing the source code, as well as in blogs, forums, presentations, small tutorials found by searching the Internet.

A lot of the changes we made to the source code that was generated from GMF, had to be applied to numerous classes. That is, the same change had to be made to many classes of the same kind (usually meaning that they inherited from the same super-class contained in a library). Eventually the developer learned to modify the GMF transformations that generated the source code to implement these kinds of changes. Of course, if the developer had been aware of these things from the start, much time could have been saved. This is also true for the GMF transformation from the meta model to the generator model. Eventually we found an alternative to the GMF transformation wizard called EuGENia (which is built on top of Epsilon [9]) which allowed us to generate the graphical configuration files from an annotated meta model. This worked very well; it was very easy to learn and the execution of the transformation was reduced to pressing a button as opposed to clicking through a series of dialogs.

Up until this point, we have argued that most of the development time was spent on modifying the generated code. However, to address the hypothesis, we must ask whether GMF shortens development time. To answer this question, it is useful to distinguish between the EMF transformation and the GMF transformation (as explained in Sect. 2). The former transformation generated code which we did not have to modify. In our view, the use of the EMF transformation clearly saved us a lot of time. This should come as no surprise, since the EMF transformation is similar to well-known parser generators which are clearly useful.

The GMF transformation is more complex than the EMF transformation. First of all, it has a lot more configuration options (e.g. for customizing the graphical constructs that should be implemented). Our initial goal was to do as much of the customization as possible on the meta model level and on the configuration level (see Fig. 1), so quite some time was spent on e.g. figuring out whether or not it was possible to specify the kind of graphical construct that we needed using the configuration files (instead of having to modify the source code). It turned out that it was not possible, and eventually the configuration files were mostly ignored in favor of source code modification.

The main difference between the GMF transformation and the EMF transformation from the perspective of time use was that the code that was produced by the GMF transformation had to be modified whereas this was not the case for EMF. As already explained, the code modification turned out to be the biggest time drain. Since figuring out how to modify the code took such a long time, it is hard to say for sure whether or not it would have been faster to write all the generated code from scratch. However, if we were to make a new graphical editor with the knowledge we have today of how GMF works, we definitely think that using the GMF transformation will be faster than writing the code from scratch. We therefore believe that the hypothesis H1 is true, but that the answer is not as clear cut as we believed it to be when we started developing the tool.

H2: The CORAS tool is more reliable when developed using GMF than it would have been if developed using the alternative approach.

As mentioned in the previous section, GMF had some bugs, but these were more of the kind that slowed us down rather than making the generated code unreliable. After having tested the CORAS tool on students, we have not found any serious error in the GMF code (apart from the copy/paste functionality). The few errors that were found were caused by us rather than the GMF code.

The generated GMF code seems to be based on a lot of standard design patterns. This is probably mostly an advantage, but not necessarily if the developer who has to modify the generated code is not familiar with those patterns. Had the developer written the code from scratch, he would have used patterns that he was familiar with and could understand, and would therefore have a much better understanding of how the code works. Furthermore, the code base would likely have been smaller and more manageable.

In general we can say this: the time and effort spent on verifying the GMF transformation (and the code produced by it) is probably greater than the time and effort we would have spent on verifying the code we would have written had we followed the alternative approach. In this sense, the generated code is potentially more reliable. However, if the generated code must be modified, then the picture is less clear. The reason for this is that modifying code that is unfamiliar to the developer and which furthermore may be based on patterns that the developer is not familiar with may cause the developer to modify the code in a way that it is not intended to be modified. However, had we followed the alternative approach, we would still have to use GEF which is based on certain design patterns that must be followed in order to use the framework properly. In fact, it is probably less likely that GEF is used incorrectly in the generated code than it is that GEF had been used incorrectly had we followed the alternative approach.

As explained in Sect. 2, the first time the GMF transformations are executed, output is generated which has to be modified. When the transformations are executed again, they will overwrite parts of the output which was generated from the previous execution, and leave other parts unchanged (presumably the modified parts). Regarding the transformations from the meta model to the configuration level, and from the configuration level to the generator model, it was a bit unclear to us what parts would be overwritten, and what parts would be changed. This is of course a potential source of error. Regarding the transformation from the generator model to the source code, it was clear which parts where overwritten and which were not. The reason for this is that the developer had to explicitly annotate methods in the generated source code to indicate that they should not be overwritten during the next execution of the transformation. However, this approach does by no means guarantee that the transformation does not generate errors in the code the next time it is run. That is, changes made in the meta model or on the configuration model could result in a modification in methods that have been specified not to be overwritten.

The considerations above are potential sources of errors, but they did not as far as we know, turn out to be any problem w.r.t. to the reliability of the CORAS tool. However, it is difficult to determine whether this was a coincidence or not.

In conclusion, we believe that the hypothesis is true. The main reason for this is that we did not discover many errors which affected the reliability of the GMF code; most of the errors we found were caused by us. Source code which is generated and should be used many times is more likely to be subjected to a more detailed verification process than the code which is written from scratch. Despite the danger of modifying the generated code in a way that violates the design patterns that are used, this danger also exists if the code had been written from scratch using third party libraries such as GEF. The possibility of modifying the output of a transformation may potentially lead to errors when transformations have to be executed several times. However, according to our experience, this did not affect the reliability of the CORAS tool to a noticeable extent.

> H3: The CORAS tool is more maintainable when developed using GMF than it would have been if developed using the alternative approach.

As explained in Sect. 3, the CORAS tool has been extended into three new tool versions. In the process of figuring out how to maintain these different versions, we discovered that code generation actually made things a lot more difficult for us. We will now explain this.

Consider the scenario in which we want to extend tool A into a tool B. By this we mean that we want to develop a new tool B that has a lot of the same functionality as A, but some of the functionality will be different. A standard solution to the problem is the following: package A into a component (e.g. a java jar file or an Eclipse plugin) that can be used by B, e.g. by invoking methods exposed by the public interface of the component or sub-classing public classes of A. The problem, however, is that this standard solution is not supported in the GMF code generation setting. To see this, consider Fig.3. Here tool A has been decomposed into two parts: $Model_A$ and $Code_A$ where the idea is that $Code_A$ is generated from $Model_A$ (the same applies for tool B). To extend A into B, it is possible to both extend the model and the code. Imagine that we try to apply the standard solution to the problem. We get the following scenario: First we package the source code of A into a component, then we make a folder/project for B and import component A into it. Suppose that the model has to be extended. Since it is not possible to package the model into a component like the source code, $Model_A$ is copied into the folder of B. The problem now is that when code $Code_B$ is generated from $Model_B$, $Code_B$ will contain much of the same functionality that is contained in package A and it would be very inconvenient to try to replace the functionality in $Code_B$ that overlaps with the package A with invocations to A.

The problem is most notable in the cases where $Code_A$ has been modified after it has been generated from $Model_A$. If all the modifications had been expressed in the transformation or in the model, then there would be no need to package A into a component. However, the problem is still present since GMF does not support the possibility of packaging models or transformations into components.

In summary, we can conclude that the hypothesis H3 is false. The standard way of extending tools is not supported in the GMF code generation setting.

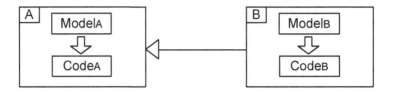

Fig. 3. Extending *A* into *B*

6   Suggested Improvements

The issues regarding poor documentation or the fact that the GMF architecture was hard to understand are not specific to transformation based development approaches. In this section, we therefore focus on the transformation aspect of the GMF framework. In particular we will focus on the GMF transformation (since we did not find any problems with the EMF transformation).

In Table. 2, we have given an overview of our main suggested improvements and the problems they are related to. In the following, we discuss each suggestion in turn.

Table 2. Summary of problems and suggested improvements

Problem	Suggested improvement
The dialog based GMF transformation did not work and was time consuming to use	Avoid human interaction during transformation execution
Unclear whether changes to generated artifacts would be preserved under subsequent transformation executions	Expose the transformation language to the end user / avoid changing generated artifacts
Lack of modularity support	Incorporate traditional programming language solutions to modularity

6.1   Avoid Human Interaction During Transformation Execution

The GMF transformation from the meta model to the graphical configuration models was wizard based, i.e. the user could configure the transformation through a series a dialogs. If the transformation was run a second time, the transformation would remember the dialog settings of the previous run of the transformation. Or at least that was the idea. This transformation did not work properly, but if we ignore that, we still think that the use of dialogs is bad. First, clicking through a series of dialogs each time the transformation is run is time consuming. Even though we had a stable meta model to begin with, we ended up generation the editor countless of times. Second, since the mechanisms of how the transformation worked was hidden from the user, it was unclear how a change in the dialog option would affect the transformation.

Based on our experience, we therefore think the use of transformation executors that require human interaction is a bad idea. As previously discussed, we eventually ended up using an alternative (called EuGENia) to the GMF transformation wizard for producing the graphical configuration model. This approach enabled us to annotate the meta-model with GMF-annotations, and then to generate the configuration files from the annotated meta-model without any human interaction. This approach worked far better than the GMF dialog based approach.

6.2   Expose the Transformation Language to the End User

The generated artifacts on all three levels had to be modified. For the GMF transformations that generated the configuration level artifacts and the generated model, it was unclear whether or not the modifications to the artifacts would be preserved upon subsequent executions of the transformations. One of the reasons for this was that the transformations were hidden from the user; without understanding how the transformation works it is also hard to understand how the transformation generates its output.

We therefore suggest that the transformation should be made visible to the user in the same manner as source code is often made available to programmers. Furthermore, we believe that for the GMF model transformations (i.e. the transformations that do not generate the source code), it is better to modify the transformations that generate the model artifacts (as opposed to modifying the generated artifacts) because this gives the user precise control of what the transformation generates.

This suggestion is made on the basis of our experience with using the language Epsilon Object Language (EOL) [8], which we used to customize the GMF transformations that produced the configuration level models and the generator model. This approach worked very well. EOL removed the need of modifying the generated artifacts, and enabled us precisely control the output of the transformation. Furthermore, it was not more difficult or more time consuming to customize the transformation than to modify the generated artifacts.

One might think that requiring the end user to learn a new language (the transformation language) could be a problem. However, our experience with EOL suggests otherwise. In fact, after only seeing a couple of examples of EOL code, we were able to customize the transformation as needed. Contrasting this to the months spent on modifying the generated GMF source code, the effort required to learn how to use the language becomes negligible.

Regarding the GMF transformation (written in Xpand) that generated the source code, it was fairly clear what parts of the code the Xpand transformation would change or leave unchanged when it was executed. This is because Xpand enables the user to annotate methods in the generated code to indicate whether or not the methods should be overwritten when the transformation is executed again. However, we believe that it would have been helpful increase the granularity and flexibility of this annotation scheme. For instance, it would have been helpful indicate that certain *parts* of a method (not just the whole method) have been modified and should not be overwritten.

W.r.t. source code generators, we do not have enough evidence to determine whether or not the need of modifying the generated source code (as opposed to modifying the transformation) is a bad idea.

6.3   Incorporate Traditional Programming Language Solutions to Modularity

The GMF transformation from the generator model to the source code is can be customized/extended as explained in Sect. 2. However, we do not believe that this manner of customization is a good one; it is essentially the same as copying the source of a library into the current project and then overwriting the code. It is better to package the library into a component which can be invoked through a public interface or extended through sub-classing public classes. We believe that the transformation language should have similar extension capabilities. After all, GMF can be seen as common library, with the difference that certain parts of the code are transformations.

7   Related Work

There are not many empirical studies on applying Model-Driven Development (MDD) in industry settings. A survey of literature reporting experiences from applying MDD in industry settings can be found in [13], but there is too little evidence to allow generalization of the results. Nevertheless, many of case studies mentioned in the surveys report about a 25% productivity gain using MDD over conventional development. The paper [13] does not address GMF in particular. Papers that do consider GMF in particular are: [1,6,10,14]. Both [1] and [14] compare GMF against other domain specific language tools. According to [1], GMF is the most difficult to use, but it generates very usable editors. The paper [14] compares GMF against Microsoft DSL Tools, and concludes that GMF seems to be better accepted by participants of their case study.

In [6], the authors report on the experiences of developing a network modeling tool using GMF. They make two main conclusions: (1) a high level of programming experience is needed to use GMF properly, and that GMF should be made easier to use by domain-experts with no particular programming experience; (2) GMF has shortcomings in providing support for modeling at different abstraction levels.

In [10], the authors report on a case study where software with identical functionality was created twice: once using conventional development without code generation, and once using GMF. The study concludes that development using GMF was about 9 times faster than conventional development, and that GMF produced much higher quality of code. A threat to the validity of the study was that the conventional development was not based on EMF or GEF, but on .NET and an, according to [10], immature graphical library.

8 Conclusion

We have presented an evaluation of GMF based on our experiences in developing the CORAS tool. Our hypothesis was that GMF shortens development time, and that it results in more reliable and maintainable systems than an alternative development approach which is not based on code generation.

Our evaluation suggests that GMF does shorten development time, but to a smaller degree than we initially expected. Furthermore, we believe that the use of GMF may result in more reliable systems, but that it results in less maintainable systems according to our definition of maintainability.

For code generators that produce code that to a little or no degree should be modified (like parser generators, compilers, or EMF to a certain extent), it is perfectly reasonable to hide the transformation from the developer; letting all the work be done at the model level and in customization files. However, we believe that this is not OK for transformations (e.g. the GMF transformation) that must be extensively modified (either by modifying the transformation itself or the generated artifact). In fact, we believe that in this case, the transformations should be pushed to the forefront of the development; that the developer should be expected and accommodated to modify the transformation. GMF does offer the possibility of modifying one of the three GMF transformations, but in GMF tutorials and other documentation, this possibility is treated more like an advanced feature than an important part of the development on par with e.g. configuration model customization. In fact, the developer was not even aware of the possibility until far into the development process. Finally, we believe that the transformations should be extended in much the same way as libraries are extended when programming. Currently, this is not possible in the transformations of GMF.

Acknowledgments. The research on which this paper reports has been carried out within the DIGIT (180052/S10) and the EMERGENCY projects (187799/S10), funded by the Research Council of Norway, the MASTER and the NESSoS projects, funded from the European Community's Seventh Framework Programme (FP7/2007-2013) under grant agreements FP7-216917 and FP7-256980, respectively.

References

1. Amyot, D., Farah, H., Roy, J.-F.: Evaluation of Development Tools for Domain-Specific Modeling Languages. In: Gotzhein, R., Reed, R. (eds.) SAM 2006. LNCS, vol. 4320, pp. 183–197. Springer, Heidelberg (2006)
2. Avizienis, A., Laprie, J.-C., Randell, B.: Fundamental Concepts of Dependability. Research Report No 1145, LAAS-CNRS (2001)
3. Eclipse. Eclipse modeling framework project (emf) (2011), http://www.eclipse.org/modeling/gmp (visited February 8, 2011)
4. Eclipse. Graphical editing framework (gef) (2011), http://www.eclipse.org/geff (visited February 8, 2011)

5. Eclipse. Graphical modeling project (gmp) (2011),
   `http://www.eclipse.org/modeling/emf` (visited February 8, 2011)
6. Evans, A., Fernández, M.A., Mohagheghi, P.: Experiences of developing a network modeling tool using the eclipse environment. In: Paige, R.F., Hartman, A., Rensink, A. (eds.) ECMDA-FA 2009. LNCS, vol. 5562, pp. 301–312. Springer, Heidelberg (2009)
7. Gronback, R.C.: Eclipse Modeling Project: A Domain-Specific Language (DSL) Toolkit. Addison-Wesley, Reading (2009)
8. Kolovos, D.S., Paige, R.F., Polack, F.A.C.: The epsilon object language (EOL). In: Rensink, A., Warmer, J. (eds.) ECMDA-FA 2006. LNCS, vol. 4066, pp. 128–142. Springer, Heidelberg (2006)
9. Kolvos, D.S.: An Extensible Platform for Specification of Integrated Languages for Model Management. PhD thesis, Department of Computer Science, University of York (2008)
10. Krogmann, K., Becker, S.: A case study on model-driven and conventional software development: The palladio editor. In: Proc. of tSoftware Engineering 2007 - Beiträge zu den Workshops, Fachtagung des GI-Fachbereichs Softwaretechnik, vol. 106, pp. 169–176. GI (2007)
11. Lund, M.S., Solhaug, B., Stølen, K.: Model Driven Risk Analysis - The CORAS Approach. Springer, Heidelberg (2011)
12. McGrath, J.E.: Groups: Interaction and performance. Prentice-Hall, Englewood Cliffs (1984)
13. Mohagheghi, P., Dehlen, V.: Where is the proof? - A review of experiences from applying MDE in industry. In: Schieferdecker, I., Hartman, A. (eds.) ECMDA-FA 2008. LNCS, vol. 5095, pp. 432–443. Springer, Heidelberg (2008)
14. Pelechano, V., Albert, M., Muñoz, J., Cetina, C.: Building tools for model driven development. comparing microsoft dsl tools and eclipse modeling plugins. In: Proc. of the Actas del Taller sobre Desarrollo de Software Dirigido por Modelos. MDA y Aplicaciones. CEUR Workshop Proceedings, vol. 227 (2007)

A Graph Query Language for EMF Models*

Gábor Bergmann, Zoltán Ujhelyi, István Ráth, and Dániel Varró

Budapest University of Technology and Economics,
Department of Measurement and Information Systems,
1117 Budapest, Magyar tudósok krt. 2
{bergmann,ujhelyiz,rath,varro}@mit.bme.hu

Abstract. While model queries are important components in model-driven tool chains, they are still frequently implemented using traditional programming languages, despite the availability of model query languages due to performance and expressiveness issues. In the current paper, we propose EMF-INCQUERY as a novel, graph-based query language for EMF models by adapting the query language of the VIATRA2 model transformation framework to inherit its concise, declarative nature, but to properly tailor the new query language to the modeling specificities of EMF. The EMF-INCQUERY language includes (i) structural restrictions for queries imposed by EMF models, (ii) syntactic sugar and notational shorthand in queries, (iii) true semantic extensions which introduce new query features, and (iv) a constraint-based static type checking method to detect violations of EMF-specific type inference rules.

1 Introduction

Model queries are important components in model-driven tool chains. They are widely used in model transformations, model execution/simulation, report generation, or the evaluation of well-formedness constraints. *Global model queries* can be evaluated over the entire model to retrieve all results fulfilling the query, while *local model queries* retrieve information specific for some given input model elements. In current industrial applications based on popular modeling frameworks (e.g. the Eclipse Modeling Framework *EMF*[1]), model queries are still frequently implemented using a traditional programming language (Java), despite the availability of more advanced declarative query languages such as OCL [2] or EMF Model Query [3].

The reasons for this are two-fold. Unfortunately, as observed in tool development practice, as well as in benchmark measurements [4], the implementation infrastructure behind these high level model query languages often has *scalability issues* when large instance models are used, which may effectively rule out the application of these technologies in certain industrial applications.

---

* This work was partially supported by the SecureChange (ICT-FET-231101) European Research Project.

J. Cabot and E. Visser (Eds.): ICMT 2011, LNCS 6707, pp. 167–182, 2011.

Additional issues include *expressiveness and learning effort*. Simple technologies (such as EMF Model Query) are not flexible or expressive enough for advanced use cases involving complex join operations, while complex – and thus significantly harder to learn [5] – languages such as OCL still lack important features despite their higher expressive power. Such important features include reusable query modularization, recursion and transitive closures, which are not easily accessible or not supported at all. Finally, there is also a practical need for the adaptation and extension of compile-time validation techniques, which are currently in very early stages of development.

In [4], we demonstrated how incremental model transformation techniques of the VIATRA2 framework can be adapted to efficiently support advanced model queries over large EMF models and proposed a new runtime model query framework called EMF-INCQUERY. Our initial investigations were focused on providing high performance for model queries, therefore, we reused the query language of VIATRA2. However, as the underlying (meta-)modeling foundations for VIATRA2 and EMF are different, the direct reuse of the VIATRA2 graph pattern language raised usability issues.

In the current paper, we present the query language of EMF-INCQUERY, which provides an EMF-specific dialect of the graph pattern language of the VIATRA2 transformation framework. This query language – having its roots in the graph transformation domain – shares proven concepts from languages of existing and very powerful tools (e.g. Fujaba, PROGRES, GrGEN, GReAT, VMTS, AGG) and is intended to integrate to the industry-standard EMF platform to reach a broader audience. By adapting the query language of VIATRA2, our goal is (1) to enable that EMF-INCQUERY inherits the declarative nature, conciseness, easy specification and comprehension of the VIATRA2 language, and (2) to ensure that the new query language is properly tailored to the modeling specificities of EMF.

In the paper, we report about this adaptation, which includes (i) structural restrictions for queries imposed by EMF models (e.g. lack of edge variables), (ii) syntactic sugar and notational shorthand in queries (like transitive closure along edges, simplified attribute conditions) that support more convenient query specification, and (iii) true semantic extensions to the existing VIATRA2 pattern language, which introduce new query features (like aggregation, indexing in ordered collections, arithmetic assignments). Finally, (iv) a constraint-based static type checking method is used to detect violations of EMF-specific type inference rules in the EMF-INCQUERY language. Compared to [4] (which introduced the runtime incremental matching framework for EMF-INCQUERY together with performance benchmarks), the current paper focuses exclusively on the EMF-specific query language itself.

The rest of the paper is structured as follows. In Sec. 2, we introduce a motivating case study and the existing pattern language of VIATRA2. Sec. 3 describes the novel language features of EMF-INCQUERY by elaborating the case study. We present the static type checking feature in Sec. 4 and discuss related work in Sec. 5. Sec. 6 concludes the paper with future research directions.

2   Background and Case Study

2.1   Case Study

Problem Domain. Our motivating scenario is from the domain of security requirements engineering in case of evolving models, inspired by the Air Traffic Management case study of the SecureChange European FP7 project. A requirements model assists security engineers to capture security related aspects of the system, to analyze the security needs of the stakeholders, and to argue about potential security threats. The concepts of a security requirements modeling language such as SecureTropos [6] typically include *actors*, *resources* (e.g. security-critical information assets) provided by actors, *goals* (functional, security, etc. requirements) wanted by actors, and *tasks* performed by actors. Relationships include tasks to fulfilling goals; trust relationships between actors; and delegation of responsibility over resources, goals or tasks. See Fig. 1 for the most important elements of the SecureChange requirements metamodel.

An important role of security requirement models is to support reasoning about security properties by formal or informal argumentation techniques [7] in an early phase of system development. To formalize static security properties, we use graph patterns as a query language in the scope of the project. On the tooling level, the EMF-INCQUERY framework provides efficient, incremental constraint evaluation and feedback for the engineers already in the early stages of requirements modeling.

Analysis Tasks. Early-stage analysis of requirements models is carried out by (local and global) model queries in the case study of this paper. Support can range from finding violations of structural semantic constraints that represent security properties of the model, to generating reports that guide the engineer to fix these problems.

One challenge where early-stage analysis is beneficial is detecting violations of the *trusted path* property. The context is the following: a valuable data asset is provided by one actor, and is eventually delivered to a recipient actor, through

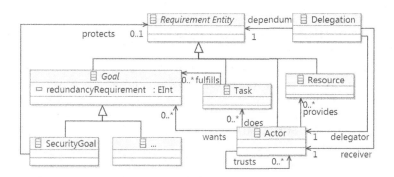

Fig. 1. Simplified security requirements metamodel

potentially unreliable intermediate actors. A security goal requires the protection of the integrity and confidentiality of this data resource. The trusted path property states that either a trusted actor has to perform an action that explicitly fulfills the goal (e.g. time-stamping, digital signature and encryption), or else the entire data path must be trusted; indirect trust is permitted. The challenge is to formulate a query which finds the violations of this security property.

A second application of model queries is related to the *redundancy* property. Redundancy is important for resilience against failures and attacks, and is therefore an integral part of security; thus requirements often have a minimal degree of redundancy associated with them. For example, the availability requirement of a service task or data asset can be augmented with the demand of triple modular redundancy, i.e. 3 replicas of data / service must be available. A goal with the `redundancyRequirement` attribute set must be fulfilled by at least this number of separate tasks (performed by trusted actors). We will formulate two queries associated with this property: (a) one to find goals whose redundancy requirement is not met, and (b) a second one that computes an actor-centric progress indicator that informs of the total number of missing replicas for all the goals wanted by a given actor.

2.2 Case Study Solution Using the Original VIATRA2 Language

VPM Models. VPM [8], the model representation of the VIATRA2 transformation framework [9], has a very generic graph structure, similarly to the concept of clabjects [10] and ontologies [11]. A VPM model is a containment hierarchy of entities (nodes) with interconnecting relations (edges), and some special relationships such as instantiation. Models and metamodels are represented uniformly in a very flexible multi-typed, multi-level metamodeling paradigm. Nodes and edges have likewise an identity of their own, with a locally unique name, and possibly attributes. A model entity, however, can only store a single (unnamed) value, and therefore multiple attributes are represented by separate relation types and local *wrapper* model entities.

Graph Patterns and Model Queries. The VTCL language [9] was originally designed to support model transformation over VIATRA2's model representation VPM. In particular, it offers graph patterns as a mechanism for querying VPM models; a graph pattern is basically a typed graph-like structure which is matched against a large model graph. The VTCL language defines graph patterns by specifying *graph pattern constraints* over *pattern variables*. The pattern variables here are the nodes and edges of the graph pattern, some of which can be made externally accessible as *symbolic parameters* of the pattern. The constraints assert the graph structure and types of the pattern (as well as some other properties). A *match* of the pattern is a mapping of variables to VPM entities and relations so that all constraints are satisfied (analogously to a morphism into the model graph).

Graph patterns support parametrizable queries by evaluating the entire match set of a pattern globally in the model, or by binding one or more pattern parameters as input elements and only retrieving the local matches of the pattern.

Listing 1. Violations of the trusted path property, original syntax

```
1 shareable pattern noTrustedPath(ConcernedActor,SecGoal,Asset,UntrustedActor)={
2   Actor.wants(WantsEdge,ConcernedActor,SecGoal);
3   SecurityGoal(SecGoal);
4   SecurityGoal.protects(ProtectsEdge,SecGoal, Asset);
5   Actor.provides(ProvidesEdge,ProviderActor,Asset);
6   find transitiveDelegation(ProviderActor,UntrustedActor,Asset);
7   neg find transitiveTrust(ConcernedActor,UntrustedActor);
8   neg find trustedFulfillment(ConcernedActor,AnyActor,AnyTask,SecGoal);
9 }
```

We now present a solution using graph patterns in the VTCL language to address the trusted path property, as the redundancy property heavily relies on arithmetic computations that are not expressible in the original VTCL language.

Basic Pattern Elements. Pattern `noTrustedPath` in Lst. 1 captures the violations of the trusted path security property using the original VTCL syntax. The symbolic parameters of the pattern are `ConcernedActor`, `SecGoal`, `Asset`, `UntrustedActor`; there are also local variables `ProtectsEdge`, `ProviderActor`, etc. The pattern constraints include a *node constraint* on line 3 that asserts that variable `SecGoal` must be mapped to a node of type `SecurityGoal`. Lines 2,4 and 5 are *edge constraints*; e.g. the first of them asserts that the variable `WantsEdge` be an edge of type `Actor.wants` (i.e. the `wants` reference of class `Actor`), leading from `ConcernedActor` to `SecGoal`. As demonstrated by line 5, edges can be navigated in both directions.

To conform to a typical engineer's intuition, patterns are normally *injective*, i.e. object variables within a pattern will be matched to different model elements; unless the pattern is declared `shareable`, when two pattern variables may store / share the same model element, or explicit variable assignment (see Line 6) is used. Here the `shareable` keyword is used in the definition of `noTrustedPath`, as the pattern must allow the special case where `ConcernedActor` and `ProviderActor` are the same.

Pattern Composition. An important type of pattern constraint is pattern composition or *pattern call*, denoted by the `find` keyword. A pattern call reuses a *called pattern* inside the body of the *calling pattern* (possibly recursively). Line 6 of Lst. 1 provides an example that asserts that the tuple (`ProviderActor`, `UntrustedActor`, `Asset`) must be a match of a pattern called `transitiveDelegation`.

The three patterns called from `noTrustedPath` are defined in Lst. 2. The *disjunctive* pattern `trustedFulfillment` finds trusted actors that fulfill a given goal. The *recursive* pattern `transitiveTrust` captures the transitive closure of the `Actor.trusts` edges. Pattern `transitiveDelegation` is also recursive, in a more complex way.

Negation. Node and edge constraints, as well as pattern calls can be prefixed by the `neg` keyword to express negation, resulting in a *negative application condition* (NAC). A match of the enclosing pattern is considered invalid if the NAC is satisfiable. Lines 7 and 8 of Lst. 1 provide examples: the pattern `noTrustedPath` matches

Listing 2. Trusted path helper patterns

```
1 pattern trustedFulfillment(TrustingActor,FulfillerActor,Task,Goal)={
2     find actorFulfillsGoal(FulfillerActor,Task,Goal);
3     find transitiveTrust(TrustingActor,FulfillerActor);
4 } or {
5     find actorFulfillsGoal(FulfillerActor,Task,Goal);
6     TrustingActor = FulfillerActor; // explicit variable assignment
7 }
8 pattern transitiveTrust(TrustingActor,Trustee)={
9     Actor.trusts(TrustEdge,TrustingActor,Trustee);
10 } or {
11     find transitiveTrust(TrustingActor,MiddleMan);
12     Actor.trusts(TrustEdge,MiddleMan,Trustee);
13 }
14 pattern transitiveDelegation(Delegator,Receiver,Dependum)={
15     find directDelegation(Delegator,Receiver,Dependum);
16 } or {
17     find transitiveDelegation(Delegator,MiddleMan,Dependum);
18     find directDelegation(MiddleMan,Receiver,Dependum);
19 } or {
20     find transitiveDelegation(Delegator,Receiver,SuperDependum);
21     find decomposeDirect(SuperDependum,Dependum);
22 }
```

only if there is no transitive trust between `ConcernedActor` and `UntrustedActor`; and there is no such `AnyActor` and `AnyTask` that `ConcernedActor`, `AnyActor`, `AnyTask`, `SecGoal` would form a match of pattern `trustedFulfillment`.

NACs do not *define* new variables in their header arguments, they are either *input or quantified*. Input variables of a NAC are those arguments that are defined somewhere else (e.g. at a positive edge or node constraint); the rest of the variables are non-existentially quantified, and are not allowed to be referenced anywhere else. The NAC states that no substitution of the quantified variables can satisfy a match of the NAC, given the value of the input variables. In the previous example, `AnyActor` and `AnyTask` were quantified variables, and the other two were obtained as input argument of the NAC.

3   The Language of EMF-INCQUERY

EMF-INCQUERY is a framework with a *language for defining declarative local and global queries over EMF models*, and a *runtime engine for executing them efficiently without manual coding*. The query language of EMF-INCQUERY reuses the concepts of graph patterns VIATRA2 as a concise and easy way to specify complex structural model queries. However, while in [4], we simply restricted the VTCL language, this paper provides a more systematic design of a graph query language for EMF models to provide high level of expressiveness but also to overcome language usability issues we experienced in [4].

After a brief introduction to EMF, we present the syntax of EMF-INCQUERY step-by-step. The new language introduces some significant semantic extensions, as well as syntactic sugar for conciseness. The two main areas where EMF-INCQUERY differs from the original VTCL syntax are the structural/navigational language elements and the handling of attributes and arithmetic expressions.

Listing 3. Violations of the trusted path property, EMF-specific syntax

```
1  shareable pattern noTrustedPath(ConcernedActor,SecGoal,Asset,UntrustedActor)={
2    Actor.wants(ConcernedActor,SecGoal);
3    SecurityGoal(SecGoal);
4    SecurityGoal.protects(SecGoal, Asset);
5    Actor.provides(ProviderActor,Asset);
6    find transitiveDelegation(ProviderActor,UntrustedActor,Asset);
7    neg Actor.trust*(ConcernedActor,UntrustedActor);
8    neg find trustedFulfillment(ConcernedActor,AnyActor,AnyTask,SecGoal);
9  }
```

3.1   Background Technology: The Eclipse Modeling Framework

The *EMF* ecosystem provides automated code generation and tooling (e.g. notification, editor) for model representation in Java. EMF models consist of a containment hierarchy of model elements (*EObjects*) with cross-references – some of which may only be traversed by programs in one direction (unidirectional references). Objects also have a number of attributes (primitive data values).

EMF uses *Ecore* metamodels to describe the abstract syntax of a modeling language. The main elements of Ecore are *EClass* (graphically depicted as a box), *EReference* (depicted as an edge between boxes), and *EAttribute* (depicted within the middle compartment of a box). EClasses define the types of EObjects, enumerating EAttributes to specify attribute types of class instances and EReferences to define association types to other EObjects. EReferences and EAttributes can be multi-valued and ordered. Some EReferences can additionally imply containment. Inheritance may be defined between classes (depicted by an arrow ending in a hollow triangle), which means that the inherited class has all the properties its parent has, and its instances are also instances of the ancestor class, but it may further define some extra features. Each instance EObject has exactly one EClass type, and the metamodel is well-separated from instance models. The ECore diagram of the casestudy metamodel is depicted in Fig. 1.

3.2   Structural Constraints

We now demonstrate the structural pattern constraints of the EMF-INCQUERY language using the trusted path property, captured in Lst. 3. The graph pattern based query language of EMF-INCQUERY references EClasses as node types, EReferences and EAttributes as edge types. Pattern variables will be mapped to EObjects of the instance model or attribute values. For example in Lst. 3, line 3 seeks for an EObject of type SecurityGoal and stores the corresponding element in variable SecGoal. Line 2 navigates from the ConcernedActor (also appearing as a symbolic parameter) along an EReference of type wants, and the EObject reached that way should be the one stored by variable SecGoal.

Two major limitations of the core EMF API are the lack of (i) efficient enumeration of all instances of a class regardless of location, and (ii) backwards navigation along uni-directional references. As seen here, the structural graph constraints of EMF-INCQUERY can provide these missing features.

Listing 4. Helper pattern dependent on EMF edge ordering

```
1  pattern directDelegation(Delegator,Receiver,Dependum)={
2      Delegation(Delegation);
3      Delegation.elements[0](Delegation,Delegator);
4      Delegation.elements[1](Delegation,Receiver);
5      Delegation.elements[2](Delegation,Dependum);
6  }
```

Binary Edge Constraints. Edge constraints in EMF-INCQUERY (lines 2,4,5 in Lst. 3) look more simple than in VIATRA2; *binary edge constraints* only use the variables representing the source and the target of the edge, and edge variables are altogether omitted from the pattern. This language design choice was made to reflect that EMF, does not assign edges an identity of their own. Instance model edges are characterized only by their source object, their EReference type (defined or inherited by the EClass of the source object) and the target object, but the reference itself does not have a corresponding EObject on instance-level.

Transitive Closure. The most frequent use case of recursion in queries is to capture *transitive closure*. For more convenient definition of queries, a concise syntax is proposed for the transitive closure of an edge type: by postfixing the type name by an asterisk (*), its transitive closure can be used without defining a recursive pattern for it. Similarly, the closure of a binary pattern can be defined in the same way, by putting an asterisk between the pattern name and arguments in a `find` clause. Such a binary pattern emulates a pseudo-edge of the graph, while encapsulating an arbitrarily complex relationship between its pseudo-source and pseudo-target. Line 7 of Lst. 3 applies the transitive closure operator to the edge type `Actor.trust`, eliminating the need for the separate pattern `transitiveTrust` (given that `trustedFulfillment` is also modified this way). However, as `transitiveDelegation` captures a more complex recursive relationship, it cannot be expressed using this shorthand.

Accessing Ordered Edges by Index. The `directDelegation` pattern called by `transitiveDelegation` hides a further layer of complexity. Delegation is a ternary relation; the metamodel includes a separate `Delegation` class with references to the delegator, the receiver and the dependum. Although Fig. 1 shows these as three distinct EReferences, in practice often there is only a single ordered EReference, and the three instance-level links are distinguished according to their order in the list. Such a solution may not be elegant, but it is still frequent (industrial) practice (e.g. with a metamodel generated from a grammar).

For this purpose, EMF-INCQUERY offers an optional *ordering index* qualifier to capture the position of the edge within the ordered collection at the source object. Pattern `directDelegation` in Lst. 4 takes advantage of this feature and binds the index to the constant values 0, 1, and 2, respectively to capture a direct delegation relation.

Listing 5. Violations of the redundancy property

```
1  pattern redundancyViolated(CA,RG)={
2      find redundantReplicas(CA,RG,DegreeOfRedundancy,RequiredRedundancy);
3  //   check (toInteger(value(DegreeOfRedundancy)) <
4  //       toInteger(value(RequiredRedundancy))); -- Old VTCL syntax
5      check (DegreeOfRedundancy < RequiredRedundancy);
6  } pattern
7  redundantReplicas(CA,RG,DegreeOfRedundancy,RequiredRedundancy)={
8      Actor.wants(CA,RG);
9      Goal.redundancyRequirement(RG,RequiredRedundancy);
10     let DegreeOfRedundancy = count with find
11         trustedFulfillment(CA,AnyFulfillerActor,AnyTask,RG);
12 }
```

3.3   Attribute and Arithmetic Constraints

We now demonstrate the attribute and arithmetic constraints of EMF-INCQUERY by formalizing the redundancy property of the case study. As defined in Fig. 2.1, the redundancy property states that a goal RG with a redundancyRequirement attribute must be fulfilled at least as many times (by trusted actors) as specified by the attribute value. The pattern redundancyViolated described in Lst. 5 identifies violations of this property, using a helper pattern. The secondary challenge is to provide an actor-centric indicator report on the number of missing replicas; the solution is shown in Lst. 6. In the sequel, we will gradually explain these patterns when introducing the new language features.

Scalar Variables and EAttribute Edges. EMF attribute values are stored directly within an EObject, as a separate member variable for each attribute type defined or inherited by the EClass. Therefore edge constraints representing EMF EAttributes immediately point to the raw data value. In case of asserting the equality of two attributes, the attribute edge constraints may simply share the same target variable. Such raw data values that are not model elements (EObjects) will be referred to as *scalar variables*, while variables that will be substituted with EObjects are *object variables*, which distinction was not originally part of VTCL. See line 7 of Lst. 5 as an example edge constraint extracting an attribute value from an EObject; RequiredRedundancy will therefore be a scalar variable (as well as DegreeOfRedundancy, MR and TMR).

VTCL includes a special type of pattern constraint denoted by check() that checks *arithmetic conditions* based on attribute values; see line 3 in Lst. 5 or line 9 in Lst. 6 for example usage.

Scalar variables are not subject to injectivity checks and can be mapped to the same value by default. This semantic distinction of scalar and object variables introduces additional static type inference challenges as well, which will be discussed later in Sec. 4.

Arithmetic Evaluation and Assignment. As scalar variables were not available previously, the pattern language of VTCL only allowed arithmetic expressions within check() pattern constraints. With the introduction of the class of scalar patterns, a straightforward semantic extension is the introduction

Listing 6. Missing replicas per actor and goal

```
1 pattern totalMissingReplicas(CA,TMR)={
2     Actor(CA);
3     let TMR = sum(MR) with find
4         missingReplicas(CA,AnyGoal,MR);
5 }
6 pattern missingReplicas(CA,RG,MR)={
7     find redundantReplicas(CA,RG,DegreeOfRedundancy,RequiredRedundancy);
8     let MR = eval(RequiredRedundancy - DegreeOfRedundancy);
9     check (MR > 0);
10 }
```

of *arithmetic expression evaluation* constraints. An eval constraint evaluates an arithmetic expression based on referenced scalar variables, and assigns the result to a scalar variable. Line 8 in Lst. 6 provides an example, where the difference between two integer scalar variables is assigned to variable MR. The result scalar variable can be used just as freely as an attribute value, e.g. it can appear as a symbolic parameter to be used externally. Note however that EMF-INCQUERY is not an equation solver, so circular references in expressions are disallowed.

Aggregation. The language EMF-IncQuery also includes an *aggregation* pattern constraint similar to e.g. aggregation functions of SQL. An aggregation is a pattern call that aggregates (counts, sums, etc.) matches of the called pattern with some given input parameters. More precisely, except for match counting, an arithmetic expression based on the match of the called pattern is aggregated over the matches. The resulting aggregate value is either specified in the calling pattern as a numeric constant, or captured in a scalar variable. For example, lines 8-9 in Lst. 5 count the number of trusted fulfillments of the goal, and store the result in DegreeOfRedundancy; likewise lines 3-4 in Lst. 6 assign TMR to the sum of the computed MR values for each goal of the actor.

The following incrementally maintainable aggregator functions are supported:

- count that returns the number of matches of the called pattern (with the given values of its referenced variables),
- sum(expr) that computes the sum of the evaluations of expression expr over each match,
- avg(expr) that returns the average of expr,
- min(expr) and max(expr) that respectively return the minimal and maximal value among evaluations of expr over the matches.

If the called pattern has no matches, count and sum(expr) return a default value of 0, while the other aggregation constraints will not be satisfied (i.e. the enclosing pattern will fail to match).

Similarly to NACs, aggregations do not *define* the variables in their arguments (except for the aggregate result), they are either input or quantified. It is worth noticing that NAC is a special case of match counting, with the aggregate value bound to 0; and match counting itself is a special case of summation, where a constant 1 is being summed over the matches.

Table 1. Language features

Intent	Feature	EMF	VPM	Origin
enumeration	node constraint	Yes	Yes	Originally available
navigation	edge constraints	Binary	Ternary	EMF adaptation
	edge indices	Yes	No	EMF adaptation
	graph structure	Yes	Yes	Originally available
	recursion	Yes	Yes	Originally available
	transitive closure	Yes	Yes	Syntactic sugar
filter	negative application condition	Yes	Yes	Originally available
	attribute checks	Scalars	Wrappers	EMF adaptation
computation	arithmetic evaluation	Scalars	Wrappers	Semantic Extension
	counting and aggregation	Yes	Yes	Semantic Extension
reuse	pattern composition	Yes	Yes	Originally available

The preceding discussion of the case study solution presented some aspects of the language design of EMF-INCQUERY. Table 1 shows an overview of some important language features.

4 Static Type Checking for the Query Language

As the EMF-INCQUERY query language uses complex structures (such as path expressions or transitive closures), it is possible to write erroneous queries that may lead to unexpected runtime behavior or exceptions. These mistakes can be detected by using static analysis techniques without the costly execution of the transformation. In the current work, we focus on *type errors* (e.g. using a pattern variable with incompatible types) that are hard to detect manually, because they may not cause runtime errors during execution, but rather result in an empty match set being returned. In our experience, such mistakes are very common (e.g. calling a pattern with invalid parameters, or parameters in an invalid order).

For example, the CA and AnyGoal parameters of the missingReplicas pattern call are switched in Line 5 in Lst. 7. In this case, the pattern is called with its RG parameter bound to a variable with the Actor type, and as a result, the pattern will never match (and the variable TMR will always contain the integer scalar 0).

To detect such problems, we propose a constraint-based static type checking framework for graph patterns, adapting a type checking approach for partially typed graph transformation programs [12]. For pattern constraints (see Table 1) expressing graph structure (e.g. in Line 2), the type information that has to be checked for consistency is always available. However, in the case of pattern composition, as pattern parameters are dynamically typed, *pattern parameter type inference* is necessary (see the call of missingReplicas pattern in Line 5). We encode type inference as constraint satisfaction problems and apply a constraint solver to propagate the available type information to calls where type inference is needed. To improve performance, the type constraints are generated and

Listing 7. Erroneous version of missing replica counter pattern

```
1  pattern totalMissingReplicas(CA, TMR)={
2      Actor(CA);
3      //Error: CA and AnyGoal parameters switched during pattern composition
4      let TMR = sum(MR) with find
5         missingReplicas(AnyGoal,CA,MR);
6  }
7  pattern missingReplicas(CA,RG,MR)={
8      find redundantReplicas(CA,RG,DegreeOfRedundancy,RequiredRedundancy);
9      let MR = eval(RequiredRedundancy - DegreeOfRedundancy);
10     check (MR > 0);
11 }
```

Table 2. Type inference in the missing replicas pattern

Line	Type Constraints	Comments
Line 8	$typeOf(CA) = $ Actor $typeOf(RG) = $ Goal $typeOf(DegreeOfRedundancy) = $ int $typeOf(RequiredRedundancy) = $ int	Inferable from pattern call, not detailed here
Line 9	$typeOf(MR) = $ int $typeOf(RequiredR) = $ int $typeOf(DegreeOfR) = $ int	eval with integer operation
Line 10	$typeOf(MR) \in \{$int, double$\}$	Number comparison

evaluated for each pattern separately (by the generating type contracts), and these partial results are combined to generate the type constraints for pattern calls.

To give an overview of the analysis framework, we demonstrate its capabilities using the erroneous patterns in Lst. 7.

The type constraints generated from the *missing replicas pattern* in Table 2. The first column selects a line from the pattern, the second describes the generated type constraints, while the third shows related comments. Aggregating the type constraints shows no contradiction and the following result is calculated for the pattern parameters: $typeOf(CA) = $ Actor $\land\ typeOf(RG) = $ Goal $\land\ typeOf(MR) = $ int.

The generated type constraints for the *total missing replicas pattern* are listed in Table 3. However, the aggregation detects contradicting constraints for the variable CA, as there is no type that is both an Actor and Goal. As a result, an error is detected and reported to the developer.

5 Related Work

Model Queries over EMF. OCL [13] is a navigation-based query language, applicable over a range of modeling formalisms. OCL is more expressive in certain cases than EMF-INCQUERY, considering e.g. the iterate construct. On the

Table 3. Type inference in the total missing replicas pattern

Line	Type Constraints	Comments
Line 2	$typeOf(CA) = $ Actor	Pattern condition
Line 4	$typeOf(TMR) \in \{$int, double$\}$ $typeOf(MR) \in \{$int, double$\}$ $typeOf(TMR) = typeOf(MR)$	Scalar variables are summed
Line 5	$AnyGoal \to CA \quad \Rightarrow \quad typeOf(AnyGoal) = $ Actor $CA \to RG \quad \Rightarrow \quad typeOf(CA) = $ Goal $MR \to MR \quad \Rightarrow \quad typeOf(MR) = $ int	Variable assignments in pattern composition

Table 4. Comparison of query language features

Intent	Feature	Model Query [3]	Xpand[15]	EOL [14]	MDT-OCL [2]
enumeration	node constraint	Yes	Yes	Yes	Yes
navigation	edge constraints	Yes	Yes	Yes	Yes
	edge indices	No	Yes	Yes	Yes
	graph structure	Tree only	Yes	Yes	Yes
	recursion	No	No	Well-founded	Well-founded
	transitive closure	No	No	No	Non-standard
filter	NAC	Yes	Yes	Yes	Yes
	attribute checks	Single node only	Yes	Yes	Yes
computation	arithmetic evaluation	No	Yes	Yes	Yes
	counting and aggregation	No	Yes	Yes	Yes
reuse	pattern composition	Yes	No	Operation	Operation

other hand it lacks query compositionality (helper operations can work around this); only well-founded recursive queries are supported this way (e.g. transitive closure of non-DAG graphs, such as the network of trust between actors, is not expressible); and the language is arguably less declarative than that of graph patterns. A precise comparison of expressivity is left as non-trivial future work.

There are several technologies that support model querying over EMF, see Table 4 for a comparison showing whether features of EMF-INCQUERY can be replicated by a given tool. The Epsilon Object Language (EOL) [14], disregarding its Javascript-like imperative features, can be considered very similar to OCL. M2T Xpand's Expressions [15] is also roughly equivalent to OCL, but it does not contain any method of reuse. MDT-OCL [2] is the canonical OCL implementation for EMF. While general recursion is still not supported, the closure construct is provided as a non-standard extension to OCL, which is essentially a least fix point operator capable of expressing certain recursive queries such as transitive closure. *Model Query* [3] has significantly lower expressivity than EMF-INCQUERY or any of the above: it cannot capture graph-like (circular) relationships, or compare attribute values; however, it can be extended by OCL.

There are also several tools [16,17,18] that adapt graph transformation concepts to EMF, although for model transformation, not as a query language. These approaches do not include any of the rich language features of EMF-INCQUERY such as composition, recursion, aggregation or edge indices. Furthermore, there is a wide range of existing graph transformation tools (e.g. Fujaba, PROGRES, GrGEN, GReAT, VMTS, AGG) which offer some of the advanced features of EMF-INCQUERY without supporting queries directly over EMF models.

Although not aimed at model-driven purposes, SPARQL [19] is an important query language. Comparison and benchmarking is planned for a future paper.

Incrementality. From a performance viewpoint, *incremental query evaluation* has a significant impact on the scalability of technologies that build on queries (model transformations, well-formedness validators, simulators etc.). In [4], we demonstrated that the supporting infrastructure of EMF-INCQUERY scales up to provide instantaneous results for queries over large models with millions of model elements. Related work on other incremental evaluators (for OCL and other query/transformation languages) is also discussed in detail in [4].

Language Specialization. An important challenge of the current paper was to adapt a general-purpose transformation language to a restricted technological domain, focusing on a well-defined feature subset, retaining the best characteristics, and maximizing usability in practical applications. While such language reusability engineering practices are well known in the domain-specific language engineering community [20] (e.g. based on software product line techniques [21]), to our best knowledge, no adaptation experience across such different modeling platforms has been reported yet for model transformation languages.

6 Conclusion

We have introduced a graph pattern based query language for EMF-INCQUERY, a technology for model queries over EMF models, with use-cases ranging from model validation to on-the-fly model synchronization. The proposed language is derived from the graph pattern fragment of VTCL and tailored to the task of querying EMF models, with additional significant semantic extensions to its predecessor. The query language is complemented by a static type inference mechanism that is necessary to guide the interpretation of queries in some cases; additionally it can detect certain classes of developer errors (and can also provide valuable information to the code generator component of EMF-INCQUERY).

The language extends a core graph pattern formalism (with nested negation) by rich attribute handling and aggregation. Query capabilities also include recursion and transitive closure, which is frequently needed but (in the general case) inexpressible in many query languages. The expressivity of the language is complemented by the beneficial performance characteristics discussed in [4].

As future work, we are planning to provide streamlined integration of the query system into a fully featured model validation framework. We also envision declarative support for incremental model transformation driven by query results, using the graph transformation formalism. Finally, we plan to extend the scope of queries from a single model state to the evolution of the model, in order to support change-driven transformations [22].

References

1. The Eclipse Project: Eclipse Modeling Framework, http://www.eclipse.org/emf
2. Eclipse Model Development Tools Project: MDT-OCL website (2011), http://www.eclipse.org/modeling/mdt/?project=ocl
3. Eclipse Modeling Project: EMF model query website (2011), http://www.eclipse.org/modeling/emf/?project=query
4. Bergmann, G., Horváth, Á., Ráth, I., Varró, D., Balogh, A., Balogh, Z., Ökrös, A.: Incremental evaluation of model queries over EMF models. In: Petriu, D.C., Rouquette, N., Haugen, Ø. (eds.) MODELS 2010. LNCS, vol. 6394, pp. 76–90. Springer, Heidelberg (2010)
5. Gilles, O., Hugues, J.: Validating requirements at model-level. In: Ingénierie Dirigée par les modéles (IDM 2008), Mulhouse, France, pp. 35–49 (2008)
6. Mouratidis, H., et al.: A natural extension of Tropos methodology for modelling security. In: Agent Oriented Methodologies Workshop. Object Oriented Programming, Systems, Languages (OOPSLA). ACM, Seattle-USA (2002)
7. Tun, T.T., et al.: Model-based argument analysis for evolving security requirements. Secure System Integration and Reliability Improvement 0, 88–97 (2010)
8. Varró, D., Pataricza, A.: VPM: A visual, precise and multilevel metamodeling framework for describing mathematical domains and UML. Journal of Software and Systems Modeling 2(3), 187–210 (2003)
9. Varró, D., Balogh, A.: The model transformation language of the VIATRA2 framework. Sci. Comput. Program. 68(3), 214–234 (2007)
10. de Lara, J., Guerra, E.: Deep meta-modelling with METADEPTH. In: Vitek, J. (ed.) TOOLS 2010. LNCS, vol. 6141, pp. 1–20. Springer, Heidelberg (2010)
11. W3C OWL Working Group: OWL 2 Web Ontology Language. Technical report, W3C (2009), http://www.w3.org/TR/owl2-overview/
12. Ujhelyi, Z.: Static type checking of model transformation programs. In: Ehrig, H., Rensink, A., Rozenberg, G., Schürr, A. (eds.) ICGT 2010. LNCS, vol. 6372, pp. 413–415. Springer, Heidelberg (2010)
13. Object Management Group: Object Constraint Language, Version 2.2. (February 2010)
14. Kolovos, D.S., Paige, R.F., Polack, F.A.C.: The epsilon transformation language. In: Vallecillo, A., Gray, J., Pierantonio, A. (eds.) ICMT 2008. LNCS, vol. 5063, pp. 46–60. Springer, Heidelberg (2008)
15. Eclipse Modeling Project: Xpand wiki (2010), http://wiki.eclipse.org/Xpand
16. Biermann, E., et al.: Precise semantics of EMF model transformations by graph transformation. In: Busch, C., Ober, I., Bruel, J.-M., Uhl, A., Völter, M. (eds.) MODELS 2008. LNCS, vol. 5301, pp. 53–67. Springer, Heidelberg (2008)
17. Giese, H., Hildebrandt, S., Seibel, A.: Improved Flexibility and Scalability by Interpreting Story Diagrams. In: Magaria, T., Padberg, J., Taentzer, G. (eds.) Proceedings of GT-VMT 2009, vol. 18. Electronic Communications of the EASST (2009)
18. Arendt, T., et al.: Henshin: Advanced concepts and tools for in-place EMF model transformations. In: Petriu, D.C., Rouquette, N., Haugen, Ø. (eds.) MODELS 2010. LNCS, vol. 6394, pp. 121–135. Springer, Heidelberg (2010)
19. W3C: SPARQL Query Language for RDF (January 2008)

20. Cleenewerck, T., et al.: Evolution and reuse of language specifications for dSLs (ERLS). In: Østvold, B.M. (ed.) ECOOP 2004. LNCS, vol. 3344, pp. 187–201. Springer, Heidelberg (2005)
21. White, J., et al.: Improving domain-specific language reuse with software product line techniques. IEEE Software 26(4), 47–53 (2009)
22. Ráth, I., et al.: Change-driven model transformations. In: Schürr, A., Selic, B. (eds.) MODELS 2009. LNCS, vol. 5795, pp. 342–356. Springer, Heidelberg (2009)

The GReTL Transformation Language

Tassilo Horn and Jürgen Ebert

Institute for Software Technology
University Koblenz-Landau
{horn,ebert}@uni-koblenz.de

Abstract. This paper introduces the graph-based transformation language GReTL. GReTL is an operational transformation language whose operations are either specified in plain Java using the GReTL API or in a simple domain-specific language. GReTL follows the conception of incrementally constructing the target metamodel together with the target graph. When creating a new metamodel element, a set-based semantic expression is specified that describes the set of instances that have to be created in the target graph. This expression is described by a query on the source graph. After a description of the foundations of GReTL, its most important elements are introduced along with a simple example.

1 Introduction

The *Graph Repository Transformation Language*[1] (*GReTL*, [1]) is an operational model transformation language. A transformation constructs the target metamodel incrementally while specifying the target graph in terms of the *extensions* (instance sets) of the target schema constituents, which is a novel concept. Transformations with pre-existing target schemas are treated as a special case.

We think that GReTL (thanks to GReQL's querying abilities) provides more expressive constructs than most other querying/transformation approaches, especially when requiring very complex, non-local matching of elements with an arbitrary distance in terms of edges in between.

Transformations work on graphs, but GReTL is by no means a graph transformation language with *match-replace* semantics. GReTL transformations are guaranteed to terminate, and running a transformation twice on the same source model produces identical target models.

GReTL is built upon a simple but complete *Java API* consisting of a minimal set of creation operations for the target schema elements. They allow for creating the target schema and corresponding target graph for a given source model[2]. GReTL transformations can either be programmed using the API or specified using a simple DSL, where this paper concentrates on the latter.

This paper is organized as follows: Section 2 introduces TGraphs and schemas and explains the compositional semantics of schemas. A minimal set of *create-operations* for schemas is derived. Section 3 explains these operations in detail

---

[1] http://userpages.uni-koblenz.de/~ist/GReTL

[2] If many source models are to be transformed in a sequence, only the first invocation creates the target metamodel, and following invocations reuse it.

J. Cabot and E. Visser (Eds.): ICMT 2011, LNCS 6707, pp. 183–197, 2011.
© Springer-Verlag Berlin Heidelberg 2011

along a complete example transformation. Section 4 relates GReTL to other transformation languages, and Section 5 finally concludes the paper.

2   Foundations

GReTL is the transformation language of the *TGraph* technological space [2], where models are represented using a very general and expressive kind of graphs. This section introduces the concept of TGraphs, their schemas, and the relation between schemas and their corresponding graphs.

Overview. GReTL is defined on typed, attributed, and ordered directed graphs (TGraphs). In this paper, the ordering is ignored. Sets of TGraphs (*Graph-Classes*) are defined by a corresponding metamodel (grUML[3] schema). Fig. 1 depicts a TGraph that conforms to the grUML schema in Fig. 2. This graph is used as source graph of the transformation example discussed in Section 3.

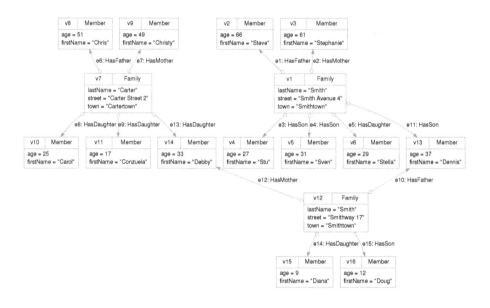

Fig. 1. A TGraph (Source Graph) conforming to the schema in Fig. 2

In Fig. 1, the TGraph properties (except for ordering) are clearly visible. All elements have a type, the edges are directed, and the vertices are attributed. For example, vertex v1 has the type Family, and its town attribute is set to the string Smithtown. It is connected to the vertex v2 of type Member via the edge e1 of type HasFather. In this example, there are no attributes on the edges.

---

[3] grUML (*graph UML*) is a large subset of UML class diagrams comprising only elements that are compatible with graph semantics. This semantics is defined in [3].

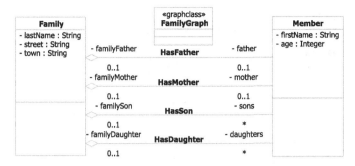

Fig. 2. A schema (Source Schema) conforming to the metaschema in Fig. 3

In Fig. 2, the vertex types (*VertexClasses*) are modeled as UML classes, and edge types (*EdgeClasses*) are modeled as associations. An additional UML class with a <<graphclass>> stereotype specifies the type of the graph (*GraphClass*). All types may contain attributes specified in the usual UML style. Supported attribute types (*Domains*) include all common basic types (booleans, numbers, strings, etc.), enumerations and records (also specified in the schema), as well as homogenous collections of arbitrary other domains (lists, sets, maps). Both vertex and edge classes may specialize other vertex or edge classes, respectively. In this example, there are no specializations.

Definitions. Unordered TGraphs consist of five components: (i) a set V of vertices, (ii) a set E of edges, (iii) an incidence function ϕ assigning a start and an end vertex to each edge, (iv) a type function *type* assigning a type to each vertex and edge, and (v) an attribute function *value* assigning to each vertex and edge a set of attribute-value pairs, according to the following definition:

Def. 2.1 (*Unordered TGraph*)

Let
- *Vertex* be a universe of **vertices**,
- *Edge* be a universe of **edges**,
- *TypeId* be a universe of **type identifiers**,
- *AttrId* be a universe of **attribute identifiers**, and
- *Value* be a universe of **attribute values**.

Then, $G = (V, E, \phi, type, value)$ is an **unordered TGraph**, iff
(i) $V \subseteq Vertex$ is a **vertex set**,
(ii) $E \subseteq Edge$ is an **edge set**,
(iii) $\phi : E \to V \times V$ is an **incidence function** assigning a start and target vertex to each edge,
(iv) $type : V \cup E \to TypeId$ is a **type function**, and
(v) $value : V \cup E \to (AttrId \nrightarrow Value)$ is an **attribute function**, where
$\forall x, y \in V \cup E : type(x) = type(y) \implies dom(value(x)) = dom(value(y))$.

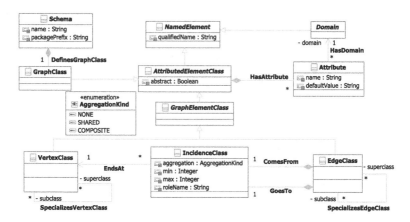

Fig. 3. grUML metaschema (core), describing all schemas such as in Fig. 2

Schemas. The structure of grUML schemas is defined by the grUML meta-schema (Fig. 3), which contains four important, non-abstract constituents[4] that define a schema S: (1) VertexClasses, (2) EdgeClasses, (3) Attributes, and (4) specialization hierarchies. Since an EdgeClass uniquely determines two IncidenceClasses, and an Attribute uniquely determines a Domain, the latter are subsumed as parts of the former. These four constituents have the following properties:

(1) A VertexClass has a qualified name and may be abstract.
(2) An EdgeClass also has a qualified name and may be abstract. It owns exactly two IncidenceClasses holding the association end properties (multiplicities, role name, aggregation kind) with respect to the VertexClass it ends at.
(3) An Attribute has a name, an optional default value, and exactly one associated Domain. Any attribute belongs to exactly one vertex or edge class.
(4) There are two separate (acyclic) specialization hierarchies defined by SpecializesVertexClass and SpecializesEdgeClass.

With these constituents, a schema describes the available vertex types (as VertexClasses) and edge types (as EdgeClasses). For each edge type, the valid start and end vertex types including their association end properties are specified. Furthermore, the schema specifies the attributes of all element classes, i.e., vertex or edge classes. The specialization hierarchies imply (transitive) inheritance of attributes and allowed incidences from superclasses to subclasses.

Defining a Graph. There may be an infinite number of instance graphs *conforming* to a given grUML schema S. Assuming S is the target schema of a model transformation, one specific instance graph has to be created as target graph for a given source graph.

To describe such a specific TGraph G conforming S, all five components (i)-(v) of G (according to Def. 2.1) have to be defined. We do this in a *compositional*

---

[4] The metaschema elements GraphClass, Schema, and Package are used for structuring grUML diagrams and are not discussed further in this paper.

way by defining the *extensions* (instance sets) of the four respective schema constituents (1) to (3) of S respecting (4).

Let $VertexClass$ and $EdgeClass$ be the sets of vertex and edge classes defined by a schema S, let *subtypes* be a reflexive function that returns all subclasses for a given class, and let G be any graph conforming to S.

Then, the *extensions* in G of the constituents of S are simple mathematical objects, namely sets and functions:

(1) There is a set $V_c \subseteq V$ for every vertex class $c \in VertexClass$,

(2) There is a set $E_r \subseteq E$ for every edge class $r \in EdgeClass$.

Assuming that r connects a vertex class c to a vertex class c', there is a function $\phi_r : E_r \to V \times V$ that assigns a tuple (u, w) to every $e \in E_r$ with $type(u) \in subtypes(c)$ and a $type(w) \in subtypes(c')$.

(3) There is a function $val_A : \bigcup_{c' \in subtypes(c)} V_{c'} \to Value$ for every attribute A defined for $c \in VertexClass \cup EdgeClass$.

If the attribute A has the domain D, and assuming that D denotes a set $T_D \subset Value$, val_A assigns only values from T_D.

Given these sets and functions, the corresponding TGraph is uniquely determined by $G = (V, E, \phi, type, value)$ with

$$V = \bigcup_{c \in VertexClass} V_c, \quad E = \bigcup_{r \in EdgeClass} E_r, \quad \phi = \bigcup_{r \in EdgeClass} \phi_r$$

$$type : V \cup E \to TypeId \text{ with } \forall v \in V : type(v) = c \iff v \in V_c$$
$$\wedge \; \forall e \in E : type(e) = r \iff e \in E_r$$

$$value : V \cup E \to (AttrId \nrightarrow Value)$$
$$\text{with } \forall x \in V \cup E : value(x)(A) = t \iff val_A(x) = t$$

The conception of GReTL is to create the new target schema operationally, and thereby specifying the extensions of each schema element in order to describe the target graph. For that purpose, GReTL supplies a set of elementary *create-operations*, one for each kind of constituent of a grUML schema: (1) CreateVertexClass, (2) CreateEdgeClass, and (3) CreateAttribute.

These functions create the constituents of the schema and their extentions. A description of the respective extensions is provided to the operations as set- or function-valued *semantic expression*, which is a query that is evaluated on the source graph. Besides that, the hierarchy information has to be given by additional operations: (4) AddSuperClass or AddSubClass.

These operations are introduced in details in Section 3.

Archetypes and Images. The semantic expressions used for the create-operations define so-called *archetype sets* for vertex and edge classes. For every member (*archetype*), a new element is created in the target graph. Every newly created vertex or edge is an *image* of exactly one archetype. It has to be stressed that there is no restriction on what may be chosen as archetype. Source graph elements may be used, as well as primitive values (numbers, strings), or composite values thereof (tuples, sets, lists).

More precisely, the semantic expressions define

(1) for each set V_c, a set of vertex *archetypes* $\overline{v}$,
(2) for each set E_r, a set of triples $(\overline{e}, \overline{u}, \overline{w})$ denoting an edge archetype $\overline{e}$ together with two vertex archetypes $\overline{u}$ and $\overline{w}$ of its start and end vertex, and
(3) for each attribute A, a function val_A assigning a value t to each archetype $\overline{x}$ for whose image the attribute A is defined either directly or by inheritance.

Thus, any target graph element is the *image* of exactly one *archetype*. During the creation of the images for an element class X, two fine-grained mappings img_X from archetypes to images and its reverse arch_X are constructed and kept in exportable hashmaps, which are accessed by other transformation operations. These maps include all *traceability* information implied by the transformation.

GReQL. The semantic expressions are described using the *Graph Repository Query Language* [4]. GReQL is a graph query language based on set theory and predicate logics, giving access to all TGraph properties and to the schema information. It is a sophisticated, dynamically typed expression language.

Two important kinds of composite expressions are *from-with-report comprehensions* and *quantified expressions*, both used in the following example query.

```
1  from a: V{Member}
2  with exists d: V{Member} @
3    a (−−<>{HasMother, HasFather} <>−−{HasSon, HasDaughter})^2 d
4  reportSet a, a.firstName end
```

This query delivers a set of tuples, where the first component is a Member vertex and the second component is the value of that member's firstName attribute. The reported members are restricted to those being at least grandparents by enforcing the existence of some descendent member d of a, who is reachable by traversing a path twice (^2), which consists of first a parent edge (to some Family) and then a child edge. When run on the source graph of Fig. 1, the query returns the tuples (v2, "Steve"), (v3, "Stephanie"), (v8, "Chris"), and (v9, "Christy").

This query highlights one of GReQL's most advanced features, *regular path expressions* [4], which allow for describing complex correlations between vertices using regular operators on edges types, e.g., sequences, options, alternatives, and iterations including the transitive closure.

3   GReTL Operations

In this section, the elementary GReTL transformation operations described in Section 2 are introduced by using a running example, which is an extended variant of the *Families2Persons* transformation used in the ATL tutorial [5]. The transformation constructs the target schema shown in Fig. 4, and it creates a conforming target graph from the example graph shown in Fig. 1.

Persons are represented as either Females or Males. Any person has a full name and belongs to some age group, either ADULT or CHILD. A marriage between a male and a female is indicated by a HasSpouse edge, and a parent is connected to his or her children via HasChild edges. Finally, every person lives at some Address.

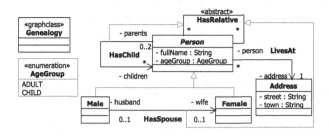

Fig. 4. The target grUML schema

The transformation creates a target graph conforming to this newly created schema and populates it using data from the family model shown in Fig. 1.

GReTL is implemented as an extensible Java API, which is not considered in this paper. Instead, the transformation is presented in the fully implemented and easy-to-use GReTL DSL. Every invocation of a transformation operation has the following form:

```
<GReTL operation> <schema properties> [ <== <semantic expression> ];
```

The GReTL operation with the given schema properties specifies the new schema element to be created[5]. Its extension is described by the semantic expression, whose result is "piped into" the operation using the arrow symbol. The semantic expression is specified in the graph querying language GReQL [4] and evaluated on the source graph (Fig. 1).

Creating VertexClasses and Vertices. There are four vertex classes in the target schema. The abstract class Person and its two subclasses Female and Male, as well as the vertex class Address.

The GReTL operation CreateAbstractVertexClass is used for Person.

```
1   CreateAbstractVertexClass  Person;
```

Because an abstract class cannot have instances, no semantic expression is provided to the operation.

Next, the concrete vertex classes Female and Male are to be created, starting with Female[6]. On the schema level, the new vertex class Female is created. The semantic expression collects those source graph Member vertices in an archetype set that are connected to at least one HasMother or HasDaughter edge. For each of those archetypes, a new Female vertex is created as image in the target graph. The mapping from archetypes to their target graph images is saved automatically

---

[5] For existing target schemas, there's a set of operations that work only on the instance level and require no schema properties except the name of the schema element.

[6] If the target schema exists, the instance-only operation CreateVertices can be used: CreateVertices Female $<==$ $<$semantic expression as above$>$;

```
2   CreateVertexClass  Female  <==  from m:  V{Member}
3                                    with degree{HasMother, HasDaughter}(m) > 0
4                                    reportSet m end;
```

by two new functions[7]: img_Female maps from source Members to Females, and arch_Female is its inverse function. These functions are available in all following semantic expressions.

img_Female is utilized in the next operation call. The archetypes for the target graph Males are exactly those source graph Members, for which no Female vertex has already been created.

```
5   CreateVertexClass  Male  <==  difference(V{Member},  keySet(img_Female));
```

In the target schema, a new vertex class Male is created. The semantic expression substracts the domain of the img_Female function, i.e., all source graph Members identified as being female, from the set of all Member vertices. For each element of the resulting archetype set, a new target graph Male vertex is created. Again, two new functions img_Male and arch_Male are made available to refer to the images and their archetypes in following semantic expressions.

The last vertex class that has to be created is Address. When looking at the source model's schema in Fig. 2, we can see that in the source model, the address is encoded with the two attributes street and town inside Families. Thus, one approach is to transform Families to Addresses. However, if two or more families live at the same address, we would end up with several Address vertices with equal street/town values. To ensure that there is exactly one address per location, the following operation is used.

```
6   CreateVertexClass  Address
7     <==  from f:  V{Family}  reportSet f.street, f.town end;
```

In the target schema, the new vertex class Address is created. The semantic expression iterates over all source model Family vertices and reports one tuple consisting of the family's street and town. Since a set is reported, duplicate tuples resulting from families living at the same location are ignored. So, for each unique 2-tuple a new target graph Address vertex is created, and again two new functions img_Address and arch_Address are made available.

This example also demonstrates that there are no restrictions for what may be used as archetypes. The usage of string-tuples as Address archetypes enables to prevent creation of elements that are considered equal based on attribute values. By choosing the archetypes wisely, we simulate QVT Relation's [6] *key* feature here without any special syntax or semantics.

---

[7] Functions are implemented as Java Maps. keySet() returns the domain of a function, values() its range, and get() the value accociated with a given key.

Creating EdgeClasses and Edges. The target schema (Fig. 4) should contain four edge classes. There is an abstract edge class HasRelative and two concrete subclasses HasSpouse and HasChild. Moreover, there is the edge class LivesAt.

The abstract HasRelative edge class is created as follows.

```
 8  CreateAbstractEdgeClass HasRelative from Person to Person;
```

This edge class is defined between Person and Person, and the default multiplicities $(0, *)$ are used. Because it is abstract, no semantic expression is provided.

The next operation creates the HasSpouse edge class between Male and Female[8].

```
 9  CreateEdgeClass HasSpouse from Male    (0,1) role husband
10                            to   Female (0,1) role wife
11    <== from f: V{Family} reportSet f,
12         theElement(f<>--{HasFather}), theElement(f<>--{HasMother}) end;
```

As discussed in Section 2, the semantic expression has to result in a set of triples where the first component is the archetype for a new edge, the second component is the archetype of the start vertex, and the third component is the archetype of the target vertex. Here, the semantic expression selects source graph Family vertices as archetypes. The Member being the father of that family is chosen as start vertex archetype, and the Member being the mother of that family is chosen as end vertex archetype. As a consequence, for each source graph family, a HasSpouse edge is created starting at the father's image (a Male) and ending at the mother's image (a Female). The mappings from archetypes (Family vertices) to their images and vice versa are made available with the new functions img_HasSpouse and arch_HasSpouse.

The next operation creates the edge class HasChild connecting two Persons. Any child may be connected to at most two parents and any parent may have an arbitrary number of children.

```
13  CreateEdgeClass HasChild from Person (0,2) role parents
14                           to   Person (0,*) role children
15    <== from e: E{HasDaughter, HasSon},
16           par: startVertex(e)<>--{HasFather, HasMother}
17       reportSet tup(endVertex(e), par), par, endVertex(e) end;
```

The semantic expression iterates over all edges of type HasSon or HasDaughter, and over the parents, which are identified by starting at the family (startVertex(e)) and selecting the vertices reachable by traversing one edge of type HasFather or HasMother. As archetypes, tuples consisting of a child Member (endVertex(e)) and one of its parent Members are used. The HasChild edges start at the parent's image and end at the child's image.

The last edge class that has to be created is LivesAt connecting persons to the address they are living at. But before doing so, two *helpers* are defined that ease the specification of an appropriate semantic expressions.

---

[8] If the target schema exists, the instance-only operation CreateEdges can be used:
CreateEdges HasSpouse <== <semantic expression as above>;

```
18   getMainFamily () := using member :
19     ( degree {HasFather , HasMother }( member ) > 0 ?
20        theElement ( member ——◇{HasFather , HasMother }) :
21        theElement ( member ——<>));
22
23   getAddressTuple () := using member :
24     let f := getMainFamily ( member ) in tup ( f . street , f . town );
```

The first helper getMainFamily() accepts one parameter member and returns its "main family". A member can be connected to at most two families, i.e., he or she is a parent of one family and a child of another. So the helper prefers the former and falls back to the latter only if that member is no parent.

The second helper getAddressTuple() also accepts a member as parameter and returns the street and town values of the given member's main family as a tuple.

Using these helpers, the operation for creating the LivesAt edge class can be specified as follows.

```
25   CreateEdgeClass LivesAt from Person (0,∗) to Address (1,1)
26     <== from m: keySet( img_Person) reportSet m, m, getAddressTuple(m) end;
```

In the target schema, the LivesAt edge class is created using appropriate multipliticies. The semantic expression iterates over person archetypes (i.e., Member vertices) and selects those as archetypes for the new edges. Each edge should start at the image of the given member m and end at the image of m's address tuple. Those are exactly the archetypes of the new target graph Address vertices.

Creating Type Hierarchies. Above, we created the abstract vertex class Person and its subclasses Male and Female, and the abstract edge class HasRelative and its subclasses HasSpouse and HasChild, without specifying the specialization relationships between them. This is done with the following operation calls.

```
27   AddSubClasses Person Male Female ;
28   AddSubClasses HasRelative HasChild HasSpouse ;
```

This has no direct effect on the instance level. However, it has an effect on the image and archetype functions, in that the functions for a supertype contain its own mappings (if any) and all its subtypes' mappings. So the two operation calls specify that

$$img_{Person} = img_{Female} \cup img_{Male}, \text{ and}$$
$$img_{HasRelative} = img_{HasSpouse} \cup img_{HasChild},$$

and the same for the inverse archetype functions.

When looking at line 26 of the example listing, the question arises how it was possible to iterate over the domain of img_Person before the AddSubClasses call occured in line 27. In fact, at this time img_Person should have been empty. The explanation is that internally, GReTL transformations are executed in two phases. The first phase constructs the complete target schema, but does not evaluate any semantic expression. The second phase creates the target graph and populates it according to the semantic expressions. Because the target schema is already finalized at that point in time, the image and archetype functions can be populated appropriately during the second phase.

It should be noted that GReTL enforces that all image and archetype functions are bijective, in order to guarantee the possibility of navigating unambiguously from archetype to image and vice versa. This implies that in any specialization hierarchy, every archetype must be unique. With respect to our example, it is forbidden to have some Member both as archetype for a Male and for a Female, because it would destroy the injectivity of arch_Person.

Creating Attributes and Setting Values. Till now, the example transformation has only dealt with creating vertices and edges. The attributes are still missing. The first attribute that is created is the fullName attribute of type string defined for the Person vertex class.

```
29   CreateAttribute Person.fullName : String
30     <== from m: keySet(img_Person)
31       reportMap m --> m.firstName ++ " " ++ getMainFamily(m).lastName end;
```

As discussed in Section 2, the semantic expression of the CreateAttribute operation has to be a function that maps archetypes of the class the attribute is created for to the values that should be set for their images. So the semantic expression evaluates to a function mapping each person archetype, i.e., a Member, to that member's first name concatenated with the main family's last name.

The other attribute of a Person is its ageGroup. Its type is the enumeration AgeGroup, which is created with the following operation call.

```
32   CreateEnumDomain AgeGroup(CHILD, ADULT);
```

Then, the attribute can be created, and its values can be set.

```
33   CreateAttribute Person.ageGroup : AgeGroup = "ADULT"
34     <== from m: keySet(img_Person) with m.age<18 reportMap m --> "CHILD" end;
```

The value ADULT is set as default. Only members younger than 18 are added to the assignment function, and for those the corresponding person's ageGroup value is set to CHILD.

The last missing attributes are street and town specifying the location of Address vertices. Here, we use the CreateAttributes operation to create both attributes in one call.

```
35   CreateAttributes Address.street : String , Address.town : String
36     <== from t: keySet(img_Address) reportMap t --> t end;
```

The CreateAttributes operation expects a function mapping archetypes to tuples with one component per attribute. Because two attributes are created here, the function maps Address archetypes, which were already defined as 2-tuples of the form (street, town), to themselves. Thus, the street attributes are set to the tuples' first component, and the town attributes are set to the tuples' second component.

In only 36 lines of transformation source code, the complete target schema shown in Fig. 4 has been constructed, and the source graph of Fig. 1 has been transformed into a conforming target graph.

Extending the Example. To demonstrate some more advanced concepts of GReQL querying and GReTL transformations, the target schema is extended with another edge class HasAffinity. It connects persons that are related by marriage. In many law systems, these persons have special rights in court, even after the marriage has been divorced, so it might be a good idea to make those relationships explicit.

```
37   CreateEdgeClass HasAffinity from Person to Person
38     <== #target# from p, a: V{Person}, s: p <->{HasSpouse}
39       with s <--{HasChild}+ -->{HasChild}* a
40         and not(s -->{HasChild}* a)
41       reportSet tup(p, a), arch_Person[p], arch_Person[a] end;
```

The first new language element refers to the fact that the semantic expression is evaluated on the target graph as indicated by the #target# marker. p and a are bound to Persons, and s is bound to p's spouse. Starting at s, his/her ancestors are found by traversing one or more HasChild edges backwards, and then zero or more HasChild edges may be traversed forward to reach relative-in-law a. Since this regular path predicate [4] also matches for the spouse s or for a being some descendant of s and p, an additional predicate excludes those real relatives.

Since the CreateEdgeClass operation expects the archetypes of an edge's start and end vertex, the arch_Person function is used to look up those by their target graph images p and a.

Finally, there should be an integer attribute for the HasAffinity edge class, which determines the degree of "affinity". Its value is set to the length of the path

```
42   CreateAttribute HasAffinity.degree : Integer
43     <== #target# from p, a: V{Person}, s: p <->{HasSpouse}
44       with p -->{HasAffinity} a
45       reportMap tup(p, a) ->
46         distance(pathSystem(s, <--{HasChild}+ -->{HasChild}*), a) end;
```

between a person's spouse and the person-in-law in question. According to that definition, parents-in-law have the degree 1, brothers- and sisters-in-law as well as grandparents-in-law have the degree 2, and so forth.

4   Related Work

Today, there is a multitude of transformation languages. Here, we only list some of the most relevant runnable and wide-spread languages and compare them to GReTL in more detail.

Some transformation languages address specific transformation scenarios, for example migration of models to new metamodel versions (e.g., Epsilon Flock [7]), while others try to provide general-purpose means to model transformation, like ATL [8] or the QVT languages [6]. Besides those MDA-style [9] languages, several graph transformation language are used to perform transformation tasks nowadays, e.g., GrGen.NET [10] or VIATRA2 [11].

In this context, GReTL should be considered as *graph-based general-purpose* transformation language. It shares with ATL and the QVT languages the property that transformations are executed *out-place*, i.e., a new target model is created from (possibly many) input models. In contrast, graph grammar approaches like GrGen.NET work by modifying the input graph in-place and have completely different execution semantics.

GReTL makes use of GReQL's *regular path expressions*. A similar concept is provided by GrGen.NET's subpatterns, which also allow for alternatives, and subpatterns may be composed of other subpatterns, possibly recursively.

While all cited transformation languages are *rule-based* with several differences in rule application semantics, e.g., imperative (QVT Operational Mapping, ATL called rules) versus declarative (QVT Relations, ATL matched rules), the concept of specifying the target graph of a transformation by defining the extensions of the target schema constituents seems to be novel.

The strict *separation of concerns* in GReTL's concept of compositional semantics with respect to the constituents of a metamodel results in a very slim set of only four transformation operations, which still suffice to perform arbitrary transformations. In contrast, languages like ATL or QVT Operational Mappings mix several concerns. A rule creates an output element for some input element and additionally sets the new element's attributes and assigns references. This may lead to duplicate code in rules creating instances of subclasses of some common superclass. Therefore, ATL and QVT Operational Mappings provide concepts like rule inheritance. Another issue that arises when trying to assign references at object creation time, is the possibility that the referenced object does not exist yet. Here, the order of rule application is crucial and has to be managed appropriately either by the transformation developer or by the (declarative) transformation execution environment like the ATL virtual machine. Another means to solve this problem is the concept of *late* or *deferred* reference assignment as it is supported by the QVT Operational Mappings language.

With respect to *traceability*, the image and archetype functions that are created automatically during the execution of a transformation are a very fine-grained traceability model. They provide the possibility for navigating from any target graph element (image) to its archetype, and the other way round. These functions can be persisted as XML file after the transformation has succeeded and loaded back later. ATL and the implementations of the QVT languages have similar traceability concepts, in that for each rule the mappings from input to output element are retained and can also be persisted. However, in GReTL the archetypes can be chosen freely and are not restricted to source graph elements.

In contrast to QVT Relations or triple graph grammar approaches like the TGG Interpreter [12] or MOFLON [13], the GReTL language does not tackle the challenge of *bidirectionality* at this time.

5   Conclusion and Discussion

This paper introduced the graph-based GReTL transformation language in its concrete syntax. Based of the concept of compositional semantics of TGraph schemas, GReTL introduces a novel concept to model transformations. GReTL transformations follow the conception of constructing the target metamodel, while simultaneously creating the target graph as an extension. GReTL allows for concise and short descriptions of transformations. The example transformation in Section 3 used only 36 lines of code.

GReTL is implemented as Java API with a special focus on extensibility [1]. Users can easily add custom transformation operations by composing the elementary operations discussed in this paper without having to touch any internals like the GReTL parser or the execution environment. In fact, GReTL provides a set of non-elementary operations that allow for example to create a complete subgraph with many vertices and connecting edges with one invocation, but even this operation is composed only in terms of the elementary operations.

First promising experiences with GReTL have been achieved when using it in a reengineering project[9], where Java software was parsed into TGraphs representing the abstract syntax of the source code. The corresponding JaMoPP schema [14] consists of 233 vertex classes and 104 edge classes. Here, GReTL transformations have been used for the extraction of state machines that had been implemented in plain Java using a set of conventions. The input graph to this transformation had about 2 million vertices and edges and could still be executed on a usual laptop in a few seconds.

Furthermore, last year's Transformation Tool Live Contest[10] was won with a combination of a first prototypical GReTL implementation and other TGraph technologies like GReQL.

GReTL is still under development. A thorough analysis of GReQL's efficiency is still missing, and further issues have to be tackled, e.g., the usage of GReTL for in-place transformations, or the inclusion of ordering information.

GReTL's concepts were derived from the formal definition of TGraphs and are aligned to the constituents that make up a grUML schema (vertex classes, edge classes, and attributes), but it seems feasible to apply the general concepts on other technological spaces like EMF [15], too. The concept of a vertex class is equivalent with Ecore's EClass, and grUML attributes correspond to Ecore EAttributes. The difference is that EMF does not consider edges as first class objects, but relations between elements are expressed as (pairs of) EReferences instead. Using EMF technology, the Object Constraint Language [16] or EMF Model Query [17,18] could be used for specifying semantic expressions.

---

[9] http://www.soamig.de
[10] http://planet-mde.org/ttc2010/

References

1. Horn, T., Ebert, J.: The GReTL Transformation Language. Technical report, University Koblenz-Landau, Institute for Software Technology (2011)
2. Kurtev, I., Bézivin, J., Aksit, M.: Technological spaces: An initial appraisal. In: Chung, S., et al. (eds.) CoopIS 2002, DOA 2002, and ODBASE 2002. LNCS, vol. 2519. Springer, Heidelberg (2002)
3. Walter, T., Ebert, J.: Foundations of Graph-Based Modeling Languages. Technical report, University of Koblenz-Landau, Institute for Software Technology (2011)
4. Ebert, J., Bildhauer, D.: Reverse engineering using graph queries. In: Engels, G., Lewerentz, C., Schäfer, W., Schürr, A., Westfechtel, B. (eds.) Nagl Festschrift. LNCS, vol. 5765, pp. 335–362. Springer, Heidelberg (2010)
5. Alliaire, F., Jouault, F.: Families to Persons. Presentation (2007), http://www.eclipse.org/m2m/atl/doc/ATLUseCase_Families2Persons.pdf
6. Object Management Group, T.: Meta Object Facility (MOF) 2.0: Query/View/-Transformation Specification v1.0 (2008)
7. Rose, L.M., Kolovos, D.S., Paige, R.F., Polack, F.A.C.: Model migration with epsilon flock. In: Tratt, L., Gogolla, M. (eds.) ICMT 2010. LNCS, vol. 6142, pp. 184–198. Springer, Heidelberg (2010)
8. ATLAS Group: ATL: User Guide (2009)
9. OMG: MDA Guide Version 1.0.1 (2003)
10. Jakumeit, E., Buchwald, S., Kroll, M.: GrGen.NET. International Journal on Software Tools for Technology Transfer (STTT) 12(3), 263–271 (2010)
11. Varró, D., Balogh, A.: The model transformation language of the VIATRA2 framework. Science of Computer Programming 68(3), 214–234 (2007)
12. Greenyer, J., Kindler, E.: Comparing relational model transformation technologies: implementing Query/View/Transformation with Triple Graph Grammars. Software and Systems Modeling 9, 21–46 (2010)
13. Amelunxen, C., Königs, A., Rötschke, T., Schürr, A.: MOFLON: A standard-compliant metamodeling framework with graph transformations. In: Rensink, A., Warmer, J. (eds.) ECMDA-FA 2006. LNCS, vol. 4066, pp. 361–375. Springer, Heidelberg (2006)
14. Heidenreich, F., Johannes, J., Seifert, M., Wende, C.: Closing the gap between modelling and java. In: van den Brand, M., Gašević, D., Gray, J. (eds.) SLE 2009. LNCS, vol. 5969, pp. 374–383. Springer, Heidelberg (2010)
15. Steinberg, D., Budinsky, F., Paternostro, M., Merks, E.: EMF: Eclipse Modeling Framework, 2nd edn. Addison-Wesley Longman, Amsterdam (2009)
16. OMG: Object Constraint Language Version 2.0 (2006)
17. The Eclipse Project: EMF Model Query, http://www.eclipse.org/modeling/emf/?project=query
18. The Eclipse Project: EMF Model Query2, http://www.eclipse.org/modeling/emf/?project=query2

Performance in Model Transformations: Experiments with ATL and QVT

Marcel van Amstel[1,*], Steven Bosems[2], Ivan Kurtev[2], and Luís Ferreira Pires[2]

[1] Department of Mathematics and Computer Science
Eindhoven University of Technology
Den Dolech 2, P.O. Box 513, 5600 MB Eindhoven, The Netherlands
`m.f.v.amstel@tue.nl`
[2] Software Engineering Group
University of Twente
P.O. Box 217, 7500 AE, Enschede, the Netherlands
`{s.bosems,kurtev,l.ferreirapires}@ewi.utwente.nl`

Abstract. Model transformations are increasingly being incorporated in software development processes. However, as systems being developed with transformations grow in size and complexity, the performance of the transformations tends to degrade. In this paper we investigate the factors that have an impact on the execution performance of model transformations. We analyze the performance of three model transformation language engines, namely ATL, QVT Operational Mappings and QVT Relations. We implemented solutions to two transformation problems in these languages and compared the performance of these transformations. We extracted metric values from the transformations to systematically analyze how their characteristics influence transformation execution performance. We also implemented a solution to a transformation problem in ATL in three functionally equivalent ways, but with different language constructs to evaluate the effect of language constructs on transformation performance. The results of this paper enable a transformation designer to estimate beforehand the performance of a transformation, and to choose among implementation alternatives to achieve the best performance. In addition, transformation engine developers may find some of our results useful in order to tune their tools for better performance.

1 Introduction

Since the introduction of Model-Driven Engineering, model transformations have become increasingly important in the software development process. Transformations are applied to problems that potentially involve huge models that need to be transformed. Examples of such problems are data translation and interoperability, refactoring of large code bases and model extraction. Transformation

---

* This work has been carried out as part of the FALCON project under the responsibility of the Embedded Systems Institute with Vanderlande Industries as the industrial partner. This project is partially supported by the Netherlands Ministry of Economic Affairs under the Embedded Systems Institute (BSIK03021) program.

J. Cabot and E. Visser (Eds.): ICMT 2011, LNCS 6707, pp. 198–212, 2011.

engines need to meet high scalability and performance requirements. In addition, transformation developers need to know the factors that determine the performance of transformations and need mechanisms to estimate and improve this performance.

Metamodels, models and transformation definitions all influence the performance of model transformations. The size and complexity of the input models are straightforward factors that affect transformation execution performance. In some model transformation languages, a certain transformation problem can be solved in multiple different but functionally equivalent ways. However, different constructs may influence the transformation execution performance either positively or negatively, and this needs to be investigated.

In this paper, we compare the performance of the transformation engines of three languages: ATL [9], QVT Operational Mappings and QVT Relations [11]. The comparison is based on two carefully chosen example transformations that are executed for series of randomly generated input models with an increasing number of model elements. For each input model, we measured and compared the duration of the transformation execution. Furthermore, we implemented one of the example transformations in three different ways in ATL, and we analyzed the effect of different ATL constructs on the performance of the ATL transformation engine. We extracted metric values from the transformation definitions and analyzed the relation between these values and the performance results. This analysis should enable developers to estimate the performance of a given transformation, and to choose among alternative transformation languages (engines) and/or transformation language constructs. The results of this study can also be used by implementors of transformation engines in order to improve the currently available tools.

This paper is structured as follows. Section 2 discusses the approach taken in this experiment. Section 3 elaborates on the metrics derived from the model transformations and their input. Section 4 gives the results of our model transformation experiments. Section 5 analyzes these results and draws some conclusions. Section 6 discusses related work. Section 7 gives our general conclusions and recommendations for future work.

2   Approach

The goal of this work is to compare the performance of the chosen transformation languages and their engines when facing input models of varying size and complexity, especially models that contain hundreds of thousands model elements. Transformation performance can be affected by several factors. In this paper we address the following factors:

Size of input model. As the number of input elements increases so does the number of the elements that are potentially matched by rules. This results in an increase of the elements to be transformed and in the overall execution time. We performed transformations on a series of models with increasing number of model elements.

Structure of input model. Models can be generally considered as graphs with a possibly complex interconnection structure of model elements. Model complexity may cause performance decrease, if complex navigation and matching needs to be done over a model. Some models may expose a simpler, tree-like structure. In order to study the impact of the structure of input models on transformations, we executed transformations over models with both simpler (tree-like and linear) structure, and more complex interconnection structures.

Transformation strategy. A given transformation problem may be solved in multiple alternative ways in a single language. Generally, different solutions may perform differently. We investigated the impact of the usage of different language constructs for a single transformation problem by implementing and executing three different but functionally equivalent solutions for the same transformation problem in ATL.

We compared the three model transformation tools that are part of the Eclipse M2M project: the ATLAS Transformation Language (ATL) [8], Query/View/Transformations Operational Mappings (QVTo) [11], and the Query/View/Transformations Relations language (QVTr) [11].

We performed two experiments: *comparison of transformation engines* and *comparison of different implementations in a single language* (ATL). Both experiments are described in the sequel.

2.1   Comparison of Engines

We implemented two transformations in each language: the SimpleClass2Simple RDBMS transformation and the RSS2ATOM transformation, both taken from the ATL zoo [12]. The input models in the SimpleClass2SimpleRDBMS transformation are graph-like class diagrams, while the input models of the RSS2ATOM transformation are tree-like. In this way we can compare how the structure of input models affects transformation execution performance.

The SimpleClass2SimpleRDBMS transformation is one of the "classical examples" of model transformations, and has been implemented in many languages. This transformation takes a simplified class diagram as input and transforms this to a relational database model. The input model consists of *packages* that contain zero or more *classes* with *associations* between them. Classes can have zero or more *attributes*. Only classes that are marked as persistent are transformed to tables. Methods and other constructs normally found in class diagrams are not supported. The resulting output model consists of *tables* that have *columns* and *foreign keys*.

For the SimpleClass2SimpleRDBMS transformation, 62 models were generated using Epsilon [1]. About half of these models correspond to a general case scenario, in which some of the input classes are not marked as persistent and therefore are not transformed. The other models correspond to a worst case scenario, in which all classes are persistent and thus have to be transformed. The input models differ in the number of classes and the number of attributes per class. Attributes are restricted in such a way that the type of an attribute cannot be the class in which the attribute is defined.

The transformation was implemented in all three languages. The result is three algorithmically identical transformations in ATL, QVTo and QVTr. The ATL transformation implementation is declarative. We ensured that the output models generated by the transformations are identical. To be able to compare the languages, we tried to use similar constructs wherever possible. For example, the matched rules in the ATL transformation are encoded as relations in QVTr and as mappings in QVTo.

Unlike the graph-like structure of Class models, Really Simple Syndication (RSS) models can be described as trees. An RSS model contains one *channel* (one root node), which in turn contains zero or more *items* (child nodes). Consequently, an RSS model contains no cycles. Items in an RSS model have certain properties, like a title, description, a category, and a channel to which they belong.

The result of the RSS2ATOM transformation is a model with a similar tree-like structure, but as an ATOM model. Like RSS, ATOM model consists of a single root node that contains *entries*. An ATOM entry is structured in the same way as the RSS item.

Similarly to the SimpleClass2SimpleRDBMS case, we implemented three functionally equivalent RSS2ATOM transformations in each language. The generated output models are identical for each of the transformations for all of the input models.

All these transformations have been executed with several input models with increasing size. Transformations were run three times and the average time was taken. There was no significant difference in times for each run. The transformation execution process considered in our experiments starts at the moment the first metamodels are loaded and ends when the resulting model has been serialized.

In our experiments, we used the following transformation engines:

ATL. ATL plugin version 3.0 for the Eclipse 3.6 (Helios).
QVTo. QVTo plugin version 2.0.1. for Eclipse 3.6 (Helios).
QVTr. Medini version 1.6.0.25263, which runs on Eclipse 3.4 (Ganymede).

We executed all these transformations on the Java Virtual Machine version 1.6 build 16, running on Microsoft Windows 7 Professional (64-bit version). The computer system was equipped with a quad core Intel Core i7 920 CPU, running at 2.67 GHz, and 6 GB of RAM.

2.2   Comparison of Implementations

We reimplemented the SimpleClass2SimpleRDBMS transformation in ATL using different implementation strategies to study the effect of different language constructs on the performance of the transformation. We choose ATL to perform this experiment since it is a hybrid language that allows several alternative functionally equivalent implementations. The two alternative transformations entail the following changes:

Move navigation to attribute helpers (Transformation ATL_a). The initial implementation of SimpleClass2SimpleRDBMS uses navigation expressions over the input model in the right-hand side of the bindings in the matched rules. In this transformation we moved the navigation expressions from the bindings to ATL attribute helpers. This causes the transformation to execute the navigation once, after which the result is cached for reuse.

Implement imperatively (Transformation ATL_b). This   transformation was implemented in imperative ATL using called rules only.

3   Metrics

Software metrics have been extensively studied in the last decades [7]. Metrics can be used to get quick insights into the characteristics of a software artifact, amongst others. We have extracted metrics from the ATL and the QVTo transformations by using the metrics collection tool described in [4] and [5], respectively. We intended to extract metrics from the QVTr transformation using the tool described in [10], but this tool was not publicly available at the time of writing. In this section, we describe the characteristics of the different transformations on the basis of the metrics extracted from the respective artifacts. We have used these characteristics to explain differences in the performance of the transformations later on in Section 5.

3.1   Metrics for ATL Model Transformations

Table 1 shows the metric values extracted from the ATL model transformations. All three *SimpleClass2SimpleRDBMS* transformations consist of five transformation rules. In ATL, target model elements can only be generated by rules. Called rules are required to generate target model elements from imperative code. Since the original ATL transformation and transformation ATL_a are both declarative, they do not need called rules. Therefore, only transformation ATL_b contains called rules. These called rules have a do-section, which are required since they provide the only way to generate target model elements from called rules. On average, there is one statement per do-section. Since this metric has a standard deviation of zero (not in the table), this means there is exactly one statement per do-section. This implies that in most do-sections nothing more is done than emitting a target model element.

All three ATL transformations contain helpers, of which at least one is an attribute helper. Transformation ATL_a only contains attribute helpers. This is expected to have a beneficial impact on the performance of the transformation, since attribute helpers are cached. One of the differences between the original ATL transformation and transformation ATL_a is the number of calls to `allInstances()`. From the metrics we conclude that these calls have been moved from rules to helpers. The `allInstances()` method is used to navigate a source model. Since navigation has been moved from rules to helpers in transformation ATL_a, this shift is expected. The average helper fan-in is higher for the

Table 1. Metrics for the ATL transformations

Metric	SimpleClass2SimpleRDBMS			RSS2ATOM
	Declarative	ATL_a	ATL_b	
# Transformation Rules	5	5	5	8
# Matched Rules	5	5	1	8
# Non-Lazy Matched Rules	1	1	0	3
# Lazy Matched Rules	4	4	1	5
# Called Rules	0	0	4	0
# Rules with an Input Filter	2	1	0	0
# Rules with a do Section	0	0	4	0
# Helpers	1	4	3	0
# Attribute Helpers	1	4	1	0
# Operation Helpers	0	0	2	0
# Calls to allInstances()	1	1	2	0
# Calls To Built-In Functions	5	5	5	1
# Elements per Output Pattern	1	1	0.8	1
# Parameters per Called Rule	0	0	0.75	0
# Statements per do Section	0	0	1	0
# Bindings per Rule	2	2	1.6	3.38
Avg. Helper Cyclomatic Complexity	1	1	1	0
# Operations on Collections per Helper	0	1	1	0
# Operations on Collections per Rule	5	3	2	1
Avg. Rule Fan-In	1.4	1.4	1.4	0.88
Avg. Helper Fan-In	3	2	1.67	0
Avg. Rule Fan-Out	2	3	2.4	0.88
Avg. Helper Fan-Out	0	0	0	0
# Calls to allInstances() per Rule	0.2	0	0.2	0
# Calls to allInstances() per Helper	0	0.25	0.25	0

declarative version than for the declarative version with the moved navigation because there are more helpers in the latter transformation.

The *RSS2ATOM* transformation is implemented differently than the ATL versions of the *SimpleClass2SimpleRDBMS* transformation, since this transformation uses more non-lazy matched rules and no helpers at all. On average, the rules are more complex since they have more bindings. However, the standard deviation for this metric is also high (3.0), indicating that this high average is caused by a small number of rules. The average rule fan-in for this transformation is also lower. This is to be expected since there are more non-lazy matched rules that cannot be invoked explicitly. Instead, non-lazy matched rules are matched on model elements by the transformation engine. Therefore, less explicit navigation is required, which explains the lower number of calls to allInstances() for this transformation.

3.2   Metrics for QVTo Model Transformations

Table 2 shows the metric values extracted from the QVTo model transformations. The metrics show that both transformations are relatively small. The *SimpleClass2SimpleRDBMS* transformation has slightly more complex mappings, since it uses conditions that consist of more sub-elements. Furthermore, the *SimpleClass2SimpleRDBMS* transformation uses a helper that is called three times by the mappings, whereas the *RSS2ATOM* transformation does not use helpers and uses more operations on collections. Apart from these differences, the metrics of both transformations are quite similar.

Table 2. Metrics for the QVTo transformations

Metric	SimpleClass2SimpleRDBMS	RSS2ATOM
# Mappings	6	8
# Mappings with Condition	5	0
# Helpers	1	0
# Calls to Resolve Expressions	3	0
# Elements per Mapping	56.33	45.25
# Parameters per Mapping	0.17	0.25
# Variables per Mapping	0.17	0
# Operations on Collections per Mapping	1.67	0.13
Avg. Cyclomatic Complexity per Mapping	1	1
# Subobjects per Helper	12	0
# Parameters per Helper	2	0
Avg. Cyclomatic Complexity per Helper	1	0
Avg. Mapping Fan-Out	1.17	1
Avg. Mapping Fan-In	1	1.25
Avg. Helper Fan-Out	0	0
Avg. Helper Fan-In	3	0
Avg. Resolve from Mapping Fan-In	0.5	0

4   Results

By executing the model transformations, we have obtained the execution time, measured in seconds, for each of the transformations for each input model. With these execution times, we can discuss and try to justify the performance differences of the transformations.

4.1   SimpleClass2SimpleRDBMS

Figure 1 and Figure 2 show the results of executing the SimpleClass2Simple RDBMS transformation. Figure 1 depicts the time the execution of a transformation required, altering the number of classes, but keeping the number of attributes per class fixed to 100. Figure 2 shows the results of varying the number of attributes and fixing the number of classes to 100. Therefore, the results on Figure 1 show the effects of increasing the size of the input model, while the results on Figure 2 show the effect of increasing the complexity of the input model. Our assumption here is that a model is more complex if it has more attributes, since attributes refer to classes (the feature *type*) thus making the model elements more interconnected, i.e., more graph-like. The results of Figure 1 and Figure 2 are also available in tabular form at [2].

Firstly, when comparing the results for the different transformation engines in Figure 1(a), we can notice that when dealing with an increasing number of classes, QVTo and ATL perform nearly identically, both having slow slopes. In contrast, QVTr has a steep slope, indicating that a high number of classes has a big effect on the performance of the QVTr tool in the general case scenario. Due to a problem in the ATL virtual machine, only three data-points are plotted for the imperative ATL implementation, which can hardly be seen in Figure 1(a) because of the other lines. This problem with the ATL virtual machine is related to the hard coded-size of the stack, which makes imperative ATL transformations very quickly result in a stack overflow. Based on our data, we can conclude that

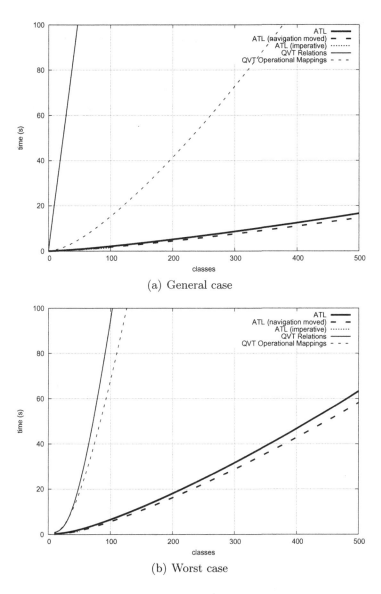

(a) General case

(b) Worst case

Fig. 1. Comparison between transformation tools, using the Simple-Class2SimpleRDBMS transformation (varying number of classes)

transformation ATL_a is the fastest, followed by the original ATL declarative transformation. Transformation ATL_b has the worst performance of all ATL transformations.

When observing the results of the worst case scenario in Figure 1(b), we observe a bigger difference between the transformations and tools. All transformations require more time to execute. The difference between the ATL and the QVT transformations has increased, where QVTo has nearly the same performance as

QVTr. The ATL transformations have the best performance, while ATL_a being the best one. As in the general case scenario, the original ATL performs better than transformation ATL_b.

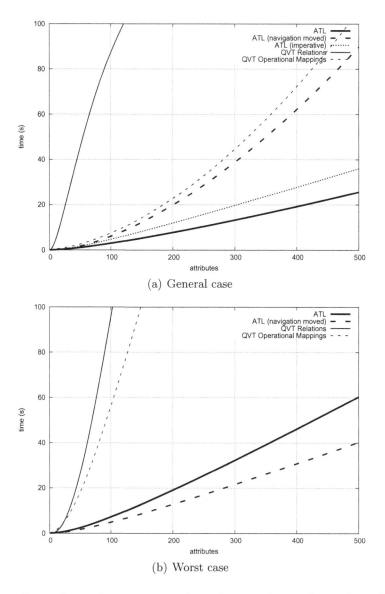

(a) General case

(b) Worst case

Fig. 2.   Comparison   between   transformation   tools,   using   the   Simple-Class2SimpleRDBMS transformation (varying number of attributes)

Figure 2 shows again different results with respect to Figure 1. Figure 2(a) shows that the original ATL transformation has the best performance of all transformations, followed by transformation ATL_b. The results of transformation ATL_a show that in this case the modification has had a negative effect on the transformation performance. QVTo has a performance similar to the performance of transformation ATL_a. Similarly to the experiment with increasing number of classes, QVTr is the transformation with the worst performance.

When comparing these results with the results from the worst case scenario depicted in Figure 2(b), we notice the same relation between the languages as in the case of Figure 1(b): the QVTo, QVTr and ATL transformations have similar performance, where the ATL transformations are the fastest.

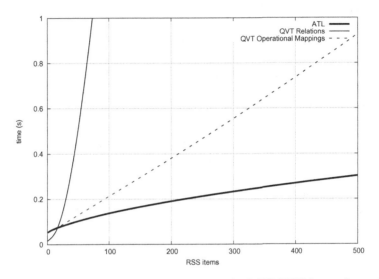

Fig. 3. Transformation tools compared using the RSS2ATOM transformation

4.2 RSS2ATOM

Figure 3 shows the results for the RSS2ATOM transformation, which are similar to the results observed in Figure 1(a). In this experiment we have only one ATL transformation written in declarative ATL. We can observe that ATL has a slow curve, while the results for QVTr and QVTo have steep curves. The difference when compared to the Figure 1(a), is that in Figure 3 ATL performs much better, with twice the speed of QVTo. However, the difference between these results remains around 500 milliseconds, putting in doubt the significance of this difference. In contrast, the time differences of the SimpleClass2SimpleRDBMS transformations are in the order to 10 seconds.

4.3 Statistical Analysis

To acquire more insights into the influence of the different implementation strategies of the *SimpleClass2SimpleRDBMS* transformation, we performed a statistical analysis to relate the metrics presented in Table 1 with the performance results presented in Section 4.1. We performed linear regression to estimate how the execution time of a transformation depends on a number of metrics describing the characteristics of that transformation.

Declarative vs. Imperative. The main difference between the declarative and the imperative implementation of the transformation is the use of called rules in the latter. The metrics presented in Table 1 show that the declarative version does not contain any called rules, whereas the imperative version contains four. Therefore, we used the number of called rules as the dependent variable in the regression analysis. The results show that there is a positive relationship between the number of called rules and execution time, meaning that performance degrades when opting for the imperative implementation. This was also concluded from the graphs presented in Section 4.1. Unfortunately, the results show a large standard error on the coefficient, meaning that they are not significant. A possible explanation for this is that there are too few subjects in the analysis, since we have only two implementations. This may be solved by considering hybrid implementations as well, e.g., with only half of the rules imperative and the others declarative.

Moving Navigation to Attributes. The main difference between the normal declarative version and the declarative version where the navigation is moved to the attributes is the number of attribute helpers. Therefore we used this metric in the regression analysis. The results show a negative relation between the number of attribute helpers and execution time, meaning that using attributes has a beneficial effect on performance. Similar to the declarative vs. imperative case, the results are not significant. Again this may be solved by considering hybrid implementations as well, e.g., with only half of the navigation moved to attribute helpers.

5   Discussion

After obtaining the metrics from the model transformations and have executed the transformations to gather performance data, we can analyze them in order to find a correlation between metric values and the speed at which the transformation can be run.

5.1   Comparison of Languages

Overall, the ATL tool implementation is the fastest performing. When increasing either the size or the complexity (the number of attributes) of the input models, the transformations run more than five times as fast as their QVTo and QVTr counterparts in the general usage scenario; these differences becomes even more apparent when dealing with the worst case scenario models. In these scenarios, QVTo performs in nearly the same way as QVTr. QVTr performs better in the worst case than in the general case scenarios. During the general case experiments, the tool medini QVT encountered `HeapSpace` problems and became unresponsive when input models have more than 100 classes or 100 attributes. These problems did not arise in the worst case models. We cannot explain this behavior due to our limited knowledge about the execution algorithm used in medini QVT.

ATL is affected by this change in input models, but to a lesser extent than QVTo. This observation is also confirmed by the RSS2ATOM transformation, where we see the same difference between the languages.

5.2   Comparison of Language Constructs

Our three implementations of the SimpleClass2SimpleRDBMS transformation in ATL all perform better than the QVT implementations. However, the performance of the implementations among themselves differ throughout the usage scenarios. When altering the size of the input models, the relative difference in performance of the transformations remains the same. However, if we increase the complexity of the input, the transformation with the navigation moved to helpers is no longer the fastest performing implementation in the general case; in the worst case, the initial order is restored: the implementation with navigation in helpers is the fastest.

The reason for this change in performance ought to be sought in the input models. If the input model does not contain elements that are visited more than once, caching the results of this navigation may have an adverse effect on the performance. However, if the elements are queried more often, the caching will have a positive effect, since the results need to be calculated only once. Considering the metrics, we cannot claim that a declarative transformation with more attribute helpers will perform better than a transformation that uses navigation in the bindings. Helpers should be defined for classes that are often matched by rules and often queried.

The imperative ATL implementation is slower than the declarative implementations when the size of models increases. However, we were unable to obtain results for all input models due to the stack size problem. If this problem is fixed we will be able to run the imperative transformation for more models and have a more reliable comparison.

Generally, declarative ATL transformations perform better than the imperative ones. There are several metrics that can be used to determine the "declarativeness" of an ATL transformation (recall that ATL is a hybrid language and both called and matched rules can be used in a single transformation program). These are the metrics that count the number of matched rules (either lazy or non-lazy or unique lazy), the number of called rules, and the number of *do* sections. The rule of thumb is: the bigger the number of matched rules is, the more "declarative" the transformation is. On the contrary, greater number of called rules and *do* sections makes a transformation more imperative-like. Table 1 confirms this intuition.

6   Related Work

Transformation Tool Contest (TTC) [3] is a series of events where solutions to transformation problems are submitted and compared. The transformation problems focus on various qualities, e.g. expressivity, evolvability, performance, scalability and the ability of the tools to solve certain problems, e.g. state space generation. The tool contest is a valuable source of insight about the strong and weak points of transformation tools. However, there is still no clear focus of achieving real comparable results, statistical soundness and relation to metrics over models and transformations. This event can be considered as a potential host for well-defined experiments.

In [6], van Amstel et al. define quality attributes and metrics for measuring them. Metrics are subdivided into size-, function-, module-, and consistency metrics. The first deals with the size of the transformation, the second deals with the complexity of functions, the third measures the complexity of modules as a whole, the last measures covers the degree to which a transformation contains conflicting information. Metrics from these four categories are related to quality attributes and their effect, either positive or negative, is mentioned. Understandability, modifiability, reusability, reuse, modularity, completeness, consistency and conciseness are named as being of importance for the quality of model transformations. The conclusion made by the authors is that the metrics should be tested through an empirical study.

Based on the quality attributes defined by the previous work, [13] defines more metrics, divided into three categories: unit metrics, rule metrics and helper metrics. The first contains the subcategories module metrics and library metrics, the second covers matched rule, lazy matched rule and called matched rule metrics, the last does not have any subcategories. In total, 81 metrics are defined. When comparing this set against the set of metrics defined in [6], the authors note that the difference in the number of metrics can be explained by the size and complexity of the ATL metamodel, from which the metrics were derived.

7   Conclusions and Future Work

We presented a comparison of the performance of the execution engines of three transformation languages: ATL, QVTo, and QVTr. We studied how the size and complexity of the input models affect the performance. Furthermore, we compared three different ATL transformations that solve the same problem in order to study the effect of different language constructs on the performance.

Overall, the declarative ATL is the fastest among the three engines. We provided metrics that can be used to measure how declarative an ATL transformation is. These metrics can be used by transformation developers when estimating the expected performance of a transformation. Our experiments run on models of up to a million of elements and give an indication of the expected time for the three transformation engines.

There are several works that define metrics over model transformation programs. However, the research on how to relate basic metric values to more abstract and complex transformation qualities is still in a very early phase.

Our work can be extended in several directions. We did not use metrics that indicate how complex a model is. Our intuition is that a graph-like model is more complex than a tree-like model. There are metrics for this characteristic and they should be correlated with our results.

We ran our experiments on two toy-like examples. To obtain more realistic results, the experiments should be repeated on real-life models that go beyond a million of elements.

Not all the language features have been studied. For example, we could have studied how usage of inheritance in ATL influences performance. The same is valid for QVTo where navigation can be separated from the mappings by the means of queries. In the experiments, all the rules contained simple source patterns. It is well known that pattern matching is a complex operation. The effect of the complexity of the source patterns needs to be studied.

The results reported in this paper are valid for the current versions of the transformation engines. Alternative implementations may produce better results. For example, some engines are implemented as a compiler and others as an interpreter. It is interesting to compare how interpreted and compiled languages affect the performance. We believe that the results in this paper will be useful to the language designers to improve the current state of their tools.

There are languages that are not covered in this paper. Our work should be extended by covering more transformation languages.

References

1. Epsilon, `http://www.eclipse.org/gmt/epsilon/`
2. Performance experiments with atl and qvt,
   `http://wwwhome.cs.utwente.nl/~kurtev/ATLQVT/`
3. Transformation tools contest,
   `http://is.tm.tue.nl/staff/pvgorp/events/TTC2011/CfC.pdf`
4. van Amstel, M.F., van den Brand, M.G.J.: Quality Assessment of ATL Model Transformations using Metrics. In: Proceedings of the 2nd International Workshop on Model Transformation with ATL (MtATL 2010), Malaga, Spain (June 2010)
5. van Amstel, M.F., van den Brand, M.G.J., Nguyen, P.H.: Metrics for model transformations. In: Proceedings of the Ninth Belgian-Netherlands Software Evolution Workshop (BENEVOL 2010), Lille, France (December 2010)
6. van Amstel, M.F., Lange, C.F.J., van den Brand, M.G.J.: Using metrics for assessing the quality of ASF+SDF model transformations. In: Paige, R.F. (ed.) ICMT 2009. LNCS, vol. 5563, pp. 239–248. Springer, Heidelberg (2009)
7. Fenton, N.E., Pfleeger, S.L.: Software Metrics: A Rigorous & Practical Approach, 2nd edn. PWS Publishing Co. (1996)
8. Jouault, F., Allilaire, F., Bézivin, J., Kurtev, I.: Atl: A model transformation tool. Sci. Comput. Program. 72(1-2), 31–39 (2008)

9. Jouault, F., Allilaire, F., Bézivin, J., Kurtev, I., Valduriez, P.: Atl: a qvt-like transformation language. In: Companion to the 21st ACM SIGPLAN Symposium on Object-oriented Programming Systems, Languages, and Applications, OOPSLA 2006, Portland, Oregon, USA, pp. 719–720. ACM, New York (2006), http://doi.acm.org/10.1145/1176617.1176691

10. Kapová, L., Goldschmidt, T., Becker, S., Henss, J.: Evaluating Maintainability with Code Metrics for Model-to-Model Transformations. In: Heineman, G.T., Kofron, J., Plasil, F. (eds.) QoSA 2010. LNCS, vol. 6093, pp. 151–166. Springer, Heidelberg (2010)

11. Object Management Group: Meta Object Facility (MOF) Query/View/Transformation Transformation Specification (2008)

12. The Eclipse Foundation: ATL Transformations, http://www.eclipse.org/m2m/atl/atlTransformations/

13. Vignaga, A.: Metrics for measuring atl model transformations. Tech. rep., Universidad de Chile (2009)

A Demonstration-Based Approach to Support Live Transformations in a Model Editor

Yu Sun[1], Jeff Gray[2], Christoph Wienands[3], Michael Golm[3], and Jules White[4]

[1] University of Alabama at Birmingham, Birmingham AL 35294
yusun@cis.uab.edu
[2] University of Alabama, Tuscaloosa, AL 35401
gray@cs.ua.edu
[3] Siemens Corporate Research, Princeton, NJ 08540
{christoph.wienands,michael.golm}@siemens.com
[4] Virginia Tech, Blacksburg, VA 24060
julesw@vt.edu

Abstract. Complex model editing activities are frequently performed to realize various model evolution tasks (e.g., model scalability, weaving aspects into models, and model refactoring). In order to automate and reuse patterns of model editing, an editing process can be regarded as an endogenous model transformation and specified as transformation rules. However, the use of traditional model transformation languages often presents a steep learning curve. Other challenges in using model transformations to automate editing tasks include insufficient support for sharing the transformations that perform the editing tasks, and a lack of automated guidance on how to use a specific transformation in some other modeling context. This paper presents a live model transformation approach that can enhance and assist model editing activities. By extending the Model Transformation By Demonstration (MTBD) approach, LiveMTBD offers users flexibility in specifying the transformation, a centralized repository to assist with transformation sharing, and a live model transformation matching engine to suggest applicable transformations during model-edit time.

Keywords: Model Editing, Live Model Transformation By Demonstration.

1 Introduction

With the ongoing adoption of Model-Driven Engineering (MDE) [1], models are emerging as first-class entities in many domains and play an increasingly significant role in every phase of software development. During the process of building models, editing operations are constantly performed in the editor to create or change the model into the desired state and configuration. For instance, a sequence of creational operations is needed to construct a typical sub-structure in a certain domain; model refactoring actions might be required occasionally to optimize the internal structure of the represented system; when errors are detected in models, operations to fix errors

J. Cabot and E. Visser (Eds.): ICMT 2011, LNCS 6707, pp. 213–227, 2011.

should be carried out in a timely manner; and with non-functional system requirements, aspect models may need to be woven into the desired locations of the base models.

The editing activities mentioned above often integrate ideas of model evolution, which involve composite editing operations on specific locations, and are very likely to be repeated in different model instances by different users. Therefore, a mechanism to automate and reuse frequently used editing patterns can benefit the model editing process. One approach to support automation and reuse of editing activities is to apply model transformation techniques. Any editing operation performed in the editor will change specific model instances, which can be considered as an endogenous model transformation process [9]. Thus, the sequence of editing operations for certain purposes can be summarized and specified as a set of transformation rules using executable Model Transformation Languages (MTLs) [4]. The rules may be directly reused in other model instances in the same domain, such that executing the rules triggers the desired editing activity automatically. However, although traditional MTLs are very powerful and expressive for specifying many editing activities, several challenges have emerged in using MTLs that prevent it from being a perfect solution:

Challenge 1. The steep learning curve of model transformation languages prevents general end-users (e.g., domain experts, non-programmers) from contributing to the editing or evolution tasks from which they have much domain experience.

Challenge 2. The abstraction gap between the concrete editing operations and the metamodel level transformation rules makes the specification of the desired editing activity challenging and perhaps even impossible for certain classes of end-users.

Challenge 3. Most MTLs and their supporting tools lack a collaborative mechanism to enable the sharing of the transformation rules among different model users, limiting the opportunity for reuse and exchange of domain-specific editing patterns.

Challenge 4. Without correctly understanding the transformation rules at the metamodel level or knowing the existence of the rules, novice users might miss the correct situations on when to reuse a specified editing activity.

To address these challenges, this paper presents an enhanced demonstration-based model transformation approach – Live Model Transformation By Demonstration (LiveMTBD). The idea is an extension to Model Transformation By Demonstration (MTBD) [2], which was designed to simplify the implementation of model transformation tasks by inferring and generating model transformation patterns from user-demonstrated behavior. The goal of MTBD is to enable general end-users in realizing their desired model transformation tasks without knowing a model transformation language or metamodel definitions. Applying MTBD to support automatic reuse of editing activities can assist end-users in avoiding the steep learning curve of MTLs and abstract metamodel definitions. By extending MTBD, LiveMTBD contains three new features: 1) *Live Demonstration*, provides a more general demonstration environment that allows users to specify editing activities based on their editing history; 2) in order to improve the sharing of editing activity knowledge among different users, *Live Sharing* – a centralized model transformation pattern repository, has been built so that transformation patterns can be reused across different editors; 3) a live model transformation matching engine – *Live Matching* has been developed to automatically match the saved transformation patterns at modeling time, and provides editing suggestions and guidance to users during editing.

The remainder of the paper is organized as follows: Section 2 explains the motivation and challenges with concrete examples borrowed from an industrial context; Section 3 presents the solution by introducing the initial work on MTBD, followed by highlighting new extensions; Section 4 discusses the advantages and limitations of the solution; Section 5 compares the related techniques, and Section 6 offers concluding remarks.

2 Motivating Example

This section overviews the challenges of specifying, reusing and automating model editing activities using MTLs. The examples used in this paper are based on the Embedded Function Modeling Language (EmFuncML), which has been used to support modeling embedded control in the automotive industry. EmFuncML enables the following: 1) model the internal computation process and data flow within functions; 2) model the high-level assignment and configurations between functions and supporting hardware devices; 3) generate platform-dependent implementation code; and 4) estimate the Worst Case Execution Time (WCET) for each function.

The top of Figure 1 shows an excerpt of the model describing functions used in an automotive system. *ReadAcc* (i.e., Read Acceleration) reads output data from *ADC* (i.e. Analog-to-Digital Converter) and sends the processed data to the *Analysis* function, which then transmits messages to the *Display* function. The input/output ports of each function are given (e.g., *ADC* has four input ports: *Resolution*, *SamplingRate*, *Downsampling*, *InterruptID*; and one output port *AnalogValue*). The hardware devices (e.g., *ADC*, *ECU*) are presented, to which the corresponding functions are assigned. A tool has been developed to estimate the WCET of each function based on the internal computation logic. For the sake of ensuring a smooth data flow and quick processing time, the WCET of each function should be less than *300ms*; otherwise it is defined as a WCET violation.

One common practice occurring in the configuration of functions in EmFuncML is that if a WCET violation occurs, a *Buffering* function can be added between the source function and the target function that receives data to ensure the correct data flow. At the bottom of Figure 1, *Analysis* sends a message data to *Display*. However, the WCET of *Analysis* is *460ms*, which is longer than the desired processing time. Therefore, a *Buffering* function is added between *Analysis* and *Display*, which serves as intermediate storage for the transmitted data.

Embedded software system engineers who are familiar with functional timing requirements may perform the *Buffering* editing activity in the editor very often whenever the WCET violation is detected. Therefore, this process can benefit from automation and reuse, which can be realized using MTLs to specify and summarize the result of the editing activity. Figure 2 shows the pseudo code of the transformation rules to accomplish the task of applying the *Buffering* function by locating functions with a WCET violation, creating the *Buffering* function, and rerouting the data flow.

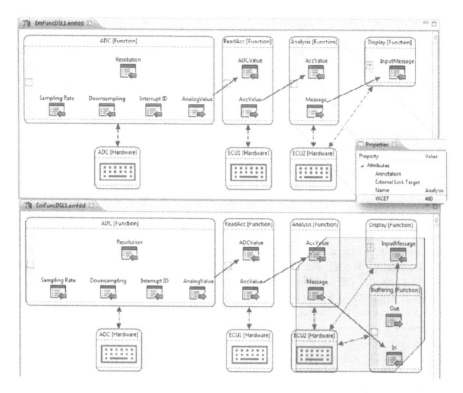

Fig. 1. EmFuncML models before (top) and after (bottom) applying *Buffering* function

A number of MTLs and tools can be applied to implement the actual model evolution task, such as ATL [3], Epsilon [20], and C-SAW [5], which support expressive mechanisms to access and manipulate models. However, using these languages requires users to learn the syntax and execution semantics, as well as some additional concepts (e.g., OCL is often used to locate model elements) and libraries. In addition, because MTLs operate at the metamodel level, in order to summarize a specific editing activity, users need to think about the whole editing process at a more abstract level and then generalize it using correct metamodel definitions. Sometimes, the difference in the execution semantics of a MTL may lead to different implementation designs (e.g., imperative textual MTLs focus on specific model manipulation steps, while declarative graphical MTLs consider the editing change as a pair of source and target graphs), which requires extra consideration for users in the specification progress.

In addition to the learning curve problem and abstraction gap when using MTLs, sharing the specified model transformations has not been taken into consideration in most MTLs and tools. For example, the left part of Figure 1 shows the *ADC* configuration, which is modeled through a sequence of approximately 20 editing operations to create the *ADC* function, input/output ports, set their names and types, and create the *ADC* hardware device with the assignment connection. Hardware engineers are more experienced than software engineers in this part of configuration.

Thus, the complex editing operation of creating an *ADC* can be specified as a reusable model transformation by hardware engineers that can be used by different colleagues in their modeling process when the *ADC* needs to be modeled in other system contexts. Clearly, if model transformations can be shared among users with different expertise or levels of experience, the reuse captured in a transformation rule can contribute to a knowledge base, improving the collaborative construction of models in the same domain.

```
foreach Output2Input connection : c
    if (c.source.parent.WCET > 300)
        create Function in EmFucnDSLFolder : tempFunc
        set tempFunc.name = "Buffering"
        create InputPort in tempFunc : tempInput
        set tempInput.name = "In"
        set tempInput.type = c.source.type
        create OutputPort in tempFunc : tempOutput
        set tempOutput.name = "Out"
        set tempOutput.type = c.target.type
        create Output2Input connection : c1 from c.source to tempInput
        create Output2Input connection : c2 from tempOutput to c.target
        create Func2HW connection : c3
            from tempFunc to c.source.parent.mappedHW
        remove Output2Input connection : c
```

Fig. 2. The pseudo code to specify *ApplyBuffer* editing activity

Finally, archiving model transformation rules does not guarantee the appropriate and correct reuse of the rules, due to a lack of suggestion or guidance about when and where to apply the transformation rules, particularly when the rules are specified by other users. For instance, it is likely that hardware engineers fail to reuse the *ApplyBuffer* transformation although it has been specified by software engineers, because they do not realize the issues involving WCET. Likewise, when software engineers are trying to configure the correct *ADC* for their system, the *ADC* creation transformation specified by hardware engineers may not be reused either, simply because the software engineers are not aware of the existence of a model transformation that can fulfill their needs directly.

Thus, the contribution of this paper focuses on providing an approach to improve specifying, reusing and automating the model editing activities.

3   Solution: LiveMTBD

Our solution to improve specification, reuse and automation of editing activities is to use a demonstration-based technique with three "live" features (i.e., active processes that monitor and respond to editing activities). In this section, we introduce MTBD in Section 3.1, and then explain the extended new LiveMTBD version in Section 3.2.

3.1 Introduction to MTBD

The key idea of MTBD is that rather than manually writing model transformation rules, users are asked to use concrete model instances and demonstrate how to transform a source model to a target model by directly editing and changing it. A recording and inference engine captures all of the user operations and automatically infers a transformation pattern that summarizes the changing process. This generated pattern can be executed in any model instance under similar circumstances to repeatedly carry out the desired transformation process. Figure 3 shows the overview of MTBD consisting of the following steps (the components with shaded background are new extensions to LiveMTBD that will be presented in Section 3.2).

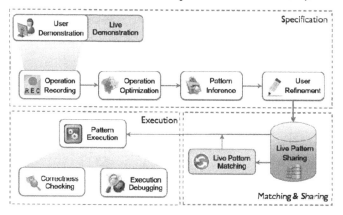

Fig. 3. Overview of LiveMTBD (components with shaded background are new extensions to MTBD) (adapted from [2])

Step 1 – User Demonstration and Operation Recording. MTBD starts from a user demonstration about the model transformation process. A desired part of a model instance is located first as the source model, after which users perform basic editing operations (e.g., add a new model element, update its attributes) to change it into the desired target model. A recording engine stores all of the operations occurring in the editor, and saves the context information for all model elements and connections involved. We illustrate the MTBD idea using the motivating example *ApplyBuffer*. On the source model shown in the top of Figure 1, users can demonstrate the process of adding the new *Buffering* function and reconnecting the data flow. List 1 shows the operations performed to complete the demonstration. The bottom of Figure 1 shows the model after the demonstration.

Step 2 – Operation Optimization. Meaningless operations are occasionally present due to a careless demonstration by the user (e.g., add one element and later remove it without using it in between). An algorithm [2] has been designed to eliminate meaningless operations. The operations in List 1 are all meaningful.

Step 3 – Pattern Inference. In MTBD, the transformation process is specified and formalized as a transformation pattern, which is a 2-tuple $<P, T>$, where P is the precondition of the transformation specifying where to apply the transformation, and T is a sequence of transformation actions specifying how the transformation is done.

Based on the optimized list of operations, an initial transformation pattern can be inferred by summarizing all the involved model elements and connections in the demonstration and generalizing their meta types and relationships. The precondition P inferred from this step specifies the minimum structural constraints where the transformation can generally be applied, and the actions T composes of all the operations from the optimized list.

List 1. Operations performed to demonstrate *ApplyBuffer*

Sequence	Operation Performed
1	Add a *Function*
2	Set *Function.name = "Buffering"*
3	Add an *InputPort* in *Buffering*
4	Set *InputPort.name = "In"*
5	Set *InputPort.type = Analysis.Message.type = "string"*
6	Add an *OutputPort* in *Buffering*
7	Set *OutputPort.name = "Out"*
8	Set *OutputPort.type = Display.InputMessage.type = "string"*
9	Connect *Analysis.Message* to *Buffering.In*
10	Connect *Buffering.Out* to *Display.InputMessage*
11	Disconnect *Analysis.Message* to *Display.InputMessage*
12	Connect *Buffering* to *ECU2*

The initial precondition shown in Figure 4 is inferred from the operations list. It specifies that two connected functions, plus the hardware, must exist to ensure that the recorded operations can be executed with correct and sufficient operands. Then, the transformation actions are generalized operations based on the precondition.

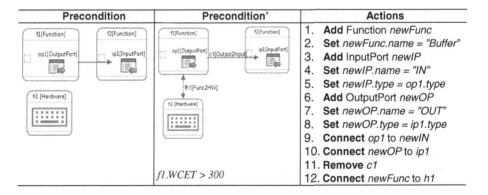

Precondition	Precondition'	Actions
		1. **Add** Function *newFunc*
		2. **Set** *newFunc.name = "Buffer"*
		3. **Add** InputPort *newIP*
		4. **Set** *newIP.name = "IN"*
		5. **Set** *newIP.type = op1.type*
		6. **Add** OutputPort *newOP*
		7. **Set** *newOP.name = "OUT"*
		8. **Set** *newOP.type = ip1.type*
		9. **Connect** *op1* to *newIN*
		10. **Connect** *newOP* to *ip1*
		11. **Remove** *c1*
	$f1.WCET > 300$	12. **Connect** *newFunc* to *h1*

Fig. 4. Model transformation pattern after Step 3 (Precondition) and Step 4 (Precondition')

Step 4 – User Refinement. The initially inferred transformation pattern is sometimes not generic and accurate enough due to the limitations of the expressiveness of a user demonstration. For instance, the precondition P only reflects the structural constraints on the elements that are touched in the demonstration, ignoring the elements that were not directly edited in the demonstration, as well as the attribute constraints. From Figure 4, it can be seen that the required assignment connection between the function *f1* and the hardware *h1* is missing, and the constraint on WCET is not specified. Thus, users can make refinements by either confirming more elements and connections to the structural precondition or specifying detailed constraints on the attribute precondition. In addition, user refinement can also be performed on the transformation actions to identify the generic operations, which should be executed repeatedly according to the actual number of available model elements and connections. The finalized transformation pattern after user refinement <*P'*, *T'*> is stored in the repository for future reuse.

In our example, two additional operations in List 2 are carried out to refine the initial transformation pattern. The containment relationship is simply done by clicking on the desired connection and confirming its existence in the pattern. The attribute precondition is given through a dialog where users can choose any model elements and connections touched in the demonstration and specify the needed constraint expressions. No refinement is performed on actions in this case. The finalized pattern is shown in Figure 4.

List 2. Operations performed for *ApplyBuffer* in the demonstration

Sequence	Operation Performed
13	Confirm the containment of assignment between *Analysis* and *ECU2*
14	Add an attribute constraint on *Analysis – Analysis.WECT > 300*

Step 5 – Pattern Execution. The transformation patterns can be reused in any model instances at any time. The execution process can be formalized as a function with two parameters: *EXECUTION (<P', T'>, I)*, where *<P', T'>* is a finalized transformation pattern, and *I* is the input candidate pool of model elements and connections to match the pattern. The execution process starts by matching precondition *P'* in the candidate pool *I*, followed by executing transformation actions *T'* in the matched locations. A back-tracking algorithm [2] has been implemented to realize the matching, and the execution of transformation actions is completed using model manipulation APIs. Users can customize the input candidate pool by either using the default full selection (all model elements and connections in the editor) or choosing specific model elements or connections. The execution of the *ApplyBuffer* pattern will match all the function pairs based on the precondition and execute the actions to reconnect them though a *Buffering* function.

Step 6 – Correctness Checking and Debugging. Because the precondition *P'* does not ensure that the execution will not violate the syntax, semantics definitions or external constraints, the execution of each transformation action will be logged and the model instance correctness checking and verification are performed after every execution. Whenever a violation occurs, all executed actions are undone and the whole transformation is cancelled. A high-level debugger is under development to help end-users to track the execution process and prevent abstraction leaks.

3.2   From MTBD to LiveMTBD

LiveMTBD consists of three new components, as shown in Figure 3. The contributions of LiveMTBD include new capabilities that improve the specification, sharing, and reuse of model transformation patterns within the MTBD framework.

Live Demonstration. Although the specification of model transformation patterns using MTBD does not require the use of MTLs or the knowledge of a metamodel definition, users must plan ahead and explicitly provide a demonstration that specifies the desired editing activity. A challenge is when a user does not realize the potential for reusing an editing activity until it is part-way through. For example, the hardware engineer configures *ADC* by performing a sequence of editing operations. After the editing is completed, the engineer may then think (post-editing) that because the *ADC* is a commonly used component in embedded systems, the editing activity just performed should be summarized and saved as a reusable model transformation pattern. Therefore, he or she may begin a demonstration and repeat exactly the same editing operations for the sake of inferring the transformation pattern. This repetition could be tedious and time-consuming if the editing activity to demonstrate is complex.

In order to enable a more flexible demonstration approach, live demonstration is implemented so that the recording engine works continuously to record every editing operation performed in the editor. Then, whenever a user realizes a need to specify and summarize a certain model transformation pattern for an editing activity, they can simply go back to the recording view and check all the operations that are related with the specific editing activity, after which the original MTBD inference engine infers the transformation from the archived editing events. Thus, users specify their desired editing activity by reflecting on their editing history, rather than by an intentional demonstration.

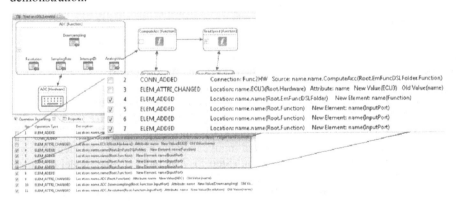

Fig. 5. Live demonstration enables demonstration by checking the editing history

As can be seen in the example from Figure 5, a user creates the whole model by adding the *ComputeAcc* function, *ADC* function and hardware, and then *ReadSpeed*. After the complete model is specified, the user may check the related operations from the recording view and then generate the transformation pattern (e.g., the *CreateADC* transformation as shown in Figure 6). This pattern can be applied to any function, and

Precondition	Actions	
 f1[Function]	1. **Set** *f1.name* = "ADC"	11. **Add** InputPort *ip4*
	2. **Add** InputPort *ip1*	12. **Set** *ip4.name* = "InterruptID"
	3. **Set** *ip1.name* = "Resolution"	13. **Set** *ip4.type* = "String"
	4. **Set** *ip1.type* = "double"	14. **Add** OutputPort *op1*
	5. **Add** InputPort *ip2*	15. **Set** *op1.name* = "AnalogValue"
	6. **Set** *ip2.name* = "Downsampling"	16. **Set** *op1.type* = "double"
	7. **Set** *ip2.type* = "double"	17. **Add** Hardware *h1*
	8. **Add** InputPort *ip3*	18. **Set** *h1.name* = "ADC"
	9. **Set** *ip3.name* = "SampingRate"	19. **Connect** *f1* to *h1*
	10. **Set** *ip3.type* = "double"	

Fig. 6. Final transformation pattern for *CreateADC*

changes the selected function into a fully configured *ADC* function by adding four input ports and one output port, as well as the corresponding *ADC* hardware.

Live Sharing. The original MTBD saves finalized patterns locally. To ease the sharing of patterns and enhance the editing activities, LiveMTBD changes the repository to a centralized repository, which can be accessed by any user at any time. The original transformation patterns are persisted as objects. The centralized repository is implemented using Java RMI, which makes the transmission of pattern objects simple and transparent.

With the patterns being stored automatically in the centralized pattern repository, they are available for all users to choose in the pattern execution step, which provides a live collaborative environment. With this feature, various categories of end-users (e.g., software engineers and hardware engineers) can exchange and benefit from each others' knowledge in model editing.

Live Matching. Without a full understanding of all the model transformation patterns, users might miss reusing the correct transformation in the appropriate situation. Although executing all the transformation patterns can automatically match the applicable editing activities, it is very expensive to restore the model if some patterns change the model into an undesired configuration state, particularly when a number of other changes happen after the pattern and undoing those operations on this part is no longer possible. To address the problem, live matching in LiveMTBD offers users guidance about applicable model transformation patterns during the editing. Live matching is a function that takes two input parameters: *MATCH(R, I)*, where *R* is the set of all available model transformation patterns <*P', T'*> in the centralized repository, and *I* is from the user-selected input candidate pool of model elements and connections. Similar to pattern execution (Step 5), *I* includes all the model elements and connections in the current editor, or a sub-part of the model based on a user's selection. The function returns all the patterns that their precondition *P'* can be satisfied in *I*, as well as the number of matched locations. Live matching requires user approval before executing the pattern.

To enable live matching, the *MATCH* function is triggered during two occasions: 1) the selected input model candidate pool *I* changes, or 2) the available pattern set *R* in the repository changes. As an example shown in the top of Figure 7, after we finalize the two transformation patterns – *CreateADC* and *ApplyBuffer*, if the users do not select any part of the model, the whole model instance is included in *I*, and live matching indicates that both patterns can be applied. Because there are five functions available in the current editor, *CreateADC* is matched 5 times; while the *ApplyBuffer* can be matched to the *ReadSpeed* function whose WCET is greater than 300. Double-clicking on any of the matched patterns triggers its execution directly.

At the bottom of Figure 7, a user may change the selections on the model from the default to the single function newly added to the model. At this point, only *CreateADC* can be matched, and the precondition of *ApplyBuffer* cannot be satisfied due to the insufficient model elements and connections in the input candidate pool. Executing *CreateADC* can automatically transform this function to a fully configured *ADC* function.

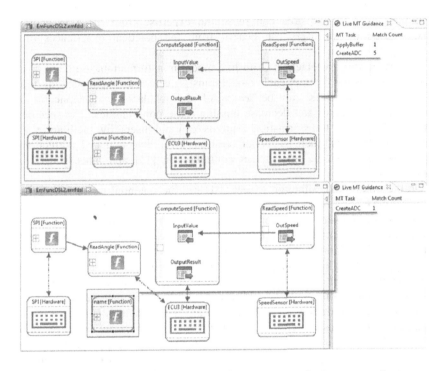

Fig. 7. Live matching suggests applicable transformations in the current selection

4 Discussion

LiveMTBD has been implemented by extending the original MTBD tool, which is a plug-in to the Generic Eclipse Modeling Systems (GEMS) [19]. Based on the challenges identified in Section 1, it can be seen that LiveMTBD offers the following advantages.

Simplified specification of desired editing activities. In LiveMTBD, users are isolated from the need to know and learn MTLs. The only steps that a user is involved are demonstrating the editing process (Step 1) and making refinements (Step 4). All of the other procedures (i.e., optimization, initial inference, generation, execution, and correctness checking) are fully automated. In addition, information exposed to users is at the model instance level in the editor, rather than the metamodel level. The generated patterns are invisible to users (Figure 4 and 6 are presented for the sake of explanation, which are not visible to users when using LiveMTBD). Therefore, users are prevented from knowing metamodel definitions and implementation details. With the live demonstration feature, the specification of model transformation patterns can be realized at any moment of the editing task by reflecting and checking the editing history, providing a more flexible environment to summarize and specify the desired editing activities.

Improved collaborative editing environment. With live sharing, different users in different distributed locations may share their modeling experience seamlessly, such that users in one area can reuse the expertise from those in another, or inexperienced novice users can benefit from the practical experiences of more knowledgeable users.

Guided editing experience. With live model transformation, users are prompted with guidance about the applicable model transformations during model edit-time, the result being that users can be aware of the available and applicable model transformation patterns and decrease missing reuse opportunities. The specified and summarized model transformation patterns can aid users by facilitating various transformation tasks, such as model creation, error detection and correction [16], aspect-oriented modeling [5], layout configuration [15] and other general model evolution tasks.

On the other hand, although LiveMTBD has the potential to improve reuse and automate the editing activities, several limitations are still present.

The need to ensure the correctness of a live demonstration. Forming the transformation pattern from the editing history is very flexible compared with the explicit demonstration, but it also leads to a possibility that the selected editing operations from the history may not be accurate. For instance, without a mechanism to guide the selection of operations related with certain model elements, extra unnecessary operations could be added accidentally to the pattern, which cannot be filtered by the optimization algorithm; or an incomplete pattern is inferred due to the insufficient operations chosen from the view. Therefore, a crucial aspect for the future work is how to ensure the correctness of the selections from using live demonstration.

Lack of a management feature in the centralized pattern repository. The current implementation of the pattern repository simply stores all the patterns together without classification. This could lead to matching transformation patterns that are not designed for the current modeling language. Therefore, categorizing the patterns is an essential part of the repository management in the future. In addition, the visibility, priority, and authorization of the patterns should also be taken into consideration.

The performance issue of live matching. Matching patterns is expensive in the current implementation of LiveMTBD, which applies a back-tracking algorithm to traverse the selected input candidate pool. This will lead to a performance issue when a large number of transformation patterns are matched by live matching in the editor. Therefore, how to optimize the matching algorithm and improve the performance deserves a deeper investigation.

5 Related Work

The challenges of using MTLs to implement model transformation have been identified previously [10]. Much work has been done to simplify the model transformation implementation processes. Model Transformation By Example (MTBE) was the first attempt in this direction [10]. With MTBE, instead of writing transformation rules manually, users are asked to build a prototypical set of interrelated mappings between the source and target models, and then the transformation rules are semi-automatically generated using a logical programming engine [11]. This approach simplifies model transformation implementation, but is not appropriate for assisting editing acitvities because: 1) it focuses on direct concept mapping between two different domains rather than changing models within the same domain; 2) MTBE does not support attribute transformation, which is an indispensible editing operation in the modeling process.

Similarly, Brosch et al. introduced a method for specifying composite operations within the user's modeling language and environment of choice [12]. The user models the composite operation by-example, changing a source model into the desirable target model. By comparing the source and target states, the specific changes can be summarized by a model difference algorithm, and transformation rules can be generated. This approach focuses on endogenous model transformation, which can be used to assist editing activities. However, attribute transformation has not been considered, and live model transformation and sharing is not currently supported in these related approaches.

Some works have been done to realize automatic model completion features to create and modify the existing model elements automatically from an incomplete state to a complete state. Sen et al. [13] proposed to transform the metamodel and associated instance models to an Alloy specification, including static semantics. Then, the partial model can be completed automatically by applying a SAT solver. This approach provides guidance to end-users in the model editors, but the limitation is that the inferred complete models are mainly based on the input constraints, rather than end-user customizations.

Mazanek et al. [14] implemented an auto-completion feature for diagram editors based on graph grammars. Given an incomplete graph (model) in the editor, all possible graphs that can be generated using the grammar production rules will be suggested to users. Although this is a runtime and live suggestion feature, the suggestions are totally dependent on the grammar, which requires users to specify a number to restrict the times of production and avoid infinite loops. Also, the graph grammar may not be fully compatible to process domain-specific modeling languages, and this approach cannot express user-customized editing activities (e.g., the *WCET* must be greater than *300*).

General MTLs, particularly graphical MTLs [9] based on left- and right- hand side patterns, can all be extended with a live model transformation feature without much modification, although this is still not a common practice. VIATRA2 [6] already supports live model transformation matching features. For instance, triggers can be defined as special rules to execute certain model transformations at modeling time. However, a suggestion or guidance before applying the transformation is not available in the editor.

Based on graphical MTLs, Rath et al. [7][8] performed a detailed investigation on live model transformations using incremental pattern matching techniques. They applied the Rete algorithm to preserve the full transformation context in the form of pattern matches that improved the performance of the live transformation. Their live model transformation was mainly aimed at supporting incremental model transformations and model synchronization between source and target models, although it could be applied to automate the editing activities as well. The full implementation of their approach is based on VIATRA2, which requires the usage of graph transformation rules at the metamodel level. Their matching technique could be helpful to improve our live matching feature.

Finally, there are also related works that support model transformation reuse. Rather than focusing on reusing the complete transformation, Iacob et al. [17] summarized a number of model transformation patterns and enabled reusing and extending these patterns in QVT; Sen et al. [18] presented a novel approach to adapt a metamodel so that an existing model transformation written for a different Metamodel can be reused.

6   Conclusion

We presented an extended model transformation environment called LiveMTBD, which supports the specification and reuse of automated model editing activities. Compared with our previous work with MTBD and other by-demonstration and by-example approaches, the main contributions of the current paper are: 1) a demonstration-based transformation inference process that allows a user to identify transformation patterns from the previous edit history using live demonstration; 2) a centralized pattern repository to enable transparent sharing of the transformation patterns; 3) a live model transformation matching engine to provide modeling-time suggestions and user guidance of reusable patterns that match the current modeling context. Our approach is fully implemented and integrated to GEMS, which is downloadable at http://www.cis.uab.edu/softcom/mtbd.

Acknowledgement

This work is supported by NSF CAREER award CCF-1052616.

References

1. Schmidt, D.: Model-Driven Engineering. IEEE Computer 39(2), 25–32 (2006)
2. Sun, Y., White, J., Gray, J.: Model transformation by demonstration. In: Schürr, A., Selic, B. (eds.) MODELS 2009. LNCS, vol. 5795, pp. 712–726. Springer, Heidelberg (2009)
3. Jouault, F., Allilaire, F., Bézivin, J., Kurtev, I.: ATL: A Model Transformation Tool. Science of Computer Programming 72(1/2), 31–39 (2008)
4. Sendall, S., Kozaczynski, W.: Model transformation - The Heart and Soul of Model-Driven Software Development. IEEE Software, Special Issue on Model Driven Software Development 20(5), 42–45 (2003)

5. Gray, J., Lin, Y., Zhang, J.: Automating Change Evolution in Model-Driven Engineering. IEEE Computer, Special Issue on Model-Driven Engineering 39(2), 51–58 (2006)
6. Balogh, Z., Varró, D.: Advanced Model Transformation Language Constructs in VIATRA2. In: Symposium on Applied Computing (SAC), Dijon, France, pp. 1280–1287 (April 2006)
7. Ráth, I., Bergmann, G., Ökrös, A., Varró, D.: Live model transformations driven by incremental pattern matching. In: Vallecillo, A., Gray, J., Pierantonio, A. (eds.) ICMT 2008. LNCS, vol. 5063, pp. 107–121. Springer, Heidelberg (2008)
8. Bergmann, G., Rath, I., Varro, D.: Parallelization of Graph Transformation based on Incremental Pattern Matching. Electronic Communications of EASST 18 (2009)
9. Mens, T., Gorp, P.: A Taxonomy of Model Transformation and its Application to Graph Transformation. In: The 1st International Workshop on Graph and Model Transformation, GraMoT 2005, Tallinn, Estonia (2005)
10. Varró, D.: Model transformation by example. In: Wang, J., Whittle, J., Harel, D., Reggio, G. (eds.) MoDELS 2006. LNCS, vol. 4199, pp. 410–424. Springer, Heidelberg (2006)
11. Balogh, Z., Varró, D.: Model Transformation by Example using Inductive Logic Programming. Software and Systems Modeling 8(3), 347–364 (2009)
12. Brosch, P., Langer, P., Seidl, M., Wieland, K., Wimmer, M., Kappel, G., Retschitzegger, W., Schwinger, W.: An example is worth a thousand words: Composite operation modeling by-example. In: Schürr, A., Selic, B. (eds.) MODELS 2009. LNCS, vol. 5795, pp. 271–285. Springer, Heidelberg (2009)
13. Sen, S., Baudry, B., Vandheluwe, H.: Towards Domain-specific Model Editors with Automatic Model Completion. Simulation 86(2), 109–126 (2010)
14. Mazanek, S., Minas, M.: Business process models as a showcase for syntax-based assistance in diagram editors. In: Schürr, A., Selic, B. (eds.) MODELS 2009. LNCS, vol. 5795, pp. 322–336. Springer, Heidelberg (2009)
15. Sun, Y., Gray, J., Langer, P., Wimmer, M., White, J.: A WYSIWYG Approach for Configuring Model Layout using Model Transformations. In: 10th Workshop on Domain-Specific Modeling, held at SPLASH 2010, Reno, NV (2010)
16. Sun, Y., White, J., Gray, J., Gokhale, A.: Model-Driven Automated Error Recovery in Cloud Computing. In: Model-driven Analysis and Software Development: Architectures and Functions, pp. 136–154. IGI Global, Hershey (2009)
17. Iacob, M., Maarten, W., Heerink, L.: Reusable Model Transformation Patterns. In: Enterprise Distributed Object Computing Conference Workshops, Munich, Germany, pp. 1–10 (2008)
18. Sen, S., Moha, N., Mahe, V., Barais, O., Baudry, B., Jezequel, J.: Reusable Model Transformations. Software and System Modeling (2010), doi:10.1007/s10270-010-0181-9
19. Generic Eclipse Modeling System, GEMS (2011),
    http://www.eclipse.org/gmt/gems/
20. Eclipse Epsilon (2011), http://www.eclipse.org/gmt/epsilon/

Author Index